Core Practices of Successful Teachers

Core Practices of Successful Teachers

Supporting Learning and Managing Instruction

Urban Fraefel

ROWMAN & LITTLEFIELD
Lanham • Boulder • New York • London

Published by Rowman & Littlefield
An imprint of The Rowman & Littlefield Publishing Group, Inc.
4501 Forbes Boulevard, Suite 200, Lanham, Maryland 20706
www.rowman.com

86-90 Paul Street, London EC2A 4NE, United Kingdom

Copyright © 2023 by Urban Fraefel

All rights reserved. No part of this book may be reproduced in any form or by any electronic or mechanical means, including information storage and retrieval systems, without written permission from the publisher, except by a reviewer who may quote passages in a review.

British Library Cataloguing in Publication Information Available

Library of Congress Cataloging-in-Publication Data

Names: Fraefel, Urban, 1953– author.
Title: Core practices of successful teachers : supporting learning and managing instruction / Urban Fraefel.
Description: Lanham, Maryland : Rowman & Littlefield, [2023] | Includes bibliographical references. | Summary: "Core Practices of Successful Teachers helps teachers develop, understand, and improve core practice—the key components of adaptive and successful teachin—to teach in the best possible way for the benefit of students. Via a variety of suggestions and exercises, teachers can engage with core practices and continually reflect on and refine them"— Provided by publisher.
Identifiers: LCCN 2022050491 (print) | LCCN 2022050492 (ebook) | ISBN 9781475869033 (Cloth) | ISBN 9781475869040 (Paperback) | ISBN 9781475869057 (epub)
Subjects: LCSH: Teacher effectiveness—United States. | Effective teaching—United States. | Individualized instruction—United States. | Communication in education—United States. | Teachers—Training of—United States.
Classification: LCC LB2832.2 .F73 2023 (print) | LCC LB2832.2 (ebook) | DDC 371.102—dc23/eng/20221228
LC record available at https://lccn.loc.gov/2022050491
LC ebook record available at https://lccn.loc.gov/2022050492

Contents

Foreword	vii
Preface	xi
PART I: READ THIS FIRST	**1**
1 What You Should Know Before Working with This Book	3
2 How to Work Successfully with This Book	11
PART II: SUPPORTING INDIVIDUAL LEARNING	**21**
3 Supporting Individual Learning: What It Is All About	23
4 Diagnostics: How Do I Find Out Where the Students Stand?	33
5 Professional Feedback to Learners: Crucial for Any Support	63
6 How to Make Feedback and One-on-One Conversations More Effective	73
PART III: MANAGING INSTRUCTION	**97**
7 Introduction	99
8 The Transparent Opening of a Lesson	105
9 Providing an Input	117
10 Guiding Discussions	131
11 Guidelines for Learning Activities	153

| **12** | Summing Up and Closing | 163 |
| **13** | Some Variations of the Basic Lesson Structure | 187 |

PART IV: WHERE DO WE STAND NOW?   211

14	A Closer Look at the Concept of (Core) Practices	213
15	Epilogue: My Own Practices	225
References		231
About the Author		245

Foreword

Becoming a teacher is a journey of a thousand steps, and the path is seldom smooth. Beginning teachers need all the supports they can find along the way, including visions of where they're headed, guideposts to mark the trail, and concrete guidance for navigating the inevitable challenges involved in such a complex journey.

Given these challenges, this workbook aimed at supporting teachers in developing a strong foundation of core practices is eminently valuable. Prof. Fraefel's deep understanding of both the importance of professional judgment and the need for practical support in learning to teach is reflected in the design of this book. He provides a map, or trail guide, for the journey to help teachers develop not only an understanding of core practices but also the ability to engage and reflect on their own practice. His hope for teachers is that they develop the kind of adaptive expertise in teaching that allows them to draw on their knowledge and practice to respond flexibly to the changing circumstances of the classroom. As he notes in his introduction to the book, "professional practices enable flexible and goal-oriented instruction, even in varying situations."

This book starts at the heart of the matter—student learning. The ultimate goal of teachers' work is to support student learning, so I appreciate that the journey starts here, with the end in view. A deep understanding of how students learn, and the diverse ways in which learning happens, is a foundational element of teachers' professional knowledge.

In his book *The System of Professions*, Andrew Abbott (1988) contends that a claim to professional expertise lies in three areas of professional practice: first, the ability to diagnose or assess the client's situation; second, the ability to reason and infer, using professional knowledge, about a client's problem; and third, the ability to treat effectively the problem or to take action on the client's behalf. In teaching, these might translate into the ability to draw on professional knowledge to assess a student's educational needs, the ability to reason about student learning when assessments are not clear-cut, and the ability to design and enact instruction in ways that support student learning—"the treatment," to use Abbott's language.

This workbook follows a similar logic, starting with an understanding of student learning and how to effectively assess where students are through diagnosis and assessment. Only once teachers have a clear understanding of where students are starting from in a particular subject area can they design instruction that is tailored to student needs. As this workbook suggests, core practices of assessment are thus crucial for beginning teachers to develop early in their careers, as these assessments form the basis that determines how best to plan and deliver instruction. These are some of the questions Prof. Fraefel poses: How are my students doing? Where are they struggling or succeeding? How can I support them? Being able to answer these questions forms the basis of pedagogical reasoning and action.

The ability to give targeted, constructive feedback represents another foundational element of teaching practice, one that research has identified as critical to supporting student learning. To provide this kind of targeted feedback, teachers must become excellent diagnosticians. As suggested in the book, teachers become better at collecting and collating information about student learning over time, just as doctors develop expertise in medical diagnosis based on their experience seeing patients over their careers. But having the tools to observe carefully and to assess learning both formally and informally is critical for beginning teachers.

The book proceeds from diagnosis to instruction—the means by which teachers support student learning. Again, Prof. Fraefel offers supportive advice to teachers about how best to plan instruction, advice rooted in research about the practices that have the best chance of helping students learn. Novice and more experienced teachers alike will benefit from exploring ways to open and close lessons and experiment with different models of instruction.

Ultimately, this workbook is designed to support teacher learning. By offering suggestions for experimentation and reflection, the book provides multiple opportunities for teachers to test their understanding and improve their practice. As Prof. Fraefel wisely states, the best way to learn is through intentional practice and reflection, coupled with constructive feedback. My hope is that teacher educators will use this book to help new teachers learn more intentionally in their practicum placements, not by simply observing but by trying out many of the ideas in this book. Organizing opportunities for teachers to deepen their learning of these core practices is the work of teacher education.

The work around core practices has been critiqued by some as an overly technical approach to teaching, one that aims to standardize instruction and rob teachers of autonomy. Nothing could be further from the truth. Every profession and craft rests on a well-specified set of practices, skills, and knowledge that novices are apprenticed into. In *The Making of a Chef*, Michael Ruhlman (2009) wrote, "I tell new students to learn the fundamentals of cooking and the rest will follow, and more, that the degree of excellence with which they master those fundamentals will very likely determine their success for the rest of their culinary careers." The same is true for the making of teachers. Mastering the foundational practices of teaching will enable teachers to develop the kind of adaptive expertise that is the mark of a true professional. These practices, coupled with professional knowledge, become the basis for continued improvement and improvisation. As any jazz player will tell you, you can't improvise if you haven't mastered the foundational chords. The goal of this book is not to provide what Michael Huberman (1983) called "recipes for busy kitchens," but instead to offer an entry into the professional practice of teaching.

I hope those of you using this book either to enter the profession or to deepen your practice will enjoy every step of this complex journey. The destination—supporting all students to learn and flourish—could not be more important.

Pam Grossman
Dean and George and Diane Weiss Professor of Education
Graduate School of Education
University of Pennsylvania
Philadelphia, Pennsylvania

Preface

Teaching is in many ways a practical profession: teachers are constantly at work, incessantly making decisions, usually visible and in the middle of the action. What could be more natural for prospective teachers than to learn exactly these practical elements of daily work?

The idea is good (and not new), the implementation more difficult than some might think. Unlike many other professions, learning to do the practical work is much more complex because the work itself is highly complex. As we now know, the most important practices—core practices—are not simply routines but clusters of elements required to successfully meet specific challenges. And ultimately, all practices boil down to the extent to which they contribute to student progress.

In recent times, a great many teacher education scholars have been engaged in practices; one can definitely speak of a movement. Therefore, a variety of approaches, concepts, and research findings are available. In the comparatively short time since core practices became a main focus of teacher education, amazing research and development has been done around the world.

This can and must be built on. This book aims not just to talk about practices but also to inspire learning, with the deep conviction that practices can only be acquired through practice but that doing so requires serious reflection, the relevant knowledge, ongoing rehearsal, and sharing with others. Therefore, the book is likely to be particularly useful to readers if they have repeated opportunities to teach, to practice, and to gain experience.

Books on teaching often have a similar structure: they usually begin with the "big" questions of meaning and goals, then gradually become more specific, and finally address assessment. Such an approach undoubtedly has its logic, but general preliminary considerations are not what prospective teachers are most interested in. They want to know how to behave in the classroom, how to teach successfully, how to deal with pressure.

It seems to me that it is advisable to start with the concrete practices when it comes to learning instruction. These are things that teachers deal with in their daily work, such as the following two areas, for example:

- How are my students doing? Where are they struggling or succeeding? How can I support them?
- In what stages am I progressing through the lesson? What is important, what less? What are the cornerstones I can rely on? How can I respond to a changing situation? How do I shape a lesson so that there is a sense of accomplishment at the end?

I have chosen to begin with those things that are probably most important to student teachers and early career teachers in their daily professional lives to ensure learning success: supporting student learning and managing instruction. However, based on these practical challenges, sources of knowledge are always drawn upon and the practical issues are reflected on from multiple perspectives.

Important things are brought up repeatedly throughout the book and are expanded on with each pass. However, this book is modular in some sense. There is nothing to stop readers from changing the order as they progress through the book.

One final point: a key part of the book is the suggestions for activities to gently urge readers to actively engage with practices. As we all know, we learn more the more intensively we do it and then reflect on it.

Part I

READ THIS FIRST

Chapter One

What You Should Know Before Working with This Book

This book is about practices, the cornerstones of professional action. This introductory chapter provides an initial clarification of what is meant here by core practices and why they are so important.

Here, however, we are deliberately limiting ourselves to the *perspective of prospective and in-service teachers*. We do this knowing that we are leaving aside for the moment many actually important differentiations that are being discussed in the community.

A BOOK FOR IN-SERVICE AND PROSPECTIVE TEACHERS

This workbook can be used individually or in practicums and internships, as well as in courses that accompany them. There is no need to work through the book page by page. The main thing is to really delve into the topics. The contents of the chapters sometimes overlap. Therefore, certain topics are examined several times from different perspectives. This is intentional and can help to create links.

EVERYONE WANTS TO BE SUCCESSFUL

Possible failure is a major concern when prospective teachers think about their profession. From the point of view of all prospective teachers, teacher education is first and foremost a preparation for a career, which should give them sufficient confidence to be able to stand their ground in their profession. This concern is completely justified and understandable and should have its place in teacher education.

DOES TEACHING "WORK" THANKS TO ROUTINES?

What do prospective teachers expect when they want to gain confidence in their own abilities? In most cases, they want to have options for action available so that they can react immediately in classroom situations. For this reason, prospective teachers are often eager to learn what has proved successful, how experienced teachers proceed, and what promising advice is available. In short, they want to know "how to do it," and they want to convert advice into routines as soon as possible. But what prospective teachers want so badly—the smooth running of lessons and the progress of students—they hardly achieve with advice and mere routines.

IMITATING SUCCESSFUL PROFESSIONALS IS NOT ENOUGH

Those who copy apparently successful routines usually succumb to a mistake in thinking. To imitate step by step what has proven successful for others can at best be a stopgap solution. A look at other professions makes it clear: physicians, cooks, mechanics, plasterers, musicians, police officers, they all perform visible actions; they perform gestures typical of their profession. But by simply copying these gestures like a recipe, nobody becomes a professional. It is not enough to imitate the visible "best practices" of the experts.

The visible actions of successful professionals are based on a great deal of knowledge and experience. Over the course of time, they have built up and internalized a solid know-how and intuitively draw on it when necessary. We call this intuitive professional knowing-how "practices." Teachers must acquire practices gradually; there is no quick fix to learn how to act professionally.

THIS IS WHAT WE MEAN BY "CORE PRACTICES" OF TEACHERS

What can prospective teachers possibly envision when we speak of the need to master a practice? We choose a very simplistic definition here: "core practices" are recurring activities that are important to support student progress in the best possible way.

Core practices like "leading a classroom discussion" are essential for teaching and learning in most subjects. Most of these core practices can be well characterized, and there is much experience, research, and knowledge about them. But ultimately, they are shaped by the teacher and therefore always have an individual coloration. If the teacher is interested in improving the practices, he or she will use them often, rehearse them, understand them better, and use them flexibly. Such practices provide a teacher with a solid foundation for his or her professional work.

YOU DO BUILD YOUR PRACTICES YOURSELF

What distinguishes practices from recipe-like recommendations? Recipes are adopted but often lack underlying knowledge and training, and a recipe rarely tells us when it is best used and with whom. In fact, we know that the plethora of well-intentioned advice constantly offered to teachers can be rather confusing and even discouraging.

Practices, on the other hand, must be developed from the ground up by teachers and continually improved through experience, contextual knowledge, feedback from others, reflection, and occasional practical advice. Over time, practices become second nature and so internalized that they can be used intuitively. Therefore, it is almost impossible to learn practices by copying or reading. Practices accumulate continuously the deeper you go into them.

And most importantly, you need to fully engage with them. Ultimately, they are *your* practices for *your* teaching. Learning practices is your personal commitment, and you are responsible for becoming a professional teacher.

FOCUS ON PRACTICES IN INITIAL TEACHER EDUCATION, BEST IN COLLABORATION

There is no fast track to build practices; this is real work. This is precisely why it has to be introduced in teacher education and not just at the beginning of a career. Teacher education sometimes offers opportunities to engage in practices in on-campus courses, but here the emphasis is clearly on practicums, internships in schools, and the formats that go with them. That is where practices can be focused, improved, flexibly designed, and properly trained. What helps is the support of experts in teacher education, the exchange of ideas with other prospective teachers, and the discussions with students.

PRACTICES NEED KNOWLEDGE AND THEORY

Prospective teachers are confronted with a great deal of knowledge in teacher education. Most of it is relevant to the teaching profession at some point. But do teachers have the relevant knowledge at hand at the right moment? Unfortunately, all too rarely. Therefore, the essential knowledge acquired on campus and online should be merged with what teachers actually *do*.

Effective practices are based not only on experience and common sense but also on the knowledge acquired on campus. It is indispensable to draw on the diverse content knowledge, pedagogical content knowledge, and educational sciences. However, it is necessary to examine which of these is useful in a specific case.

PROFESSIONAL PRACTICES ENABLE STATE-OF-THE-ART PROFESSIONAL TEACHING

The aim is to establish *practices for the best possible professional teaching*. Teachers should ask themselves habitually whether their practices are achieving the best possible effects and whether they are up to date with relevant knowledge. Researchers in the disciplines of learning and teaching and educational science are constantly researching and reviewing how schools, classrooms, and society are evolving, what concepts are promising in particular contexts, what (side) effects they have, and so on.

Prospective teachers have easy access to knowledge, because experts in teacher education teach and explain the concepts, and the experts can be consulted at any time.

PROFESSIONAL PRACTICES ARE FLEXIBLE

Those who have acquired professional practices can adequately assess a situation and "see" what is going on in the first place, then make quick and appropriate decisions depending on the situation. Take, for example, "identifying and understanding students' learning difficulties": Those who are familiar with this practice will be attentive to the students and will perceive the specifics of the present situation. They intuitively notice what is to be paid attention to, and they have the appropriate knowledge and know different ways of reacting, because they have studied and trained promising strategies.

Teachers who are familiar with the practice in question know immediately what to do and what not to do. In this way, they can quickly make the best possible decisions for the benefit of the students. In short, professional practices enable flexible and goal-oriented instruction, even in varying situations.

PROFESSIONAL PRACTICES TAKE THE PRESSURE OFF THE TEACHERS

Time and again, early career teachers report that the daily challenges of school overwhelm them because they have to think about so many things they hardly had to worry about in teacher education. The professional reality is unrelenting: the teacher is constantly faced with new challenges. The pressure of time and the pressure to (re)act immediately at school triggers constant stress, which can push especially those starting out on their careers to their limits.

This is where practices help. In contrast to mere routines and rigid recommendations, they provide teachers with options to act appropriately and professionally even in stressful situations. And that is why it is so important that professional practices are rehearsed.

ONLY GOOD PRACTICES HELP TO ACHIEVE EDUCATIONAL SUCCESS

Last but not least, not all practices have quality. There are also suboptimal or even harmful practices. Some practices are patterns that were not consciously designed but have formed with increasing routine. Possibly, they are not serving the goals at all. They may support the teacher in coping with everyday life, but they can also be unprofessional and counterproductive. The crucial question is, Do the practices help the teachers to fulfill their tasks as well and professionally as possible? And above all, *do they contribute to the students' progress?* Those who develop a practice with these questions have taken an important step on the way to becoming professional teachers.

Textbox 1.1 ACTIVITIES AND SUGGESTIONS

DO YOU HAVE ANY IDEA WHAT "PRACTICES" ARE YET?

Skim again the twelve points of this chapter, and read in particular the preliminary definition in the fifth point. Describe in a few keywords the difference between the teacher's practices and the teacher's

- skills
- knowledge
- routines
- recipes
- habits

Learning Through Imitation

Learning through observation of models is an everyday strategy to learn things. The question is whether it is also enough to imitate those teachers you remember best. Your opinion on this:

Ask the same question regarding other professions, such as property manager, farmer, doctor, pilot, or piano teacher.

A Core Practice

Imagine a practice that seems particularly important to you personally. Which one is it?

Name some characteristics of this practice.

Chapter Two

How to Work Successfully with This Book

This book is primarily intended for prospective and in-service teachers but is also helpful for cooperating teachers and teacher educators who want to actively support their student teachers in developing professional practices. It is important to note that the book works best when the prospective or in-service teachers find or create sufficient *opportunities to rehearse practices* repeatedly. This chapter clarifies that the book has an impulse character and unfolds its effect above all when people work with it actively and with commitment.

COMMITMENT HELPS

Anyone who wants to become a better teacher is committed. Countless studies and experience have shown that progress is most likely to be made when it is pursued with commitment.

Therefore, this book will be more effective if you develop the will to change and become a better teacher. This book makes a concrete suggestion: look at your current practices, improve them, and use them skillfully in the service of your own and your students' success.

THIS IS NOT JUST A TEXTBOOK

All textbooks on teacher training have in common that they aim to structure and make available a body of knowledge in an understandable way. Working through a textbook means following the authors' train of thought and understanding the facts and concepts. Of course, there is nothing wrong with that.

However, this book does not aim to provide a complete overview of relevant knowledge, even though it contains numerous references, quotations, and summaries of useful expert knowledge available elsewhere to prospective and in-service teachers. A well-informed expert will miss much and may caution that some things are too condensed. Many topics are touched on that are presented in much greater detail and sophistication in other works; that is inevitable.

But the central aspect is *practices*: What can less experienced teachers do to teach professionally and with confidence so that students benefit? What bodies of knowledge (besides practice) might be helpful? Hopefully the references will encourage readers to investigate further.

THIS IS A WORKBOOK

So this is not just a textbook, nor is it a book that accompanies an on-campus course, but it is a workbook in the strict sense of the word: you are supposed to work with it. Reading alone is not enough. Numerous tasks and suggestions will ask you to do something, to become active. In this way, you not only receive; you create. The intention is always to encourage you to engage in anything that can improve your practices as a teacher.

Do not flip through the highlighted activities and suggestions, but take the time to engage with them. This workbook can be particularly helpful to you if you are open to the suggestions and, in some ways, let yourself be guided by them. At the end of longer sections, you will find such activities and suggestions.

And always turn back. Some things only become clear at second or third sight, and some connections you only recognize afterward.

DIG DEEPER

A productive exploration goes beyond the texts and suggestions in this book. Deepen the impulses you get. Take the initiative and continue researching. If a concept is presented only in a short summary, look for more detailed descriptions and also controversial discussions. Identify references in textbooks or search for online sources. Ask experts such as lecturers or competent colleagues or peers. In other words, develop a high level of cognitive activity to get to the bottom of things.

NO PRACTICES WITHOUT PRACTICE!

To develop practices, you need practice. Therefore, combine the suggestions in the book with practical activities in schools and classrooms, for prospective teachers mainly in a practicum or school internship, but also in part-time jobs. The book will be particularly effective if you make the connections in both directions, from mental preparation to practical action and vice versa: from experience to reflection.

Experience is a very important source to be taken seriously. "Experiencing" is more than just acting. It is also about thinking about action, analyzing it. "Analysis" means questioning what has been experienced and learning from it: How did I implement this and that? How did the

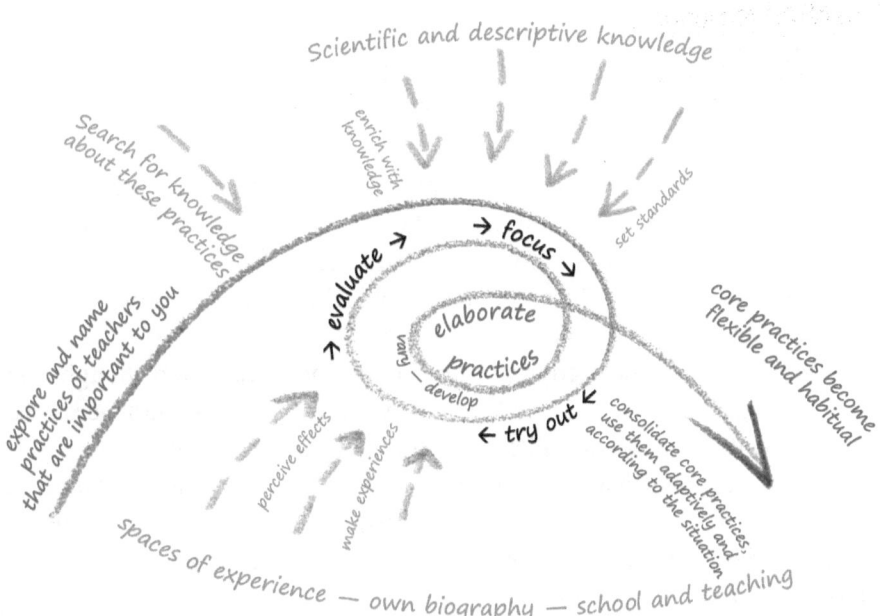

Figure 2.1. Cyclic development of practices: Slowly follow the spiral line. *Author created.*

students react? Did it help them? When exactly did the difficulties arise, and what could be the reason? How could I unblock a muddled situation? How should I do it differently?

WRITE YOUR OWN HANDBOOK

Thoughts are fleeting. Write them down and visualize them. Use the medium of your choice; this can be a blank notebook or a collection of loose sheets, your tablet, or any other digital medium. Do not spare this book; write in it. If you are currently going through teacher training, you may be writing a portfolio. Use it as a storage place for notes, sketches, and overviews.

The goal is to create your own handbook that contains successful procedures, remarkable facts, interesting findings, essential insights, experiences, checklists, references, hints, variants, conclusions, concepts, and so on concerning your practices as a teacher. Write and design it so that you would like to read it again and so that it will be useful and inspire you later.

COMBINE INTO A CLUSTER WHAT YOU HAVE EXPERIENCED, READ, AND THOUGHT

Although there have been helpful attempts to reorganize professional knowledge (starting with Shulman, 1986), it does not change its vastness. Ultimately, knowledge is only useful if the teacher absorbs it and links it in a variety of ways. In other words, only internalized knowledge can become professionally effective.

The sources of knowledge are on the one hand read and thought, on the other hand also experienced (i.e., they are conscious experiences). To absorb all this knowledge like a sponge or to attract it like a magnet is very important, but it is not enough; things have to be put in relation to each other, to be linked. Over time, a cluster with numerous interrelated elements develops around a topic (e.g., a cluster like "managing a meaningful classroom discussion").

Therefore, visualize things, draw clusters, and make lists to understand what is related to what. Use mind maps, concept maps, Venn diagrams, and whatever you are familiar with. Revise these visualizations from time to time, and you will find that they become richer and more focused.

REPEAT AND PRACTICE

A sudden insight or a unique aha experience can be illuminating, but it is not enough. Rehearsal and training in daily practice are also important. At work, situations always vary a little bit, and that's exactly why you need a lot of practice to act appropriately. In this way you learn to react to changing situations in the best possible way.

Even more, make rehearsal and training a firm habit in your practicum, your internship, or your professional life. Take up certain practices again and again and improve them, as professionals in all professions do.

NETWORK, COOPERATE

As in all professions, there are networks of professionals or those who are on their way there. They show each other what they are working on, exchange ideas, challenge each other ("critical friends"), give each other feedback and advice, and are hungry for understanding and improvement. The same applies to teams in the schools. Make professionalism an issue among peers.

REMAIN CRITICAL

One can always see things differently, and usually for good reasons. In this book you will find points of view and arguments but no conclusive truths. Take a critical look at the positions. On your way to professional practices, you will share or criticize these positions, take up or reject the suggestions, examine the fit with your experiences, and draw your own conclusions.

There is no fixed doctrine about your professional practices as a teacher. But there is a clear goal: *develop your professional practices to support students as best you can, and do so in a friendly atmosphere.*

> Textbox 2.1 FURTHER INFORMATION AND RESOURCES
>
> ## THE SELF-DETERMINATION THEORY: OR WHAT MOTIVATIONAL THEORIES HAVE TO DO WITH THIS BOOK
>
> The more motivated you are to work with the suggestions in this book, the more you will benefit. But does it depend on whether we are motivated? The following excursus on three components that contribute to motivation could shed light on this.
>
> *Why We Do What We Do*: this is the title of a book by the motivational researcher Edward Deci, who, together with Richard Ryan, developed the self-determination theory, one of the most influential motivational theories of the last fifty years (Deci & Flaste, 1995). Why do we do what we do? What drives us? Motivations are often opaque; understanding them is not always easy. Among the numerous explanations and theoretical models of motivation, however, there is one approach that is plausible for most people, especially with regard to school learning: the self-determination theory. Its central statements are very briefly summarized here.
>
> The impetus for action comes from three sources:
>
> - Physiological needs, drives (e.g., hunger)
> - Emotions (e.g., fear, longing)
> - Psychological needs (e.g., experience of competence, autonomy, relatedness)
>
> The researchers Ryan and Deci (2000) have devoted particular attention to the third area—psychological needs.
>
> ### Psychological Needs that Drive Action
>
> > Self-determination theory focuses primarily on three innate [psychological] needs: the needs for competence, relatedness, and autonomy (or self-determination). Competence involves understanding how to attain various external and internal outcomes and being efficacious in performing the requisite actions; relatedness involves developing secure and satisfying connections with others in one's social milieu; and autonomy refers to being self-initiating and self-regulating of one's own actions. . . .

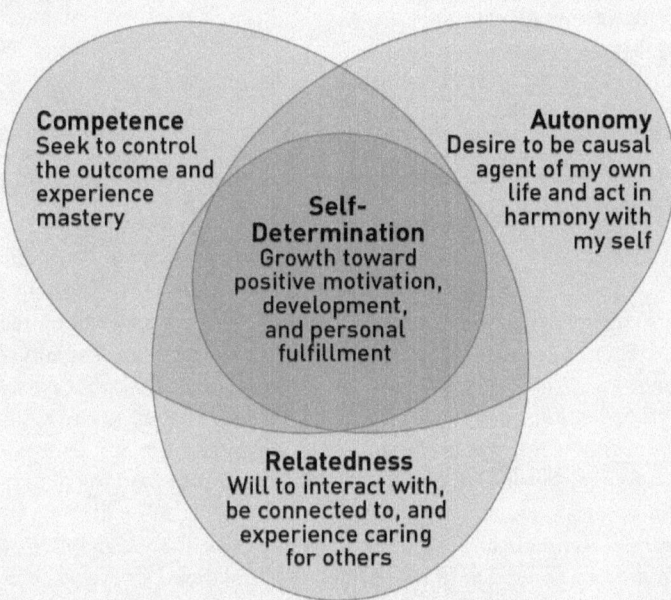

Figure 2.2. Self-determined action. *Author created.*

The concept of needs . . . allows one to specify the contextual conditions that will facilitate motivation, performance, and development. Simply stated, motivation, performance, and development will be maximized within social contexts that provide people the opportunity to satisfy their basic psychological needs for competence, relatedness, and autonomy. Opportunities to satisfy any of these three needs contribute to people's being motivated (as opposed to amotivated); however, opportunities to satisfy the need for autonomy are necessary for people to be self-determined rather than controlled. (Deci, Vallerand, Pelletier, & Ryan, 1991, pp. 327–328)

What may seem somewhat abstract can be well explained with an example: Why is working in project groups usually motivating?

1. In projects, participants shape their work together and are thus socially related.
2. In projects, participants make decisions independently and are proactive and autonomous.
3. In projects, participants achieve a self-imposed goal; they experience their competence.

This can be seen clearly in music, for example. Many highly motivated people make music together (e.g., in a choir, a rock group, or a string quartet). There they experience precisely these three dimensions of social integration, autonomy, and competence.

Promoting Self-Determined Motivation

Deci et al. (1991) summarize the importance of promoting self-determination as follows:

> We believe that promoting self-determined motivation in students should be given high priority in educational endeavors. The key elements are what we refer to as autonomy support and interpersonal involvement. When significant adults—most notably, teachers and parents—are involved with students in an autonomy-supportive way, the students will be more likely to retain their natural curiosity (their intrinsic motivation for learning) and to develop autonomous forms of self-regulation through the process of internalization and integration.
>
> Autonomy support by adults begins with taking the child's frame of reference. By understanding a child's motivational and cognitive starting point, we can relate to him or her in a way that encourages internal motivation for engagement in the education enterprise. The specific supports for self-determination we suggest include offering choice, minimizing controls, acknowledging feelings, and making available information that is needed for decision making and for performing the target task.
>
> With a general attitude of valuing children's autonomy and by providing the type of autonomy support just mentioned, we stand the greatest chance of bringing about the types of educational contexts that facilitate conceptual understanding, flexible problem solving, personal adjustment, and social responsibility. This is so whether one's analysis focuses on the classroom, the school system, or society. (p. 342)

Textbox 2.2 ACTIVITIES AND SUGGESTIONS

SOME THOUGHTS ON SELF-DIRECTED WORK WITH THIS BOOK

About the Ten Hints for Successful Working with This Book

How do you see it? Which of the above ten points do you fully agree with? List your reasoning in a few keywords.

And which of the above ten points do you see rather critically? Again, provide a brief rationale, and seek an opportunity to discuss these objections with a professional.

"Writing Your Own Handbook"

This workbook suggests that you actively engage in professional practices, including in section 6, "Write Your Own Handbook." If you are in training to be a teacher, this can also be combined with a portfolio. Note in bullet points the form in which you find it most useful to write your "handbook."

Self-Determination Theory

According to Deci and Ryan's theory, self-determination is very motivating. Connect the theory to your past experiences (in school and out of school).

Think about when you have been in a self-determined situation where you experienced the three motivational factors of competence, autonomy, and relatedness. Write down at least five examples in note form.

Part II

SUPPORTING INDIVIDUAL LEARNING

Teachers have an educational mission, and this includes, above all, helping young people to develop and enabling every student to progress. They need teachers who set challenging goals but who can also identify where support is needed, what the next steps are, and how to help those who have not understood a subject or are discouraged.

Teachers, therefore, need the *core practices of learning support*, particularly the challenging practices of diagnosing and providing feedback, which are eminently important in everyday school life.

These practices are introduced, described, discussed, and explored in depth.

Chapter Three

Supporting Individual Learning

What It Is All About

FROM "DESIGNING INSTRUCTION" TO "DESIGNING STUDENT LEARNING"

The central goal of school and teaching is the progress of the students. Even though this goal is self-evident, it is sometimes lost sight of in everyday school life. Why is that so?

For a long time, many teachers have considered one of their main tasks to be designing and delivering lessons. The underlying reasoning is, "If the teaching is good, the students will learn something." That may be true most of the time; there is nothing wrong with that. "Good teaching" is, in a sense, the medium through which a capable teacher can support student learning.

Nevertheless, this strong focus on "good teaching" also has a problematic side: well-designed instruction is *not the goal, but an important means to an end*. The goal, as stated earlier, is student progress. The teacher should do everything to help students progress, learn, improve, or understand something more deeply, even if at times he or she focuses solely on preparing and designing lessons. *Teaching is not an end in itself, but it should have an effect.* To put it pointedly, the overriding question is not so much "How do I design instruction?" but "How do I design student learning?"

Of course, many factors contribute to successful learning. Relevant practices are addressed in every chapter of this book. This chapter is about how teachers can support individual student progress.

EVERYONE LEARNS DIFFERENTLY—
LEARNING IS ALWAYS INDIVIDUAL

No two people learn the same way, which is sometimes forgotten: prior knowledge, interests, ability to concentrate, language skills, comprehension, memory, and much more vary from person to person. The big challenge is to make sure that time at school is productive for everyone and not wasted for anyone, that everyone can take something with them, not just in general but actually every day, every hour!

This "right to learn" must be guaranteed by the schools. The focus is therefore on the individual growth and development and also on the particularities of the individual students. If you perceive them as distinctive individuals and recognize where they stand at the moment, you can accompany them individually and help them to take the next step. The term "scaffolding" has become established for this.

One could argue that the really good teachers hardly need to provide individual support because the instruction is so very clear. It's true: the teacher can be confident that *some* students can overcome learning difficulties on their own or challenge themselves further when underchallenged. They can even work on gaps in their knowledge independently, or they can occupy themselves meaningfully if they are underchallenged. In other words, they can make the most of what good teaching has to offer.

But not all students are able to help themselves, no matter how good the teaching. For many learning processes, students need a counterpart who challenges them, recognizes difficulties and potential, and offers appropriate support, encouragement, or new challenges when needed.

THE TEACHER SHARES RESPONSIBILITY
FOR ENSURING THAT LEARNING TAKES PLACE

For a long time, the notion has been prevalent in the school tradition and even in research on learning that the teacher is supposed to design lessons that are technically correct, clear, and comprehensible and that it is the students' responsibility to derive benefit from these opportunities. Underlying this approach is the idea that one cannot really influence what is learned; that the receptive and learning abilities of the learners can be changed little; that the cognitive abilities, the willingness to make an effort, and the "diligence" of the students would be crucial, and that all this is not in the hands of the teacher. So much for a widespread conventional notion in the past.

But only offers that are accepted have an effect. Therefore, in recent decades there has been a growing consensus that teachers also bear a share of responsibility for whether and how students use what teachers offer. "The teacher understands how learners grow and develop": this is the first sentence of the first standard of the well-known InTASC standards, which have been regularly updated since the early 1990s (CCSSO, 2013, p. 13). And the second standard makes it unmistakably clear what is expected of teachers: "The teacher uses understanding of individual differences and diverse cultures and communities to ensure inclusive learning environments that enable each learner to meet high standards" (p. 17).

Today, it is generally assumed in schools that, on the one hand, the offer is to be designed optimally and that, on the other hand, the use of the offer by the students is to be promoted and supported. The research on teaching and learning of the last decades has provided numerous findings that learning progress depends to a large extent on the use of learning opportunities. The relations between opportunity and use are sometimes depicted in opportunity-use models, as shown in figure 3.2.

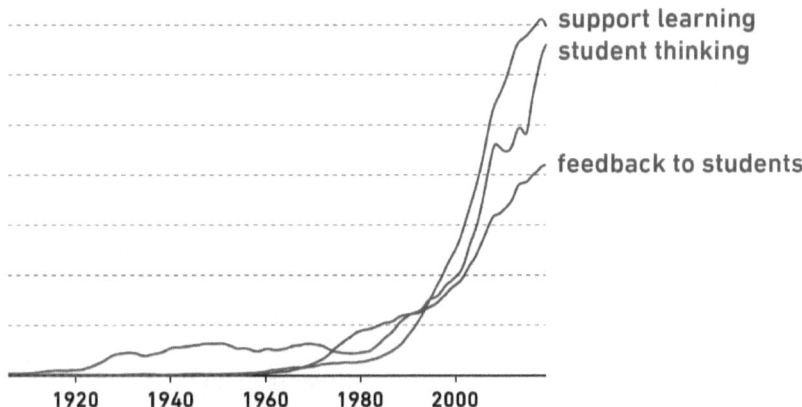

Figure 3.1. Relative proportion of mentions in American English texts. An indication of the increasing importance of learning support is the number of mentions in the professional literature. The graphs show the relative shares of the three phrases in the total stock of Google Books (American English by 2019). *https://books.google.com/ngrams/*

In short, a professional teacher is not only good at teaching but also actively supports the learners in finding access to the content. This turn is reflected not least in some terms that have increasingly seeped into professional vocabulary (see figure 3.1).

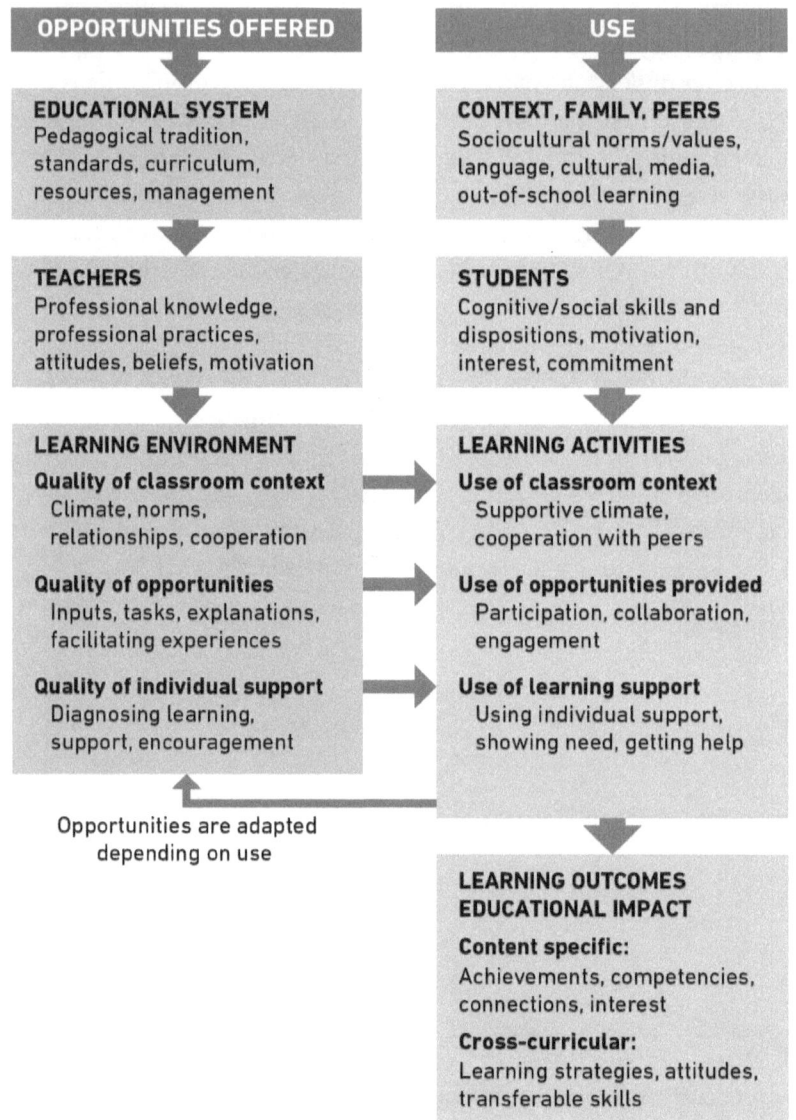

Figure 3.2.   Only what is used is of use: Opportunity–use model. *Adapted based on several sources (e.g., Fend, 1998; Reusser & Pauli, 2010). Author created.*

Textbox 3.1 ACTIVITIES AND SUGGESTIONS

TWENTY MINUTES THINKING ABOUT OPPORTUNITY AND USE IN THE SCHOOL AND CLASSROOM

Teaching Versus Supporting

"Classroom instruction, schedules, and timetables in today's school prioritize delivering lessons." Note here in keywords the extent to which you have experienced this to be true and whether you think the statement is true in this form.

Being completely honest, what concerns you more the next time you teach: the design of the lesson or the students' learning? Give reasons for your answer.

Two Statements for Discussion

Write down in keywords your thoughts on the following two statements:

- Statement 1: "Designed lessons are the most important learning environment for students. Therefore, the teacher should focus on the planning and implementation of lessons."

- Statement 2: "The sophisticated design of lessons is overrated. In the end, the only thing that matters is that as many students as possible enjoy learning as much as possible."

Unused Opportunities: What Was the Reason?

Your own experiences in school make it easier to take the learner's perspective. Think of two to four teaching situations from different phases of your school time in which you missed the boat. Looking back, what would it have taken to get back on track?

WHAT IS NEEDED FOR SUCCESSFUL SUPPORT OF INDIVIDUAL LEARNING?

The practices of individual learning support are complex. Teachers need a diverse repertoire on different levels. Here you will have the opportunity to get to know the elements, to deal with them, and to link them together. Especially when it comes to the topic of learning support, it is important that you actively look for opportunities to practice. Over time, you will learn to use and orchestrate the elements flexibly.

The Social Construction of Knowledge: A Look at the Learning Psychology Approach of Lev Vygotsky

The importance of this approach for all learning in and out of school cannot be overestimated. "Social construction of knowledge" means that people need other people to learn something and to be able to internalize the knowledge in the end. Hardly anyone learns to speak or read or knit or play a musical instrument without other people. The Russian researcher Lev Vygotsky (1896–1934) was the first to intensively research and describe it, which, along with Jean Piaget, earned him a permanent place among the pioneers of learning psychology. He stated that in the cultural development of a child, everything happens first on a social level before it takes shape within the child. All higher mental functions, according to Vygotsky, are based on real relationships between people.

Vygotsky's approach is significant for all learning. With the so-called zone of proximal development, Vygotsky created a plausible metaphor for learning in a social context. It can simply be called the "learning zone." Vygotsky takes it to mean the distance between what a child can accomplish on his or her own and what he or she can master with adult guidance or with more capable peers (Vygotsky, 1935/1978, p. 86). This is illustrated in figure 3.3. Between what is learned and what is unattainable you find the zone in which people can learn something and need more or less support. One could compare the zone to a flashlight beam at night: the zone of next development extends as far as the flashlight shines.

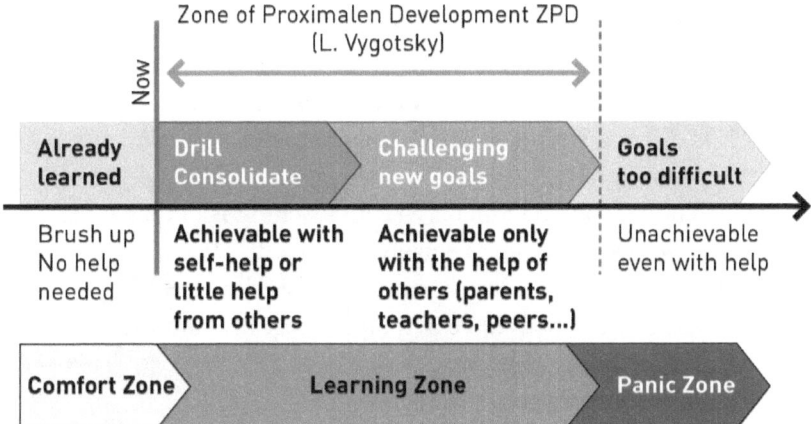

Figure 3.3. Illustration of the zone of proximal development (see also Hattie & Clarke, 2018; Tharp & Gallimore, 1991). *Author created.*

The Relevance of the Zone of Proximal Development for Learning in the Classroom

When it comes to a particular learning content, *all students have their own zone of next development* or *learning zone* where progress is possible. If the challenge is too low ("comfort zone") or too high ("panic zone"), they will learn nothing. In a classroom setting, the teacher always faces students who are in vastly different places when it comes to a particular thing. Some can't follow because it's too difficult, some are underchallenged and don't make progress, and some are lucky that the demands of the lesson are right in their zone of next development. Only those students can benefit if they want to.

An important factor is *time.* Classroom instruction is usually well paced, leaving limited time for those who have missed out. Some students would be quite successful if they had a little more time or could briefly catch up or practice something they missed. But as it is, they risk missing the boat.

In addition, there is another difficulty: there is not just one subject in a lesson; rather, numerous different subjects overlap. Depending on their abilities and prior knowledge, not all students are addressed in the same way. A student may do well on one topic and fail shortly thereafter, and the opposite is true for the next student. In other words, *teaching never fits in the learning zone for all students*. One time it fits for these, another time for those. Figure 3.4 illustrates this fact. A teacher can never reach all students of a learning group at the same time, no matter how flexible and skillful the teaching may be: student 1 is constantly in panic mode, students 8 and 9 are simply underchallenged, and only students 2 and 6 can benefit in an optimal way.

One could now conclude that classroom teaching is outdated. However, this is by no means the case. Precisely because the teaching of an entire learning group is so demanding, it should be conducted in a highly professional manner, and teachers have a great interest in establishing, training, and further developing effective practices for this purpose. This will be the subject of further chapters.

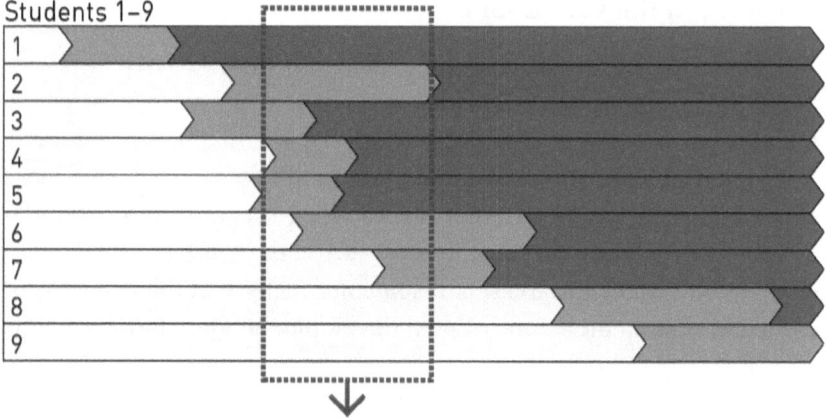

Supporting **a whole group** never reaches all students in the learning zone. Some students stay in the comfort zone, others are in the **panic zone**.

Figure 3.4. Illustration of the different zones of proximal development of the students in a learning group. *Author created.*

Textbox 3.2 ACTIVITIES AND SUGGESTIONS

FIVE SUGGESTIONS ON HOW TO APPROACH THE TOPIC OF LEARNING SUPPORT IN YOUR DAILY PRACTICE

1. **Provide Learning Support to Students**

   You should be able to connect what is explained and discussed here with actual experiences that do not go back too far.

   Continually seek opportunities to support learners. A few hints:
   - If you are teaching alone, use periods of individual or partner seatwork to support particular students as needed.
   - If you are in an internship, focus entirely on learning support during periods of co-teaching and leave classroom teaching to others.
   - Support students outside of class, such as in private tutoring.

   Help students within your circles of friends and acquaintances with their homework.

2. **Keep a Record of How You Support Learning**

   Conversations between students and teachers are fleeting, so you should collect traces of your learning support:
   - Keep, copy, or photograph what is written down during conversations.
   - Make an audio recording with your smartphone if the student agrees.
   - Have a third person record you on video if everyone involved agrees.

3. **Become Aware of Your Practices (i.e., How Your Learning Support Currently "Works")**

   In the following pages, you will learn about many aspects of learning support. In each case, you will be asked to consider and analyze your experiences with learning support from that particular point of view. Then, on the next occasion, you can pay special attention to the selected aspect.

4. **Observe Yourself**

   Even at this stage, you will probably notice how you intuitively design learning support.
   - Do you know exactly where the difficulty lies?
   - Do you ask questions to find out what the student can or cannot do?
   - Do you explain? Or do you ask questions first and foremost?
   - Do you ask several questions in a row?

- Do you ask questions to encourage the student to solve the problem him- or herself?
- Do you explain with examples?
- Do you explain by showing something?

5. **Note in Your "Handbook" What Is Remarkable, Learned, or Insufficient**

    Experiences and insights are quickly forgotten if you do not record them. Use your "handbook" in whatever form you prefer. You might read again the recommendations for the handbook in chapter 2.

Chapter Four

Diagnostics

How Do I Find Out Where the Students Stand?

DIAGNOSING IS INDISPENSABLE

Teaching and learning support are a blind flight if one does not know where the students stand. Teachers may set tasks that are too difficult, or they may expand on things that students have long understood. Diagnostic skills are therefore absolutely central for teachers.

Diagnostics requires explanation. When a teacher diagnoses, he or she obtains *relevant information about the current state of learning, the learning processes, and the special conditions of a student in order to be able to support him or her in a targeted and effective way.*

Some experts also speak of "professional vision" (see textbox 4.1). The teacher tries to find out or visualize where a child currently stands, how he or she is progressing in learning, where difficulties arise, and what could slow down or help progress. This is the condition for the teacher to be able to influence learning in a positive and solution-oriented way. Diagnostics therefore means first of all that the teacher learns something about the state of the students. The goal is to *accurately identify each student's learning level, difficulties, and potentials*, especially in the classroom.

Teachers should not only find out what the learners can do and have understood but also *why* this is so. Only then can the teacher provide meaningful support, if necessary. However, this requires a relatively quick assessment of the situation using simple procedures; the diagnosis of the causes of the problem must be *immediate*.

> Textbox 4.1
>
> ### PROFESSIONAL VISION—NOTICING—REASONING
>
> Professional vision has been identified as an important element of teacher expertise that can be developed in teacher education. It describes the use of knowledge to notice and interpret significant features of classroom situations.
>
>> It is important for pre-service teachers to develop professional vision—the ability to use professional knowledge to notice and reason about specific aspects of teaching and learning processes in classroom situations. . . .
>>
>> A teacher's ability to attend intentionally to classroom events that are important to the processes of teaching and learning, for example, events that influence student learning in a positive or negative way, is referred to as noticing. . . .
>>
>> Reasoning involves the process of making sense of what has been noticed by linking observed situations to knowledge, in this case, about teaching and learning. Thus, knowledge is used to explain noticed situations as well as to predict further learning processes. (Schäfer & Seidel, 2015, pp. 35–38)
>
> For more on this, see Sherin, Russ, Sherin, and Colestock (2008), Rosaen and Florio-Ruane (2008), Seidel and Stürmer (2014), Nilssen (2009, "The Habit of Seeing"), Wallach and Even (2005, "Hearing Students").

DIAGNOSING AS PART OF FORMATIVE ASSESSMENT

The term "formative assessment" has become common. Using the word "assessment" could give the incorrect impression that testing is involved. Hattie and Clarke (2018) therefore suggest that it is more appropriate to use the term "formative evaluation." In this book, the terms "assessment" and "evaluation" are used largely interchangeably.

All information available about student learning—observations, tests, written work, and so on—can be used formatively and summatively. Mistakenly, summative evaluation is often associated with grades and selection. This is not correct. Summative evaluation simply provides information about what students are able to do on a topic, what they have learned and what they have not learned, in order to plan next steps on this basis.

How teachers give selective grades is an entirely different matter and must not necessarily be linked to formative and summative evaluation.

According to Wiliam and Thompson (2008), five elements make up formative evaluation, of which feedback occupies a particularly important position (see figure 4.1).

Black and Wiliam (2009) summarize what formative evaluation consists of and cite numerous research findings to support their model. Admittedly, the model is not obvious at first glance. However, it accurately depicts the two main dimensions of formative evaluation:

1. Read from top to bottom, it shows that everyone—teacher, peers, and individual learners—has a responsibility for learning. All are expected to contribute actively and cooperatively to learning success in their respective roles, and thus learning in the classroom becomes a collaborative project.
2. Read from left to right, it shows the "standard process" in learning support:
   - What is to be achieved in the first place? (Goals)
   - Where are we now, or where are difficulties? (Current status)
   - What needs to be done to move forward? (Next steps)

	Where the Learner is Going	Where the Learner is right now	How to Get There
Teacher	**1** Clarifying learning intentions and sharing and criteria for success	**2** Engineering effective classroom discussions and tasks that elicit evidence of learning	**3** Providing feedback that moves learners forward
Peer	Understanding and sharing learning intentions and criteria for success	**4** Activating students as instructional resources for one another	
Learner	Understanding learning intentions and criteria for success	**5** Activating students as the owners of their own learning	

Figure 4.1. Relating strategies of formative assessment to instructional processes. *Wiliam & Thompson, 2008, p. 63.*

Hattie and Clarke (2018) choose a similar model. Addressing teachers directly, they list five factors that are important in formative evaluation. The factors are stunningly simple, plausible, and apparently highly effective in improving learning outcomes. In terms of content, they are almost congruent with Black and Wiliam's analysis, to which they refer, but they add another aspect, according to which *formative evaluation affects motivation and self-esteem*. These are their five factors:

1. The provision of effective *feedback* to students
2. The active *involvement of students* in their own learning
3. *Adjusting teaching* to take into account the results of assessment
4. A recognition of the profound *influence assessment has on the motivation and self-esteem* of students, both of which are crucial influences on learning
5. The need for students to be able to *assess themselves* and understand how to improve (p. 9)

Thus, diagnosis and feedback are key components of formative evaluation. Although the two go hand in hand, for clarity we focus first on diagnostics and then on feedback in the next chapter.

DIAGNOSES: QUICK AND/OR THOROUGH?

Quick and spontaneous diagnoses can be fuzzy, arbitrary, or even irrational and can lead to blatant misjudgments. This poses a dilemma for teachers. On the one hand, the teacher often has to make a decision quickly and act swiftly. His or her reflex diagnosis then runs the risk of being superficial and one-sided. On the other hand, if the teacher wants to know exactly, he or she must take time for a thorough, systematic examination of the student's learning status and, if necessary, his or her learning difficulties, for example by conducting a test, analyzing the student's work, or questioning him or her more thoroughly. However, this latter systematic diagnostic is not the issue here, even though it is sometimes useful in a summative assessment.

The question arises: Are there only these two alternatives—spontaneous and sometimes unconscious assessment (also called "implicit diagnostics" or "everyday diagnostics"), or systematic diagnosis along defined procedures and criteria (also called "explicit diagnostics" or "professional diagnostics")?

Well, there should be a *third option*, because the sheer number of professional teachers who can diagnose both quickly and accurately proves it. There is a *practice of accurate diagnosing*; Ruiz-Primo (2011) also calls it "informal formative evaluation." It forms the link between spontaneous judgment and analytical diagnosing. The key to this practice is a *sharpened intuition*.

INTUITIVE DIAGNOSES: IMPORTANT, CHALLENGING, LEARNABLE

The term "intuition" is hardly associated with a reliable procedure but rather with a "gut feeling." However, the highly developed intuition can be very precise and accurate. It is one of the most important skills for a teacher to have in order to act professionally in everyday life, and it is a necessary part of all practices. Observations and decisions based on intuition usually proceed quickly, yet deliberately, and they still leave room for brief reflection. In many pedagogical situations, there is no time for elaborate procedures.

Experienced teachers recognize quickly and precisely where the shoe pinches or where an opportunity opens up. In doing so, they rely largely on their intuitive judgment. To put it in a nutshell, accurate intuitions are neither spontaneous ideas nor a vague gut feeling, nor do they arise from an innate gift. "Intuition is grounded on knowledge that is developed by explicit and implicit processes of professional learning, but not on innate capabilities" (Harteis & Gruber, 2008, p. 75).

Accurate intuitions are something that people can train in themselves with knowledge, practice, and experience: "Intuition is the result of learning" (Hogarth, 2010, p. 339). Intuitions are neither unconscious nor irrational. For several decades, psychologists and neurologists have been researching how intuitive judgments are formed and how reliable they are.

Zander, Öllinger, and Volz (2016), for example, see intuition as sensitivity to unconscious information that can lead to productive insights.

Most researchers agree that intuition arises from one's tacit knowledge (Polanyi, 1966) and must be learned if it is to be coherent, especially in the teaching profession (e.g., Sipman, Thölke, Martens, & McKenney, 2019). Thus, the more the teacher has knowledge and experience about analogous situations and has been able to learn from them, the more reliable the intuitive judgments tend to be. In this regard, *learning experiences in professional contexts are absolutely crucial for the development of intuition* (Harteis & Billett, 2013).

Textbox 4.2

MICHAEL POLANYI (1891–1976)

Polanyi, born in Hungary, studied chemistry in Germany and, after Hitler's rise to power, took a position in England, where he worked throughout his life. He was active in many fields (chemistry, philosophy, economics). The contributions Polanyi made to the social sciences include an understanding of tacit knowledge. "Tacit knowledge," as distinct from explicit knowledge, is an influential term developed by Polanyi to describe the idea of know-how, or the ability to do something without necessarily being able to articulate it or even being aware of all the dimensions, for example, being able to ride a bicycle or play a musical instrument. Polanyi opened his book *The Tacit Dimension* with the following words:

> I shall reconsider human knowledge by starting from the fact that we know more than we can tell. This fact seems obvious enough; but it is not easy to say exactly what it means. Take an example. We know a person's face, and can recognize it among a thousand, indeed among a million. Yet we usually cannot tell how we recognize a face we know. So most of this knowledge cannot be put into words. (Polanyi, 1966, p. 4)

For many researchers of intuition, Polanyi's concept of tacit knowledge has proved very fruitful.

Textbox 4.3 FURTHER INFORMATION AND RESOURCES

INTUITION: THE SYNTHESIS OF REFLEX AND ANALYSIS

Pure routines and reflexive reactions do not have a good reputation; they hardly leave time for reflection and for situation-appropriate action. In teacher education, therefore, conscious analysis is often proposed and practiced as an alternative. This is possible and useful with student teachers because accompanying formats and time are provided for it. But we all know that thorough analytical reflection can only happen outside of teaching, *not during teaching*.

In a way, intuition is the link between reflex and analysis. It is both a short reflection and a quick decision. Intuition combines the advantages of the other two approaches—on the one hand, the practiced action, and on the other hand, the insights from a thorough analysis and reflection.

The crucial point is that coherent intuition can only develop with the help of the other two approaches. It needs both a repertoire of routine actions and the analytical, critical, and informed view from a temporal distance. This means that both have to be practiced intensively and repeatedly, both the routine action and the critical and well-informed analysis.

Trained and sharpened intuition helps one to perceive correctly, to decide appropriately, and to react effectively, and this happens directly in the classroom.

	Reflex	Intuition	Analysis
How rapid is the reaction?	Instant	Rapid	Deliberative
How is the situation captured?	Pattern recognition	Rapid interpretation of the current situation	Thorough review involving discussion and/or analysis
How is a decision made?	Reactive	Intuitive	Deliberative, with some analysis or discussion
What is done?	Routinized action	Routines punctuated by rapid decisions	Planned actions with periodic progress reviews

Figure 4.2. Three modes of cognition: Reflex—intuition—analysis. *Adapted and extended based on Eraut, 2004, p. 260.*

TRAINED AND SHARPENED INTUITIONS COMBINE CONFIDENCE AND FLEXIBILITY

Precisely because teaching is complex, teachers need practices that give them confidence. However, these practices must not be rigid and schematic but should adapt flexibly to the circumstances.

The ability to intuitively recognize, decide, and act conveys *confidence* (e.g., "I know this," "I know that it can work this way," "I have recognized this as right/wrong many times before"). But at the same time, intuitively controlled processes still leave room for pausing and brief reflection—that is, intuitive action control is characterized by *flexibility*.

BETTER JUDGEMENTS THROUGH MORE KNOWLEDGE, PRACTICE, AND EXPERIENCE

It is especially the less experienced teachers and student teachers who are often wrong with their intuitive impressions, assessments, and actions and, moreover, do not always realize it. This is a well-known phenomenon in all subject areas and professions. In contrast, it is known from extensive research on experts (e.g., in chess) that the accuracy and correctness of intuition increases with experience and relevant knowledge and that rapid perception and smooth processing are characteristic of experts' intuitive actions (e.g., Gobet & Chassy, 2009; Ropo, 2004). This novice problem of inaccurate intuitions can be addressed in several ways.

INFORMATION IS NEEDED ABOUT LEARNING PROGRESS AND PROCESSES AND ABOUT BACKGROUND

Teachers and student teachers sometimes rely on their more superficial impressions and do not adequately determine what the situation is really like, whether in a whole class, in a group, or with particular students. So, they lack information. It takes a close look, open listening, engagement in conversations or dialogues, and also a sure instinct to learn more about students' learning progress or state of mind. And it takes remembering things of the past that form the basis of the current situation.

In order to support children or young people, one should also know something about their development. This knowledge cannot be gained in an instant but can only be built up over a longer time. On the basis of past events, an understanding of the current situation may emerge.

Observation and listening—two key sources of information—and their training will be discussed later.

Knowledge

On the one hand, there is a need for content knowledge in the subject matter. Anyone who wants to solve a mathematics problem must be able to identify the cause of the difficulty, and to do this, the mathematics and the specific task must be precisely understood. On the other hand, we need basic knowledge about how students learn and develop. For example, we know how long, say, an elementary school student can listen intently and absorb information, or we know about the turbulence of puberty, or we know about favorable or inhibiting social processes in the classroom. With this knowledge, causes of difficulties can be narrowed down or ruled out.

The stock of knowledge in the form of texts, books, online sources, and so on cannot be tapped during the lesson. Knowledge acquisition is a longer process that happens before or after class. Teacher education offers numerous learning opportunities for this, especially in courses on teaching and learning of subject matters, educational sciences, and professional practice. Locating and linking illuminating sources is undoubtedly part of building professional practices and, in this case, is indispensable for *training* accurate diagnoses.

Practice and Experience Interacting with New Knowledge

However, it would be a mistake to think that teachers must always have their theoretical knowledge mentally present in the classroom. That is simply impossible, and that is not the point; rather, the point is the *training and sharpening of intuitions* on the basis of continuously building implicit or tacit knowledge. The essential thing about learning processes—also with adults!—is that what is learned is deeply anchored in the person. They can dispose of it freely, without ruminating, without straining to remember. The previously processed knowledge has an indirect effect.

Now that the learning process toward intuition has been initiated, acquired knowledge increasingly becomes a part of intuition; it seeps into the practices of intuitive diagnosis, so to speak.

This learning process of student teachers and early career teachers requires systematic practice. As stated earlier, the coherence of intuitions increases primarily with experience. It is therefore important that this process begins in teacher education: through productive learning situations in internships, through conversations and (self-)observations, and through purposeful practice, for which this book provides ample guidance.

But if practice is not targeted, skepticism is warranted. Hascher (2012), an Austrian researcher who has studied practice in depth, found in a major study of internships that "in practice, something is always learned somehow," but specific skills are not developed. She continues,

> Students often jump from one situation to the next, and a systematic shaping of their learning process rarely takes place. Rather, they discover something new every day that they consider highly relevant to the situation, but too rarely integrate it into their competencies and recognize its relevance to their own learning. Fundamentally, therefore, the question must be asked as to how field experiences become learning processes. (Hascher, 2012, p. 122)

Here again, the need for diligent practice is evident. School practicums and internships offer outstanding opportunities for individual practices to be worked on systematically and continuously. In this way, the practices can be developed and internalized to such an extent that they are permanently available, even under stress.

Back to the question of how intuitive diagnoses and decision-making can be improved. Figure 4.3 shows schematically from which resources a decision is fed and where one could start to improve the quality of decisions. When teachers perceive something and make an intuitive assessment, they usually do not consciously draw on knowledge resources but must be confident that they have learned to assess correctly; they use their *tacit knowledge*. And like any learning process, this one needs a lot of completions before it reaches a professional level.

But as already said, intuitions still allow a brief moment of pause to interpret the current situation; otherwise, one would act purely reflexively.

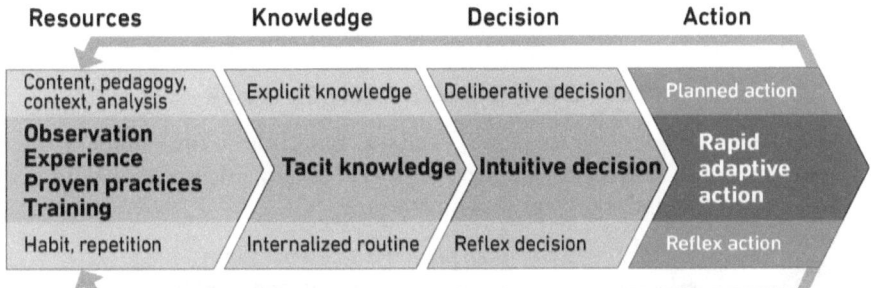

Figure 4.3. Intuition, fed by tacit knowledge, as the most important source of situational decisions. *Author created.*

In this brief moment of review ("Is this right? Am I on the right track?"), the teacher may recall information that he or she has dealt with before. Depending on the situation, it may be professional or psychological knowledge, prior knowledge of the student's history, and so on. Thus, this learning process is never complete, because there will always be slightly different situations and new knowledge that can enrich and improve the practices.

BETTER JUDGMENTS THROUGH MORE COMMITMENT AND HUMILITY

Engagement to Better Understand Learners

Less experienced teachers and student teachers in particular are inevitably so busy with teaching that they cannot always engage with student learning and sensitivities of the students. While understandable, it is still a problem. Those who are in the "designing instruction" mode have less of an eye for the learners. Therefore, switching to the "designing student learning" mode must be done constantly and consciously. It is a matter of practice, will, and even professional ethics to always take the learners' perspective as well.

It is impressive that John Hattie, author of the meta-study named after him (Hattie, 2009), concludes after reviewing all the substudies that the committed teacher is the critical factor in student success.

> Textbox 4.4
>
> **PLEA FOR THE DEDICATED TEACHER**
>
> In his final chapter, Hattie (2009) outlines, based on a large number of impact studies, *the profile of a good teacher*. For him, this is a person who has a favorable influence on student learning.
>
> 1. Teachers are among the most powerful influences in learning.
> 2. Teachers need to be directive, influential, caring, and actively engaged in the passion of teaching and learning.
> 3. Teachers need to be aware of what each and every student is thinking and knowing, to construct meaning and meaningful experiences in light of this knowledge, and to have proficient knowledge and understanding of their content to provide meaningful and appropriate feedback such that each student moves progressively through the curriculum levels.
> 4. Teachers need to know the learning intentions and success criteria of their lessons, know how well they are attaining these criteria for all students, and know where to go next in light of the gap between students' current knowledge and understanding and the success criteria.
>
> Teachers need to relate and then extend multiple ideas such that learners construct and reconstruct knowledge and ideas. It is not the knowledge or ideas, but the learner's construction of this knowledge and these ideas, that is critical. (pp. 238–39, abridged)

Less Overconfidence: Overcoming Unconscious Incompetence

Of course, anyone who has spent over ten thousand hours in school must know something about teaching, at least that is what many student teachers think. Paradoxically, this is not true at all, because from the perspective of their memories of school, they only see a small section of the teacher's tasks, and these are not always of the best quality. Thus, many superficial clichés of teaching are imprinted. In sum, these memories are not really helpful in acting professionally as a teacher. This phenomenon is called "unconscious incompetence" (see textbox 4.5).

As unpleasant, mortifying, and sometimes painful as this realization is, student teachers must first recognize how challenging it is to do right by students. They have to learn to admit that they do not yet understand much of it.

Textbox 4.5 FURTHER INFORMATION AND RESOURCES

UNCONSCIOUS INCOMPETENCE? OVERCONFIDENCE AMONG FIRST-YEAR STUDENT TEACHERS

Over several years, Hartmann and Weiser (2007) studied how prospective teachers at the very beginning of the teacher education program assessed their own teaching competencies. They were asked to comment on the following statement: "Given enough time for lesson preparation, I could deliver lessons in the following subjects at least as well as my former teacher." The results were very surprising: in content knowledge, over 50 percent considered themselves more competent than their former teachers, and with regard to teaching and climate, over 70 percent believed they could do a better job than their former teachers.

Hartmann and Weiser (2007) interpreted the result by referring to the so-called Dunning-Kruger effect. It states that incompetent people tend to systematically overestimate their abilities. This effect was presented and scientifically proven by two American researchers in a highly regarded study (Kruger & Dunning, 1999). They tested three groups of subjects in one area each: assessment of humorous situations, logical thinking, and grammar. Subsequently, test participants were asked to assess their competence in each area. While the competent participants assessed themselves rather critically, the self-assessments of the weakest test participants were always even higher than the overall average; in other words, they massively overestimated themselves. Only after extensive training in the respective area did the weakest succeed in accurately assessing their competencies.

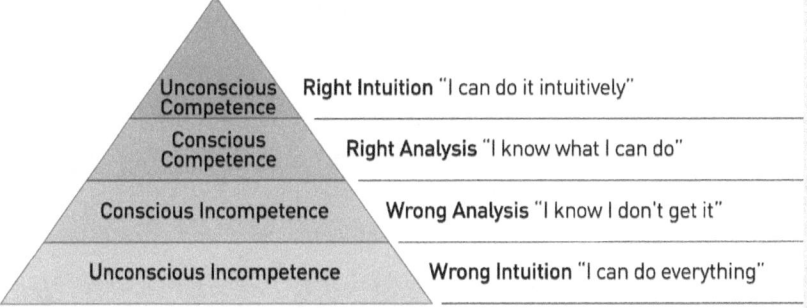

Figure 4.4. From unconscious incompetence to unconscious competence. *The first description of this model is found in Broadwell (1969). Since then, it has been presented and varied in many forms.*

Hartmann and Weiser recognize this phenomenon in their student teachers:

> In our supervision of student teachers after the initial practicum, we experience similar changes. The student teachers assess their competencies lower after the practicum, because the overestimation of themselves has been corrected in confrontation with practice, even if this can be painful. For example, one student teacher who was very convinced of his abilities in the course described his experience after the practicum as follows: 'I think it's a madness that we have to get a bloody nose in the practicum.' The sometimes painful process of becoming aware of one's own incompetence and the subsequent learning processes can be explained with the model of conscious incompetence. (p. 39)

Textbox 4.6 ACTIVITIES AND SUGGESTIONS

A "SELF-EXPERIMENT" AND SOME SUGGESTIONS FOR THINKING ABOUT THE ENGAGED TEACHER

What Do You Actually Know About Your Students?

Engage in a little self-experiment. Imagine two students from a class you have recently taught. Write down exactly how they learn and where they have difficulties, strengths, and idiosyncrasies. Write a half page to a full page each about what you know about these students. Afterward, consider these questions:

- What did you base your assessment on: observations, documents, grades, conversations, feelings, or something else?
- What information are you missing?
- Have you done justice to the two students with your descriptions?

Next, seek a casual and informal conversation with each student to learn more and adjust your assessment if necessary. This is possible at all levels, from kindergarten to grade 12.

The Profile of a Dedicated Teacher

In textbox 4.4, some key points are cited that, according to John Hattie, belong to the profile of the dedicated teacher.

1. Do you agree with the first three points? If not, why not? Note where you agree and where you have reservations (e.g., in your "handbook"), and discuss them with peers or professionals.

> 2. If you have reservations about the second point, comment again after you have worked through part III of this book, "Managing Instruction."
> 3. For the first three items, assess the extent to which you match the descriptions (on a scale of one to ten).
>
> Check your assessment again in a few weeks.
>
> **Conscious Incompetence**
>
> In the previous text on unconscious incompetence, it is suggested that becoming aware of one's own incompetence is an important first step toward competence.
>
> 1. Are there areas where you felt competent, but upon closer scrutiny you begin to doubt your competence? Which areas?
> 2. Write down at least ten areas of teaching in which you feel really incompetent.
>
> Assign each area to one of the following groups:
>
> - Classroom organization and behavior management
> - Climate and social contacts
> - Providing inputs and explaining
> - Supporting and assisting learners
>
> In this way, you can identify where you personally see the greatest need for development. However, it is important that you discuss this with someone who can give you feedback.

Empathic Observation—Listening—Discovering Traces of Thinking

For most preservice teachers, observation is a rather strenuous thing. In particular, passive observation of classroom teaching, criterion-guided and systematic observation, and logging of what is happening is a little-loved activity. However, that is not what it is about; the point is to gain additional information about specific students *while you are teaching yourself.*

Take Some Time

Does a teacher have time to observe in class at all? Yes, when he or she reserves moments to simply watch and notice—and no, when the entire focus is on controlling what happens in class. Observing students does not mean controlling them. Observers are wide awake, but they let things go for a moment to see what is happening and what helpful information they can glean from what is happening.

Good teachers are genuinely interested in recognizing and understanding how the learners feel about the subject matter at hand. Moreover, they need to exercise empathy, because without it the teacher will hardly be able to comprehend what the students are also emotionally concerned about. Reusser and Fraefel (2017) put it this way:

> Take time to sit down next to a student and look closely at how he or she thinks, what is going on in his or her head, and what problems he or she is having with the assignments. Getting very close to learners' learning processes is . . . the core of the pedagogical activity that teacher education should aim at in a straightforward way. (p. 27)

Create Opportunities

Opportunities for observation can be deliberately created by the teacher:

- No lesson should be so packed that the teacher can never take a step back. Especially *during periods of student activity*, there is an opportunity to simply absorb what is happening.
- *Walking around* the class is a good way to observe and notice things.
- The teacher pays attention to a *specific* student or group of students.
- Many additional possibilities arise when—as is often the case in teacher education and in internships—teaching is done in the form of co-teaching (i.e., when a second or third person is also present). In this way, more time can be spent on observation.

Focus on Specific Situations and Associated Traces of Thinking

The focus of the observation usually results from the teaching situation. For example, if there are math problems to be solved, the teacher will observe how students are progressing with the tasks, what they are writing, where they seem irritated, what signals their body language is sending, and what they are discussing with each other. Whenever possible, teachers should take a look at the written evidence already available—screens, worksheets, notes, sketches, texts, constructions, and so on. These offer insight into thinking patterns and state of mind. In this way, the teacher may be able to follow the thinking steps or blockages in a text or an arithmetic problem, or the teacher may be able to see at which point the student breaks off, or perhaps the form of presentation already gives clues to the state of mind.

Relate to the Personal Development of the Student

Observations are focused on the moment: What am I seeing now? What is observable? The "now" provides a lot of information if you are willing to read it. But every action also has an antecedent; there are *reasons why students behave the way they do*. We can only understand them if we have an idea of the stage of development they are in, at every level.

The context matters. For example, the teacher knows what academic problems the child has been struggling with, or the teacher knows that the student hates open-ended tasks with no clear and obvious way to solve them, or the teacher knows that this boy is struggling to manage his time well, and so on. When the current observation can be placed in a larger context, new possibilities for understanding arise.

Textbox 4.7 FURTHER INFORMATION AND RESOURCES

TRAINING TO OBSERVE WITH THE HELP OF VIDEOS

Observing by means of videos is very effective. Where else in real professional life can you simply stop and scroll back? Videos help to sharpen one's own perception outside the classroom, to check one's own interpretations and decisions, and to think through better variants if necessary.

Since digital videos are so easily accessible and their production and distribution has become very simple, the threshold for their use in teacher education is lower. While the analog videos of the last century were still very cumbersome to use and were mainly used in research, instructional videos are becoming more and more common and are used in courses and workshops in education and training. One can work with ready-made ("foreign") videos for training purposes, most of which are already well selected and instructive. Or videos of one's own teaching can be analyzed, which takes some getting used to at the beginning but is very productive overall, because one also has a lot of background information that is not visible in the video.

Since about 2000, there have been increasing reports of experiences, recommendations, and research findings on the use of instructional videos in teacher education. Here, a widely tested process in four steps is proposed, based on various sources (Biaggi, Krammer, & Hugener, 2013; Santagata & Guarino, 2011).

The instruction relates to a course in teacher education. It is done *with third-party videos* (i.e., not with videos of the student teachers themselves). All student teacher activity is supervised and supported by a teacher educator. However, the procedure can also be adapted to other settings.

Step 1: Clarify the Encountered Teaching Situation and the Expectations for the Students

First, clarify what the scene is about and what the students are supposed to do and learn. Ideally, the student teachers first work on the tasks and assignments given to the students themselves, then discuss different ways of solving them.

Step 2: Observe the Students (Behavior, Learning, and Thinking Processes)

It is crucial to first take your eyes off the teacher and shift your perspective to the learners. The focus of attention should be on the students' behavior. One must try to understand what is going on with the students, what they are actually doing, how they are doing it, and what they might be thinking.

That's not always easy, because you don't see what is happening in their heads, and sometimes you don't even see the products (e.g., texts, calculations, notes). So it is all the more important to understand, at least in one scene of the video, what exactly is going on in order to develop an understanding of this student.

Step 3: Analyze the Teacher's Actions and Their Effects

Next, the teacher is in view, especially how he or she may or may not be influencing the students' learning. One can make assumptions about whether there are connections between the teacher's actions and the students' learning activities. If possible, connections are also made to theoretical knowledge, such as instructional concepts or knowledge about learning, and of course content knowledge.

Step 4: Propose and Reason for Alternatives

The goal of the last step is for the student teachers to develop suggestions to optimize the lesson, which they can also rationalize by establishing links between their suggestions and knowledge on content, educational science, and learning and developmental psychology.

This approach has been developed for teacher education courses, but the basic structure can also be carried out without a teacher educator—alone, in pairs or in small groups, and also with videos of their own teaching. The advantage of such a structured and streamlined procedure is that it prevents you from judging too quickly and forces you to observe from the learners' perspective. Without this change of perspective, the yield is lower, since it should be primarily about the students' learning processes and not about the teacher's performance.

ENGAGING IN CONVERSATIONS— AND ABOVE ALL, LISTENING

Students are your partners. With them, you have a common interest, which is to move forward. Certainly, there will be differences about how and when and where the journey should go. It is therefore important to understand what the students are concerned about.

No Pseudo-Conversations with Stilted Questions

The obvious thing to do is talk to the student—not classroom talk but dialogues with a student, occasionally with a group. But watch out! Many teacher-student conversations are one-way: the teacher asks questions and provides stimuli, and the students respond in monosyllables, if at all. Stilted teacher questions are poison for a real dialogue. Most adults would become quite annoyed if you tried to get them to talk with pseudo-questions. So, it's not surprising that students would be reluctant to engage.

The project that unites you and the learners is called "making progress"—in all areas, not just in the subject that is currently in demand. Therefore, develop within yourself a genuine interest in the learners and express it. On this basis, authentic conversations can emerge. These do not have to be long and grave; often giving the student a brief sign of understanding directly in class is enough.

Let the Students Talk—They Give You Unique Insights

Most teachers talk a lot, explain, offer solutions and strategies, and want to help. But are they listening as well? Stephen Burt introduces his book *The Art of Listening in Coaching and Mentoring* this way: "Listening is the heart of coaching. . . . Not only is listening a core skill and an essential enabler, it can also resolve issues and generate solutions" (Burt, 2019, p. 1). Those who listen learn a great deal, and they also do the other person a favor by giving him or her the opportunity to express him- or herself. Therefore, let the students talk.

But the important thing is that the students can express themselves freely; they do not have to follow any rules of conduct for one-on-one conversations. The starting point of such conversations is usually a real learning problem, and that's a good thing. If you simply listen without trying to sell anything, chances are good that you will find your way into a genuine conversation. What you learn can help you and the learner navigate the realities of school learning, uncover difficulties, solve a specific problem, set meaningful goals, rediscover interest, adjust pace, try new things, and so on.

In addition, the students always give you feedback—whether openly or "between the lines." In this way, you learn what the students want to tell you directly or indirectly. It may concern the learning material, the tasks, the difficulty of the objectives, the climate, or your way of teaching or even your person. Talking to learners without fear therefore gives you

---

Textbox 4.8

STUDENT-TEACHER FEEDBACK

Student feedback or student-teacher feedback can also be understood as a written survey of the students about the lessons and/or the teacher. There are now many proven and standardized instruments available for classroom evaluation and student feedback. While such methods can supplement the teacher's own observations, they are usually time-consuming and often provide only averaged scores with not too much significance.

important clues as to how you should go about developing lessons and learning opportunities.

FIND OUT WHICH LEVEL IS INVOLVED

Anyone who carries out observations must also be able to do something with them, must be able to make sense of them. Most people have a quick hand with interpretations. Often incidents are even interpreted hastily without knowing enough. Therefore, one should learn to narrow down the information to focus on what one is dealing with at the moment. This is explained by an example.

Textbox 4.9

FOUR LEVELS: AN EXAMPLE

In a foreign language class, the teacher is watching a student during seatwork. Suddenly, the student violently pushes away his worksheet and says he doesn't understand. The teacher wonders why he is giving up in frustration. Here are four likely causes.

First Possibility: The Student Has a Problem with the Subject Matter

It's the task he's not getting anywhere with. It may be too difficult for him or too unclearly formulated. Or he has forgotten the crucial vocabulary and cannot make sense of it. Or he does not know how to form the corresponding tense.

Second Possibility: There Is a Lack of Strategy

The student realizes that he is having trouble, but he doesn't have a plan for how to go about it. He doesn't quite know what the problem is. Possible strategies (e.g., rereading the example sentence, looking up the forgotten words, asking a neighbor for help) do not occur to him, or he cannot decide how to proceed.

Third Possibility: He Cannot Organize Himself

He wants to get the task done as quickly as possible and doesn't take any time. He is already thinking about other things again and is distracting himself. He is only aware of his displeasure and does not notice, for example, that the untidy table robs him of his concentration or that the thought of the next unfinished task distracts him.

Fourth Possibility: Something Personal Absorbs Him

He is totally absorbed in something else and has no interest in learning at all. He may not even be aware of it. It might be something pleasant (he is looking forward to a date) or something stressful (he is having a heated argument with a colleague) or something family related that is nobody's business here.

What Should the Teacher Do Now?

It would be pointless to explain a fact of grammar if a personal problem haunts him; it would be pointless to recommend a learning strategy if he can no longer cope with the clutter on his desk. If the teacher wants to help him, he must hit the level.

The Four Levels According to Hattie and Timperley (2007)

The above four possibilities (in textbox 4.9) correspond to the four levels identified by Hattie and Timperley (2007) in their groundbreaking essay "The Power of Feedback":

Level	*Challenge*
Task	Coping with the current task on the matter level
Process	Strategies needed to understand and accomplish the task
Self-regulation	Supervise, direct, and regulate own activities
Self	A personal situation that overrides everything else

The teacher's support only makes sense if he or she knows at which level the challenge is to be placed. Otherwise, we talk past each other and risk confusion and frustration. The correct identification of the levels is a basic prerequisite for successful learning support. And therefore, the teacher needs the necessary information.

Textbox 4.10 ACTIVITIES AND SUGGESTIONS

OBSERVING AND LISTENING IN CLASS: SUGGESTIONS FOR TRAINING

Below are several suggestions on how you can practice observing and listening. Pay attention to the following four things in each suggestion:

Try to Understand

Observing and listening means gaining information. Observation can be trained—not passive observation, but active effort to understand what is going on with a student.

Train and Share

It is important to invest time in the training of observing and listening and to exchange ideas with peers and experts, and also directly with the students when an informal opportunity arises.

Combine Training Variants

You can change the order of the following training variants or combine them.

See the Learning Processes and the Individuals

The processes, difficulties, and successes around learning are one thing, but also see the individuals—that is, the person's peculiarities, strengths, weaknesses, motives, frustrations, and yes, perhaps crises. Do not judge, but simply perceive and feel into the person. One sentence that helps is "How would I feel in his or her place?"

Observing and Listening: Practicing While Teaching Yourself

1. Try to find out by observation and without asking questions whether the class has been able to follow the topic of the lesson. Try to identify exactly who is having difficulties and who is underchallenged. Make notes and check at a later time to what extent you were correct in your assessment.
2. Look around the class and pay attention to students who don't really stand out to you, who don't make themselves known and who don't

talk much. Observe these students closely during the next phase of work. Pay attention to their expressions and try to find out where they stand in relation to the topic of the lesson.
3. Try to find out which student needs your support the most now.

Observing and Listening: Train While Others Teach

First inform the teacher that you will be moving around the classroom.

1. Ask the teacher what he or she wants you to observe during this lesson. Then observe exactly the same thing and compare your perceptions after the lesson.
2. Try to figure out what was missed and how to prevent it from happening in another lesson.
3. Observe which students are attentive or distracted or absent, and pay attention to when each changes. Make guesses as to what influences the changes in attention and discuss it with the teacher afterward.
4. Observe *one* student for an extended period of time; listen to what he or she says, and try to put yourself in his or her place.

Observing, Listening, and Diagnosing: Train with Particular Students

You work with particular students, for example, during seatwork or in a tutoring session, or even when you are helping your own or a neighbor's children at home. This setting is particularly suitable for practicing listening skills.

1. Create a relaxed atmosphere so that the student does not become stressed.
   - Ask the student to explain in as much detail as possible where the problem is.
   - Have the student explain what he or she already knows about the issue.
   - Talk as little as possible.
2. Practice categorizing into the four levels according to Hattie and Timperley. Then try to find out carefully in the conversation whether you are right with your assumption.
3. If you hear covert or overt criticism of the school, the lessons, the tasks, the learning content, or yourself, do not react defensively; simply take note of it as a "description of the state" of the learners and imagine how you would feel in their place. Don't react hastily but take your time to think about it carefully.

> **Analyze and Diagnose: Train with Documents**
>
> Examine student work, such as exams and tests, worksheets, notes, essays, videos, drawings, exercise books, and so on. If possible, place multiple documents from a single individual side by side.
>
> - Try to understand the student's thinking and sensitivities when creating the documents.
> - Try to identify the student's development needs.
> - Assign these to the four levels according to Hattie and Timperley.
> - Get a holistic picture of this person.
>
> **Observe and Analyze: Train with Third-Party Videos**
>
> Follow the instructions for working with videos (see textbox 4.7). Adapt the instructions for your purposes, as they are designed for a teacher education course. Nevertheless, stick to the four steps.
>
> **Train with Self-Recorded Videos**
>
> Usually, short sequences recorded with a smartphone are enough to analyze a situation in more detail. Keep in mind that you have to respect privacy when recording videos and find out exactly which consents you need and how the video material may be stored.

THOROUGH ANALYSES SHARPEN PERCEPTION AND COHERENT INTUITION

For the training of intuitive and accurate diagnoses, the analytical eye with which things are viewed from a distance is needed, for example, in a retrospective video analysis or a review of the lesson, alone or with peers or other teachers. In teacher education, courses accompanying internships are the preferred place for systematic analyses and linking with bodies of knowledge. Some of the analyses are strictly rule-governed in order to uncover one-sidedness and blind spots of perception and, if necessary, to arrive at insights that are both unexpected and illuminating.

In other words, building professional learning support practices also requires the careful analysis of evidence of teaching (videos, texts, student work, reports) preferably with other teachers or peers, and drawing on third-party insights—in other words, referring to what student teachers commonly call "theory," which is really a vast storehouse of knowledge, insight, and experience. It would be foolish not to make use of it.

All of this serves the ability to make timely diagnostic assessments in the classroom. Perception must be sharpened and trained; one learns to interpret, prioritize, and process information quickly and intuitively in order to then respond appropriately. In short, all of this contributes to building, improving, and making more effective professional learning support practices.

Textbox 4.11 FURTHER INFORMATION AND RESOURCES

OBTAIN AND ACCEPT FEEDBACK: A KEY TO YOUR OWN DEVELOPMENT

It is the preservice or in-service teacher's own responsibility to work on practices that are professional and that produce the expected educational effects in students. This workbook seeks to support just that: taking responsibility for "self-professionalization."

Feedback from Others as a Guide to Professional Development

It's fine for teachers to want to develop their own practices. But one can raise a legitimate objection: How is it actually ensured that their practices end up being *professional*? Using the example of diagnosing: Will the teacher interpret professional situations appropriately and draw the best conclusions from them? It is true that situations can always be interpreted in different ways, but how can it be avoided that the teacher draws obviously wrong conclusions, has blind spots, or follows counterproductive intuitions? These concerns need to be taken seriously, especially since teachers often have to work alone and without mentoring.

The key point is that professionalization is *never possible without feedback from others*, especially in this profession. Without feedback, teachers risk developing their practices in problematic directions or even risk deprofessionalizing. Paradoxically, practices are always being built; teachers cannot be without practices if they are to meet daily workplace challenges. The question is who or what guides the development of these practices in a desirable professional direction.

How to manage one's own learning as a teacher through feedback from others is the topic of the next few sections. Then, in the next chapter, we turn to the feedback that teachers give to learners.

Implicit Feedback from Students

Implicit feedback is not directly expressed feedback from students. Such feedback can also reflect effects of one's own actions: a student who is confused, a class that seems apathetic, a child who does not know what to do, an achievement test that yields devastating results, body postures that express state of mind, and so on.

Teachers are expected to take note of these signals and to interpret them. Not every signal of this kind has to do with the teacher; therefore, it must be soberly analyzed to what extent it directly affects the teacher. Perhaps the cause lies elsewhere, it settles itself, or the teacher discreetly puts the matter right, and that's that. One should think twice before such implicit feedback is openly verbalized, and if it is, then by no means in a confrontational tone but rather showing interest in order to understand things better. Sometimes, however, especially when it comes to personal matters that can affect you, a conversation with a colleague is the better way to go.

Of course, students occasionally give explicit feedback, especially at the factual and motivational level ("I didn't understand that," "That's boring"). Sometimes, however, the feedback is directed at the teacher, at his or her behavior, style of teaching and explaining, and so on. Again, a gentle, nonconfrontational approach is advisable.

In short, implicit feedbacks are suggestive messages for which the teacher will develop a sensorium. He or she must take the signals seriously and see them as a help. The teacher should not overreact but rather put the messages into context and react in a proportionate and solution-focused way.

Explicit Feedback from Colleagues and Professionals

An important control and correction mechanism is collegial feedback or peer feedback as well as feedback from experts. To succeed, there are a few things to keep in mind:

Talk About the Effect of Action on Learning

The outside perspective from other student teachers, teachers, or faculty is helpful when it is *focused entirely on student learning and progress* (and not primarily on how well the teacher did). Unfortunately, colleagues and professionals sometimes take the teacher's behavior first; they immediately see what could and should have been done differently. Therefore, one should always look at the students first and find out what is going on with them, and only in a *second step* consider to what extent the teacher has a favorable or inhibiting influence.

Maintain a Friendly Attitude

Equally important is a *friendly attitude* on the part of the peers and experts. These are not examiners who judge good and bad; they see themselves as "critical friends" who do not nag the teacher but help to support the students in their progress in the best possible way.

Encourage a Trusting Atmosphere

Those who receive feedback show themselves to be *vulnerable*. Even implicit feedback can be unpleasant, indeed painful, for teachers. Understandably, they may overlook, ignore, suppress, or downplay it. Explicit feedback can also be overheard, ignored, or dismissed. Therefore, a *trusting atmosphere* is needed in which the teacher in question can overcome his or her sensitivities and lay the cards on the table. Conversely, the teacher can expect collegial confidentiality from the professionals. In this way, building professional practices becomes a collaborative project in which *practices are improved* rather than individuals are judged.

Some in-service teachers may probably be reluctant to open up entirely to other colleagues in the school. That's understandable if they fear that this openness might have negative consequences for their position in the school or even for their employment. Therefore, it is important to find colleagues who can be trusted completely. If there is a climate of openness and respect in this school anyway, all the better.

Keep Everything on the Table

Peers and professionals need *information and access to what is happening*. Selective insights, for example during classroom visits, reveal little. If the experts are not on site, they need to obtain information that is as authentic as possible—not personally colored reports but hard facts: documents, videos, students' work, and so on. If the experts are on site, they can participate in the daily work (e.g., by helping with planning and preparation or by simply shadowing).

Again, the most insidious trap in feedback is judging the other person. Feedback from peers and professionals makes the most sense when those involved ask themselves together: How can we increase the educational impact on children and young people?

Textbox 4.12 ACTIVITIES AND SUGGESTIONS

SUGGESTIONS ON HOW FEEDBACK FROM PEERS AND PROFESSIONALS CAN HELP YOU MOVE FORWARD

There is no shortage of professional and advice literature on feedback that can be consulted as needed. In all feedback situations with peers or professionals, focus on the following points. These are only four points, but they are very important if feedback situations are not to end in frustration and discouragement.

1. Make sure that the *starting point* of the conversation is never yourself but rather the question, How can we fulfill our mission even better? How can we further support student progress, learning, motivation, cooperative behavior, and so on?
2. If possible, talk about particular students and look for ways to support or encourage them.
3. Talk about your practices, but only insofar as they are relevant to student learning and progress. If design issues of instruction and tools do not contribute to desired effects, put them on the back burner and talk about something else.
4. Certainly, feelings such as anxiety, discomfort, or anger can overshadow all work. Therefore, sometimes it is important to address the specifics of the person but talk about aspects of yourself only if you mutually agree that it is significant in this context, and again, only if confidentiality is guaranteed.

Chapter Five

Professional Feedback to Learners
Crucial for Any Support

FEEDBACK TO LEARNERS

The following sections show how to provide professional feedback to students. Here, the focus is almost exclusively on *feedback from the teacher to the learner* with the *goal of supporting progress*. At the end of the chapter, your own learning process will not be finished; this practice is demanding and needs to be continuously developed in order to be able to act flexibly and professionally in new contexts and on different content. So, here you will not find simplifying rules and checklists for feedbacks but rather basic information and training suggestions.

FEEDBACK INCREASINGLY IN FOCUS

At least since the first decade of the 2000s, teachers have come to believe that feedback in the classroom is hugely important. Over the past decades, numerous publications and concepts have been presented, research findings have been reported, and many recommendations for classroom practice have been derived. Two papers, one by Kluger and DeNisi (1996), "The Effects of Feedback Interventions on Performance," and the other by Hattie and Timperley (2007), "The Power of Feedback," are still groundbreaking today. Both have been cited over five thousand times each in scholarly texts alone. The first paper summarizes the research findings on feedback up to 1996, and the second adds more recent findings and presents the four-level model already mentioned. A differentiated presentation of the concepts and research findings on feedback cannot be provided here. However, some significant aspects and findings are summarized very briefly, and reference is made to some relevant literature.

One can interpret the great resonance of the topic of feedback as indicating that classroom researchers, teachers, and teacher education have widely recognized the importance of feedback to and from learners. Its supportive effect is *indispensable* for progress in learning and development and has become an integral part of all professional teaching.

And yet, research findings cannot be translated into rigid rules. Most findings indicate tendencies and probabilities about the effect. How feedback works depends on the situation. Above all, it is uncertain how learners respond to feedback, whether they accept it or possibly even reject it, and how, in turn, the teacher responds.

What does that mean in consequence? Feedback is one of the most challenging practices; the practice of feedback requires a lot of training and experience but also a lot of expertise and understanding of learning processes. The aspects described below on feedback are a starting point, nothing more. What must follow is a deep, persistent exploration of how student learning can succeed.

GOOD FEEDBACK: ESSENTIAL FOR PROFESSIONAL TEACHERS

Feedback is virtually a unique feature of the professional teacher. Feedback can hardly be replaced by anything else, and when it is absent (or useless), the learning processes of many learners stall or go astray. The teacher is concerned that the learning processes of all students are kept on track. So the teacher intervenes at the right moment in the best possible way to initiate a good turn of things toward better learning, more confidence and motivation, and deeper understanding, but sometimes also soberly noting an aberration. It is to do the right thing at the right moment, which is not so easy because the window of opportunity for decisions is short—perhaps a few seconds, rarely more.

It's pretty obvious that teachers must have a lot of knowledge and experience to be successful at it. What, then, allows them to do the right thing right now? It is the *elaborated practices based on knowledge, expe-*

rience, and sharpened intuition. The following aspects provide only hints; integrating them into one's own practice is the work of student teachers and teachers.

BETTER FEEDBACK THROUGH DETERMINATION TO MAKE A DIFFERENCE

At times, the determination to help children and young people make progress is not always sufficiently developed. After all, teachers with less experience are often busy just ensuring that the lessons run smoothly in the first place. The more intensively the teacher deals with the particular student, the more determined he or she is likely to become to achieve the maximum and to help everyone on their way through school. This is actually a given; it is at the core of the teaching profession, but this professional ethical attitude must also be nurtured. It is in the individual case, with a desperate student, a lethargic adolescent, an enthusiastic child, that it becomes apparent whether the teacher is committed or not.

The following excerpt reports on a feedback study in England. It suggests the developmental process that teachers go through when they turn their attention to student learning. Teachers realized that their previous strategies and feedback were inadequate; they initially wanted only to improve their feedback, but they triggered a series of changes, established an entirely new relationship with their students, and designed their teaching to be increasingly learning and goal oriented, and teachers developed new and improved practices to do so.

> We suggested to teachers that feedback would be more effective if, as well as indicating whether results were correct, the feedback also identified what students should do to move their learning on. To our surprise, they found this very difficult. . . .
>
> A few months into the project, the teachers asked us for some formal information about the psychology of learning. At first, this too surprised us, but perhaps we should not have been so surprised. We had asked them to provide feedback that their students could use, and to do that, they needed models of their students' thinking. Despite the fact that most of the teachers had substantial teaching experience (well over ten years in most cases), they had managed—and indeed in many cases been regarded as highly effective

teachers—without any clear idea of what was happening in their students' heads.

The teachers also began to think much more carefully about the tasks they set their students. They had realized that to provide effective feedback to their students, they needed to find out more about their students' thinking, and that the tasks they routinely used varied considerably in the extent to which they provided useful, instructionally tractable, information about student achievement.

That, in turn, led teachers to an awareness that they needed much greater clarity about the aims of their instruction, in order to be clear about what kinds of questions or tasks would be most appropriate. While the project had focused originally on feedback, real implementation of these ideas required attention to the ways in which evidence of learning was elicited, which in turn necessitated clarity about the learning goals.

At the same time, the kinds of practices that the teachers were adopting in their classrooms placed much greater responsibility for learning on the learners. Put bluntly, changing what teachers were doing in classrooms also required changing what students were doing. In particular, harnessing the power of assessment and feedback to improve learning involved greater use of students assessing their own work and that of their peers. (Wiliam, 2018, pp. 20–21)

BETTER FEEDBACK THROUGH KNOWLEDGE ABOUT FEEDBACK AND ITS EFFECTS

Of course, teachers need a solid, deeply understood, and internalized *knowledge of how feedback can work*. Certain feedbacks are almost always counterproductive; they are a no-go. Those who use them are probably simply not professional. With other feedbacks, the good effect is proven by solid findings, and with still others one is inclined to say, "Maybe it works; it depends." There is a lot of research on this, and some of the key findings and mechanisms on feedback are discussed in textboxes 5.1, 5.2, and 5.3.

Textbox 5.1 FURTHER INFORMATION AND RESOURCES

THE POWER OF FEEDBACK

Numerous studies have been done on feedback to students as far back as the last century. The first major survey study was by Kluger and DeNisi (1996). Hattie and Timperley (2007) supplemented the updated findings with a framework on feedback in school situations. John Hattie's (2009) well-known study, based on numerous meta-studies, summarized the state of research at that time. The data are continually updated and are available for public access (www.visiblelearningmetax.com). Table 5.1 shows some selected effect sizes of factors on learning success, especially factors related to feedback.

Table 5.1. Factors Influencing Learning Success

Factors influencing learning success		Effect size d
Feedback (reinforcement and cues)		0.92
Setting success criteria		0.88
Teacher clarity		0.84
Interventions for students with learning needs		0.78
Help-seeking by students		0.72
Distributed practice (instead of mass practice)		0.65
Metacognitive strategies		0.60
Suspension/expelling students		−0.20
Student's screen time		−0.29
Presence of mobile phones		−0.34
Student's anxiety		−0.36
Effect sizes relating to types of feedback		*Effect size d*
Correct feedback	"It is correct"	0.43
	"It is incorrect"	0.25
Task feedback about changes from previous trials	Yes	0.55
	No	0.28
Task feedback designed to discourage the student	Yes	−0.14
	No	0.33
Praise feedback about the task	Yes	0.09
	No	0.34
Number of times feedback was provided	Lots	0.39
	Little	0.32
Task complexity	Very complex	0.03
	Not complex	0.55
Goal setting	Difficult goals	0.51
	Easy, do your best goals	0.30
Threat to self-esteem	Much threat	0.08
	Little threat	0.47

Sources: www.visiblelearningmetax.com (retrieved May 13, 2022); Hattie and Timperley (2007); Kluger and DeNisi (1996).

What Does "Effect Size" Mean?

The effect size (d) is a statistical measure that can be used to indicate how large the effect of a single measure or an influencing variable is, compared to before or compared to a situation without this influencing variable. The effect size is particularly well suited as a measure for comparing different studies.

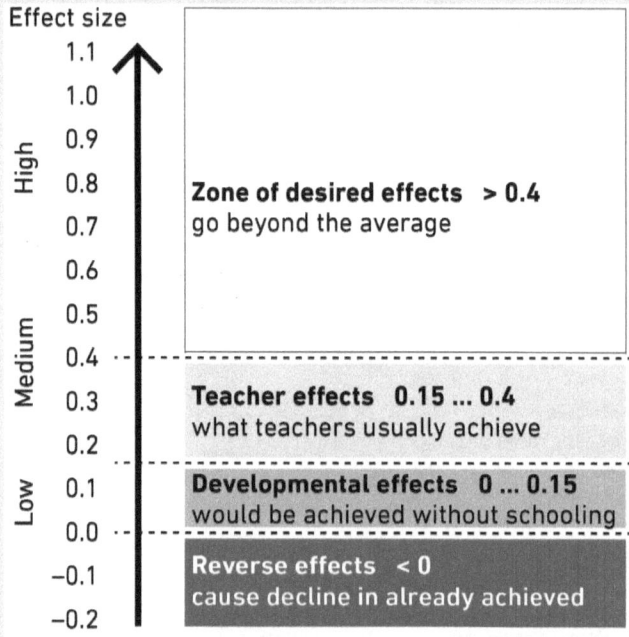

Figure 5.1. Influence of a factor on student achievement, displayed on the effect size scale. *Based on Hattie, 2009, pp. 18–20.*

How Are Effect Sizes to Be Interpreted?

In studies on effects in the field of education, it must be taken into account that people always learn, even without school (up to d = 0.15) and that the average of all school-based measures is d = 0.4. Thus, a really good effect is above 0.4, while effects below 0.4 do not stand out from the ordinary. Hattie (2009) positions the effects he compiled on an effect size scale (figure 5.1). Only effects in the highest range (d > 0.4) make a difference compared to conventional teaching and learning.

There are also findings on the effect of individual feedbacks. Feedback refers to *all teacher interventions that support and assist individual learning*. The selected results in table 5.1 provide an initial insight into the mechanisms of feedback

According to Kluger and DeNisi (1996), feedback is more effective

- if it does *not* focus on the learner *as a person*,
- if it provides more than just information about the correctness of the answers,
- if it provides guidelines—but not instructions—on how to accomplish the task and thus encourages active thinking (i.e., no instructions that do not require learners to think for themselves), and
- if it is immediate and not delayed, especially when it concerns more demanding and complex tasks.

The effects of some feedbacks are surprising and counterintuitive, such as the small effect of praise (if it is not linked to further information) or the large effect of demanding goals with little complex tasks, or the fact that a lot of feedback has no greater effect than little feedback.

In the majority of cases, feedback on (individual) goals and on changes compared to earlier is obviously effective; it contains information about the learning process and helps students to assess where they stand, what they have already learned, and what they still have to do.

However, it is important to be aware of the limitations of this short and very generalized list of effective and less effective feedback. These few references will not be sufficient to serve as the only guidelines for professional teachers, but it is a start (see bibliography on feedback).

Textbox 5.2 FURTHER INFORMATION AND RESOURCES

HOW PRESCRIPTIVE CAN THE RECOMMENDATIONS OF EDUCATIONAL RESEARCH BE? A CRITICAL LOOK AT THE "FEEDBACK" EXAMPLE

The English educational researcher Dylan Wiliam (2019) takes the firm position that empirical evidence on learning, teaching, and schooling should not be generalized as universally valid recommendations for action, because (1) the results are never completely unambiguous and show a scattering, and in individual cases opposite effects also occur, and because (2) the local conditions where a recommendation is to be applied are always different from those in the respective studies. He concludes, "In educational research, 'What works' is usually the wrong question because almost anything works somewhere, and nothing works everywhere. A better question is, 'Under what circumstances does this work,' which is why using research to improve education cannot be achieved by slavishly following a recipe dictated" (p. 137).

Similar critical positions toward so-called evidence-based educational programs are held by the following authors:

- Gert Biesta (2010, "Why 'What Works' Still Won't Work")
- Catherine Snow (2015, "Rigor and Realism: Doing Educational Science in the Real World")
- Anthony Bryk and collaborators (2015, *Learning to Improve*)

The implication of these authors is not to discard evidence from studies but always to consider the extent to which they are valid under local conditions and how recommendations should be differentiated to achieve the best effect. Studies may indicate beneficial effects, but in many individual cases, the recommendations have exactly the opposite effect.

Wiliam illustrates this with the example of feedback. Kluger and DeNisi (1996) found in their careful review that feedback significantly increased achievement on average. Based on this and his own findings, John Hattie suggested that "the simplest prescription for improving education must be dollops of feedback" (Hattie, 1999, p. 9).

However, although Kluger and DeNisi showed an average positive effect, about 38 percent of the total 607 effect sizes were negative. In other words, in more than one-third of the cases they studied, it would have been better simply not to provide feedback at all. Looking at the overall benefits, Hattie's recommendation is understandable. But in the many cases where performance-inhibiting feedback is constantly practiced, the recommendation is counterproductive, and it is of little help that the overall benefit across all studies appears rather favorable. Wiliam (2019) concludes,

> What this means, I think, is that the entire project of evidence-based education can never be successful. Any claims about "what works" are necessarily local, in that they are limited to the participants and contexts actually studied, and judgement will be needed to apply them in other settings. Moreover, such claims will be provisional, in that new findings, insights, and understandings will bring previously credible interpretations of research studies into question. (pp. 135–136)

Textbox 5.3
A SELECTION OF PUBLICATIONS ON THE TOPIC OF FEEDBACK

Some of the literature on feedback takes the perspective discussed here much further. Well-founded contributions are provided in particular by the books in which John Hattie is directly or indirectly involved (Hattie & Clarke, 2018).

- Archer, J., et al. (2016). *Better Feedback for Better Teaching: A Practical Guide to Improving Classroom Observations*. San Francisco: Jossey-Bass.
- Brookhart, S. M. (2017). *How to Give Effective Feedback to Your Students*. Alexandria, VA: ASCD.
- Dann, R. (2018). *Developing Feedback for Pupil Learning: Teaching, Learning and Assessment in Schools*. London: Routledge.
- Hattie, J., & Clarke, S. (2018). *Visible Learning: Feedback*. London: Routledge.
- Lipnevich, A. A., & Smith, J. K. (Eds.) (2018). *The Cambridge Handbook of Instructional Feedback*. Cambridge: University Press.
- Pollock, J. E. (2012). *Feedback: The Hinge that Joins Teaching and Learning*. Thousand Oaks, CA: Corwin.

Chapter Six

How to Make Feedback and One-on-One Conversations More Effective

ACCURATE DIAGNOSES AS A PREREQUISITE FOR GOOD FEEDBACK

Feedback must be linked to the specific situation. The decisive *prerequisite is an accurate diagnosis* of what is mainly at stake. Diagnosis is not a purely rational act in which the situation at hand is systematically examined; diagnoses, as we know, are strongly guided by intuitions. Intuitions, in turn, are increasingly refined and sharpened through knowledge, practice, and experience. Feedback is successful when the *developmental stage of the child or adolescent* is taken into account.

As we know, part of a solid diagnosis is identifying the *level of the challenge* at hand. Feedback is most effective when it addresses the level at which the problem is located. In the context of diagnostics, the four levels suggested by Hattie and Timperley (2007) have already been discussed.

Level	Challenge
Task	Coping with the current task on the matter level
Process	Strategies needed to understand and accomplish the task
Self-regulation	Supervise, direct, and regulate own activities
Self	A personal situation that overrides everything else

We focus on the first three levels; addressing the fourth personal level in classroom situations is delicate, so we leave it out for now.

BETTER FEEDBACK BY STARTING AT THE RIGHT POINT IN THE LEARNING PROCESS

Feedbacks do not have to do solely with support for stalled learning processes; that would be a blatant misunderstanding. Feedback concerns the entire cycle of a learning process. This cycle can be illustrated by learning tasks, which are known to be a dominant element of teaching. Teachers use them to initiate learning processes, to provide practice opportunities, to move students forward with challenging problems, and so on. Every learning task has its "lifetime": it begins (1) with the *task*, then follows (2) *processing and problem solving*, and finally (3) *what happens next*. The teacher, as well as the student, must be aware of this cycle. Depending on where one stands with a task, the problem is different. In addition, the problem presents itself differently at each level. This can be explained using the Hattie-Timperley model: the "timeline" can be divided into three stages, analogous to the formative evaluation mentioned earlier (Wiliam, 2018).

Goals	→	Status now	→	Next steps
"Where to?"		"How is it going?"		"What next?"

Individual Goals: Expectations for Learning Progress

Formulating expectations and setting individual goals will be discussed later. Here, only the perspective of feedback is of interest.

Teachers are often unclear about what a task is supposed to do. In many cases, they follow a given teaching material, assuming that its tasks are well constructed and selected. But as we know, not all students are at the same level. So the teacher or sometimes the student must figure out what task might now be appropriate and effective.

Teachers and Learners Must Correctly Assess the Level of Difficulty

If you set general goals for the whole class, you also know that not all learners will reach these goals and that some will even be underchal-

Four options for learners: They...		Feedback shows learners that...	
		...the current performance falls short of the set goal	...the current performance exceeds the set goal
...change their behavior	→	**They increase the effort**	They reduce the effort
...adjust their goal	→	They reduce the aspiration	**They increase the aspiration**
...abandon the goal	→	They decide goal is too hard	They decide goal is too easy
...reject feedback	→	They ignore the feedback	They ignore the feedback

Figure 6.1. When feedback shows learners where they stand: Possible responses to such feedback. The highlighted options are the learners' optimal response in terms of the learning process. The other six options slow down the learning process. *Based on Wiliam, 2018, p. 15.*

lenged. As a rule, the goals and the tasks must be differentiated. Only solvable tasks can move learners forward—that is, the goals and tasks must be in the zone of proximal development, the learning zone, but not in the comfort zone or the panic zone. Several researchers have already pointed out the problem that even with the best feedback, the learning process can stop if the goals are too challenging or too easy (Hattie & Timperley, 2007, p. 89; Kluger & DeNisi, 1996, p. 278). Not all learners view difficulty as a stimulus; some give up or simply drop out. Wiliam (2018, p. 15) summarizes the ways of reacting to goals that are too difficult or too easy this way:

Teachers and Learners Should Ensure That Individual Goals Are Well Accepted

In addition to the difficulty of the goals, it is also important that the goals are accepted. It doesn't matter whether the goals and tasks were given by the teacher or chosen by the students themselves. The latter should understand what a goal is for and what a task is useful for. Transparency is a necessary condition for acceptance. Even if students may not explicitly say so, they want to know if the effort is worthwhile, and they want to know what is in it for them.

Teachers and Learners Must Set Individual Goals according to the Level

The starting point is usually a goal at the subject level that relates to the subject matter in question. But students should also learn strategies and be able to deal with problems. Since Mager (1962) at the latest, we have known how important transparent goals are. Teachers are well advised to routinely formulate and transparently communicate two goals at different levels—one at the subject level and another at the strategy level (this will be explored in more depth later in the book).

The Current Status and Next Steps

Once the goals have been clarified, the learning processes are tracked and, if necessary, supported in order to then initiate the next steps (i.e., formulate new goals). The following table provides an overview of this. It combines the levels (from top to bottom) and the process (from left to right).

GOOD FEEDBACK AND EXPLAINING REQUIRES UNDERSTANDING THE SUBJECT MATTER

It goes without saying that the teacher understands the subject matter, not only in the context of feedback but also when setting tasks or providing input. However, when giving feedback, the teacher usually does not have time to become knowledgeable if he or she has difficulties with the content. Therefore, for good feedback, *the teacher must thoroughly understand the issue at hand*. No matter what the topic is—a ball toss, an arithmetic problem, correctly reading a map, understanding a foreign language sentence, a historical context—the teacher should have explored the matter from several perspectives and know several paths that lead to a result. This is often a great challenge for student teachers; they know little of the teaching materials, have possibly never taught this topic before, and are busy with other things. Nevertheless, there is no way around it: the matter should be understood. It is fatal if the teacher only pretends to have a grasp of the subject—he or she often misleads the students, creates confusion, and wastes valuable learning and living time.

Table 6.1. A Feedback Model That Considers Levels and Process (based on Hattie & Timperley, 2007)

	Individual Goals: "Where to?"	Status Now: "How is it going?"	Next Steps: "What next?"
Task Level Coping with the current task on the matter level	Is it clear what is to be done, and is the task purposeful?	Do the learners cope with the task? What, if anything, is the factual problem? How can I keep the learning process going?	How can learners apply or build on what they have learned? Next steps?
	e.g., clarify what the task is; why it is worth solving it	e.g., observe where the specific problem lies; make factual corrections; give practical advice on how to liquefy the learning process	e.g., show a specific task that can be accomplished with the new skill
Process Level Strategies needed to understand and accomplish the task	What are the strategies to learn here?	How do learners use intended strategies? How can I support learners to optimize strategies?	What does the strategy learned enable the learner to do? Next steps?
	e.g., discuss with the student why the learning process repeatedly stalls and formulate as a goal that a suitable strategy is to be found	e.g., suggest a procedure for detecting and correcting specific errors yourself	e.g., suggest as a next step to make the acquired strategy even more effective by means of a more challenging problem
Self-Regulation Level Supervise, direct, and regulate own activities	What steps toward appropriate self-regulation need to be taken?	Is more or appropriate self-regulation successful? How can I support the learners in this?	What do the acquired self-regulation strategies enable you to do? Next steps?
	e.g., determine that more focused, active help-seeking should be learned	e.g., show where successful help-seeking usually fails	e.g., finding out together what enables even more independence in learning in addition to successfully seeking help
Self Level Feedback that relates to the learner as a person, combined with feedback on tasks or strategies	Quality criterion of feedback on the person: Does a statement about the learner's person also contain any information that helps the learner to do (even) better in the future?		
	e.g., "That's very good, and I think it's great that you were able to successfully solve the problem with this new strategy." In contrast, feedback on the personal level, such as praise or disapproval, is virtually ineffective if it does not contain concrete statements about the respective tasks or strategies (cf. Hattie & Timperley, 2007).		

Textbox 6.1 ACTIVITIES AND SUGGESTIONS

FIND THE BEST STARTING POINT FOR EFFECTIVE FEEDBACK: A QUESTION OF TRAINING

Everything said so far remains dead letters if it does not become professional practices. Professional practices rely on internalized tacit knowledge that comes from a combination of experience, training, explicit knowledge, and deliberate engagement. Training is absolutely essential; good feedback practices do not come naturally.

Therefore, the following suggestions mainly concern training and the use of experience.

1. **Obtain audios and videos of feedback situations.**
   Perceptions and memories can be misleading. Therefore, document feedback dialogues.
   - The easiest way is to record audio with your smartphone. This is usually quite sufficient to be able to follow a dialogue afterward. Find out about regulations on digital data in your institution.
   - Taking your own video recordings provides more information and shows the activities of the participants. These recordings are technically easy to produce but usually require another person to do so, unless you use video glasses with a built-in camera. However, questions of data privacy must be addressed.
   - Third-party video recordings are increasingly available; there are databases accessible online. The disadvantage: the recordings rarely match what one wants to practice or analyze, and the search effort is not to be underestimated. Therefore, third-party videos are particularly suitable for teacher education and continuing education, where lecturers make a good selection.

2a. **Analyze audio or video according to specific criteria.**
   A general impression of a feedback dialogue can lead to false conclusions. Decide on certain criteria when analyzing audio or video. Here are some aspects you should focus on. Focus on one aspect at a time.
   - Diagnosis: Try to find out if the teacher is really trying to understand where the problem is, and if so, how he or she is going about it. Also consider whether you are identifying a different problem than the teacher.
   - Right level: Pay attention to whether the teacher wants to hit the right level. Remember, very often it is the factual level and, problem-

atically, the personal level (praise and reprimand without content), less often the levels of strategy and self-regulation. Make assumptions about which is the right level in this case.
- Goal—status now—next steps: See where in the learning process the specific situation stands. It can be about clarifying the goal, finding the current difficulty, or planning the next step.
- Flexibility and authenticity: Pay attention to how the teacher responds to the student—whether he or she adjusts his or her explanatory strategy, changes levels, or asks (genuine) questions. Assess how authentic or contrived the dialogue is.
- Relationship and commitment: You can usually sense the extent to which the teacher is interested in the students' progress. Look for signs of contact between the participants that is promoting learning and signs of the teacher's commitment.

2b. **Train in real situations.**
Train exactly this aspect, which you have analyzed under 2a, again in real teaching situations.

3. **Exchange information with others.**
Always look for opportunities to share with peers about it as well.

Thus, content knowledge does not mean the academic knowledge about the underlying discipline but the *deep understanding of those learning contents that the students are supposed to learn.*

Textbox 6.2 FURTHER INFORMATION AND RESOURCES

WHAT IS MEANT BY "UNDERSTANDING THE CONTENT"?

Teachers must have in-depth mastery of facts and context at the student level. They have penetrated the learning content from a wide variety of perspectives and are also familiar with different solutions, variants, and explanations. The following example comes from the highly regarded and consequential COACTIV study, which examined the relationship between teachers' competencies and students' progress in lower secondary mathematics. One of the results is highly sobering, if not shocking: for a moderately difficult task at the lower secondary level, teachers were able to give an average of just 1.15 different ways of solving it—and about one in seven teachers failed to come up with a solution at all.

Below is an excerpt from the aforementioned COACTIV study:

> Teachers should not only be able to solve tasks they use in lessons themselves, but also know different possible solutions, among other things, in order to better understand students when problems arise and to be able to provide them with adequate individual support. This was also one of the three facets of the COACTIV teaching test: generating as many possible solutions to given tasks as possible. In the following, we show one such sample task from the test. A general instruction was given in the prelude, and the neighboring numbers task was then the last of four given (see task in the box).
>
> Task for Testing Teachers' Pedagogical
Content Knowledge in Mathematics
>
> "Lucas claims that the square of a natural number is always one greater than the product of its two neighbors. Is Lucas's claim true?"
>
> Please name as many different solutions as possible. Note: It is not about guessing which solutions students would choose but about all possible solutions that you yourself see for this task.
>
> Two obvious solutions for neighboring numbers are, first, an algebraic reasoning with variables and, second, a geometric approach. The list below shows how many possible solutions to the neighboring numbers task were written down by teachers in the COACTIV test:
>
> | | |
> |---|---|
> | wrong solution or no solutions | 16% |
> | one correct solution | 55% |
> | two correct solutions | 27% |
> | three correct solutions | 3% |
>
> The average number of correct solutions generated by teachers was 1.15. About one in seven teachers could not indicate a correct solution at all.
>
> Results such as this exemplify the fact that teachers' professional content knowledge appears to vary widely; other such tasks have revealed similar or even greater differences. (Blum, Krauss, & Neubrand, 2011, pp. 329–331)

GOOD EXPLAINING IMPROVES FEEDBACK

Explaining is undoubtedly one of the core practices of a teacher. It can be many things: imparting knowledge, demonstrating, assisting in knowledge building, offering strategies, and much more. Here, for the time being, it is only a matter of quickly clarifying a point, usually to an individual student—in other words, providing supportive feedback at the matter level. But the ability to explain things well and understandably is important in all phases of teaching.

Explaining in Alternation of Rule and Example

One of the most common explanatory strategies is the alternating use of examples and rules. This applies to explanatory texts as well as to oral explanations. Usually, this is also a change of level from the actual operational level (What is to be done?) to the strategic level (What is the underlying principle?) or vice versa. Research findings suggest that it does not matter so much whether one starts with the example or with the rule (cf. summarizing Leinhardt, 2001; Stein & Kucan, 2010).

Sometimes one explanatory element is already sufficient, and sometimes it is a two-step, often a three-step, explanation. Crucial, as already mentioned, is the flexible change between example and rule, as needed. The strategic level of the rule is particularly important for transfers; it facilitates application in other, similar situations.

Here are six explanation patterns with up to three elements. In oral explanations, attention should be paid to brevity and conciseness. Explanations can be stopped immediately if the matter has been understood or if the explanation obviously does not lead to success.

Explaining Through Modeling

Demonstrating is something that teachers are very familiar with. It can also be applied to mental (cognitive) activities. The teacher then demonstrates not a physical action but rather thinking steps by speaking aloud and commenting on what he or she is thinking. The teacher "models" the process *and* the thinking about this process (cf. example of subtracting below)—in other words, he or she switches between the factual and the strategic level.

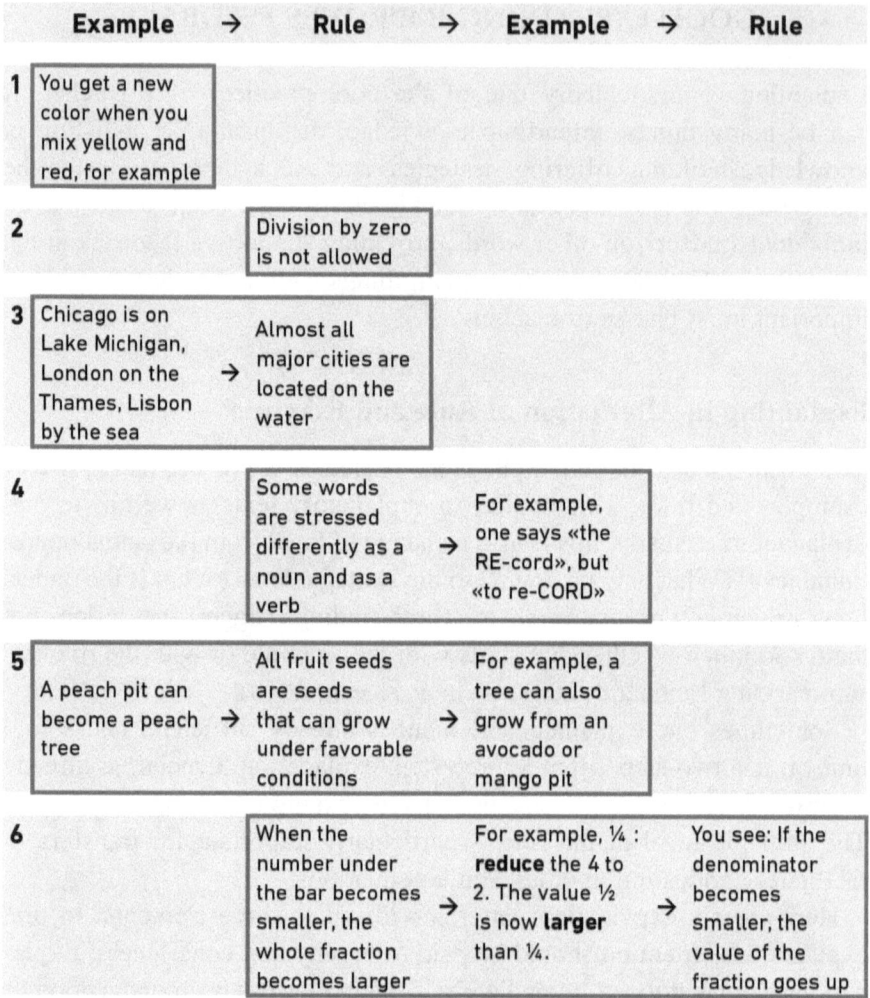

Figure 6.2. Six patterns of explanatory strategies with alternating use of examples and rules. *Author created.*

Thinking about thinking is called metacognition. Metacognition helps students improve their learning strategies (e.g., Martinez, 2006).

Modeling by thinking aloud is shown in figure 6.3 with two examples. In the first example, a new procedure (in this case, subtraction according to the European or Austrian method) is shown and commented on by thinking aloud, and in the second example, thinking aloud refers to the strategy of problem solving—in other words, being aware of how one

Modeling a procedure (Example: Subtraction with the "Austrian" method)

$$\begin{array}{r} 549 \\ -284 \\ \hline \end{array}$$

	Thinking aloud and commenting
Now I want to subtract this number from the upper one.	Well, I have to make sure that the ones, the tens, etc. are exactly below each other. I start at the bottom right.
4 and how much is 9? 5. So I write 5.	Done. Now I move one place to the left to the tens.
8 and how much is 4? I can't.	Aha, I have to use a trick: I don't complete to 4, but to 14! So, if it doesn't work, you just put a 1 in front of it.
8 and 6 makes 14. I write a 6 below.	But do not forget: I have only borrowed a 1 of the number 14, I have to give it back. I write very small a 1 under the next place, here under the 2. In this way I give the 1 back again. So, and now the hundreds.
There is actually not a 2 but a 3.	The 2 and the borrowed 1 add up to 3.
3 and how much is 5? 2. I write 2 and I'm done: It's 265.	$$\begin{array}{r} 549 \\ -2\,\underset{\scriptscriptstyle 1}{8}4 \\ \hline 265 \end{array}$$

Modeling problem solving (metacognition on the example of an equation)

	Thinking aloud and commenting
$6x = x + 10$	For which values of x is this equation true? I want to find it out systematically, not by tinkering or guessing.
$6x = x + 10$	There the x occurs twice, I want to simplify that first, because it is difficult to determine x if it occurs in several places.
$6x = x + 10 \quad / \quad -x$	I take away an x on both sides: I subtract x. I am allowed to do that, because both sides of the equal sign still have the same value—less, but still the same.
$5x = 10$	The equation already looks simpler... but I would like to have it even simpler. Only x should remain on the left. What can I do?
$5x = 10 \quad / \quad :5$	I just divide both sides by 5. Thus: both sides by 5...
$x = 2$	... on the left, x remains and on the right I get 2. Now it is clear: For x I must insert 2, so that the equation is still correct (2 = 2)

Figure 6.3. Modeling by thinking aloud: Two examples. *Author created.*

thinks while solving problems. It is to be expected that, as with demonstration, students will mimic the process and use metacognitive cues to solve the problem and to better understand the process of solving it (cf. Collins, Brown, & Newman, 1989). Thus, this process leads from modeling a thinking process to supported self-doing to independent mastery of the process by the students.

Textbox 6.4 ACTIVITIES AND SUGGESTIONS

CORRECT AND PEDAGOGICALLY OPTIMAL EXPLAINING AND MODELING

Do not underestimate the importance of careful and correct explanation. Your responsibility is great because wrong or inadequate explanations lead students down wrong paths. They get confused, or worse, they practice something wrong, which prevents them from progressing. So, take this fundamental task of a teacher very seriously.

Solve All Tasks Yourself That You Have Not Already Thoroughly Mastered

In internships, the division of labor with peers and teachers helps student teachers to have enough time for professional preparation. Therefore, it is a good and important habit to *work through all tasks and assignments by yourself*, if you are not already well versed.

Search for and Test Solution Variants Yourself

Explore the breadth and depth of the tasks and assignments. This way you can better appreciate the different ways students approach the problem.

- In well-structured tasks (e.g., often in mathematics and science, also in foreign languages and physical education) different ways can lead to the goal, sometimes also different ways of representation.
- In the case of ill-structured tasks (e.g., writing a text, planning an event, designing a website), you as a teacher are especially challenged to anticipate and appreciate a wide range of different and meaningful ways to do things.

Watch Yourself and Others Explain

Students often ask for help: "How does this work?" "I don't understand" "What do I have to do here?" Usually, the teacher responds with an *expla-*

nation sequence or a *modeling sequence*. Try to observe yourself while explaining how you proceed:

- Do you really explain or just ask questions?
- Do you simply show how to do it, or do you explain the strategy? Observe the change between the two levels.
- To what extent does time pressure play a role? When there is a rush, there is a tendency to give purely operational explanations ("Do it this way").
- Use your video or audio footage to analyze a few sequences.
- See if you are using modeling at all (thinking aloud when solving a task).
- Get brief feedback from students each time: "To what extent was I able to help?" "Where are there still unanswered questions?"

Now do the same by observing another teacher or other student teachers explaining and modeling.

SUSTAINABLE LEARNING THROUGH MONITORING AND GOOD TIMING OF FEEDBACK

It would be a great mistake to think that students only need feedback when they have visible learning difficulties. Regardless of performance, all have the need and also the right to have as many productive learning opportunities as possible.

Sustained learning processes usually need to be gone through at least three to five times, and sometimes significantly more, depending on the subject matter and context (see textbox 6.5).

Don't Forget the Fast Learners and the Silent Learners!

Even learners who are at work without noticeable problems must remain in view. Their learning processes can also be incomplete or misguided. For the fast and powerful, it is not enough to state that they "can" do it. They, too, need multiple executions until the thing sinks in. Those who quietly make mistakes may remain "under the radar"—they practice the wrong things (it is known that it takes twice as much effort to get rid of them). So, the teacher should be in the right place at the right time, giving a nudge here and there, so that the learning processes are sustainable. This is what is meant by "timing" (Hattie & Clarke, 2018). However, it is not easy to keep track of all students in a class. True, monitoring all learning is nearly impossible. But this is where the teacher comes in with perfected practices of diagnosis and feedback. A capable teacher will notice where the need is greatest and who should not be overlooked. The likelihood of someone falling through the cracks diminishes, and that's a good thing.

Textbox 6.5 FURTHER INFORMATION AND RESOURCES

LEARNING, REMEMBERING, AND FORGETTING

Undoubtedly, the notion that remembering facts is the essence of cognitive learning and knowledge has lost its relevance. The concept of knowledge is now much broader (e.g., Anderson & Krathwohl, 2001). Nevertheless, it is interesting and important to know what factors plays a role in whether and how long people can remember things and how this memory process can be influenced.

The functioning of learning, remembering, and forgetting facts and skills was one of the main topics of psychological research in the late nineteenth and twentieth centuries. Here are examples of some very basic findings, which are also deepened in common textbooks on the psychology of learning.

Performance Depends on the Number of Repetitions

As a general rule, all learning is increased and reinforced by repetition. The initial course of a learning curve can vary. Initial or start-up difficulties may cause a slow rise until the moment when the learning process gets going and the curve lifts. In other cases, the first attempts bring the greatest learning progress. In any case, the rate of progress decreases over time.

Distributed Practice Is More Effective than Massed Practice

The potential power of repetition is reduced by a certain amount due to fatigue and saturation. Learning stagnates at the level already achieved. During the learning pause, fatigue disappears. When starting "fresh," the effective performance equals the potential performance. Distributed practice leads to faster learning and better retention of memory material and movement sequences than massed practice (Cepeda, Pashler, Vul, Wixted, & Rohrer, 2006).

The Forgetting Curve of Ebbinghaus

Already in the nineteenth century, Ebbinghaus (1885) had found that the speed of forgetting has certain typical courses. One forgets most in the first days after learning the material. Then the "forgetting curve" flattens out—that is, the losses per unit of time become smaller and smaller. In certain cases, the curve gradually reaches zero (complete forgetting); in others, a faint trace of what has been learned remains for years and even decades.

Numerous Other Factors Determine Learning, Retention, and Transfer

Various researchers have further pointed out that meaningful and understood material is forgotten less quickly than meaningless material that was not well understood. Not only is it better remembered, but also the transfer is increased—that is, it is more easily applied to new situations in a meaningful way.

Learning and forgetting depend on many other factors that are not discussed in depth here, such as interest, emotions, content, type of knowledge (declarative, procedural, metacognitive, with appropriate differentiations), context, and especially subject context: foreign languages, music, mathematics, and so on. The psychology of learning, educational psychology, and knowledge about teaching and learning provide a differentiated picture in this regard.

Further Reading

Easy-to-understand and accessible summaries of learning in general and in the school context are provided by the two books *How People Learn* (Bransford, Brown, & Cocking, 2000) and *How People Learn II* (National Academies of Sciences Engineering and Medicine, 2018). They can be downloaded free of charge (https://www.nap.edu, search "how people learn").

THE RIGHT AMOUNT OF SUPPORT AND ENCOURAGEMENT

No "Over-Feedback"

Especially when there are several teachers or student teachers in the classroom, it can happen that "over-feedback" occurs. The adults overwhelm, even bully, the learners with well-intentioned feedback. They should be aware that their intervention may interrupt a productive process or be perceived as annoying or even threatening.

Dosing Feedback Properly

It would be a fallacy to believe that more feedback is always better. The main criterion is, *Does an intervention help learners to achieve clarity, to progress, and to foster interest?* The case is clear if the intervention is urgent (e.g., for challenging tasks, because otherwise there is a risk of dropout if learners practice something obviously wrong), but in all other cases the teacher should pause briefly to consider *what* kind of intervention is now the most helpful and whether it is needed at all.

There are definitely reasons not to jump right in. Here are a few examples:

- The student is about to break through
- The student is now unresponsive
- The student still needs time
- The peer next to the student may as well help
- The time for explanations would be too short
- Nothing to give feedback on—the student is well on the way

Feedback as Encouragement

Learners need *encouragement*, not empty praise that has no positive effect, as we know, but signs that strengthen motivation, perseverance, and willingness to work hard. Sometimes a nonverbal gesture, a nod, a smile—in short, signs of sympathy and empathy—can help.

Earlier, we talked about *self-determination theory*, related to the learning processes of student teachers and teachers. But the approach of self-determination theory is also very pertinent in the classroom. Feedback can strengthen students in any of the three areas:

- Experiencing competence and effectiveness
- Sense of social relatedness
- Autonomy and self-determination

As we know, these are three deeply rooted psychological needs. When they are satisfied, people usually flourish; they are motivated and willing to get involved.

Textbox 6.6

STUDENTS TELL YOU IF THEY NEED SUPPORT. BUT HOW?

In a fear-free learning atmosphere, students have no problem saying they're stuck and need help. But additional tools can help students get noticed more easily. A simple tool is a *traffic light they place on their desk*:

- Green means "Things are going well."
- Amber means "I'm getting along, but I have a question."
- Red means "I'm stuck and need help."

The teacher can see from a distance who is having difficulty and who can continue working on their own. So, she or he can turn to where the most help is needed.

No complicated devices are needed: three plastic cups in the colors green, amber, and red do the trick, or a not-too-small cube with these three colors on its sides.

Be Careful About Student Self-Assessment!

You might think that the traffic lights could also be used for self-assessment: red would mean "all understood," amber would mean "more or less understood," and red would mean "serious difficulties." Self-assessment (e.g., with the traffic lights) can serve a purpose if you have the type of classroom that values mistake-making and a growth mindset and is psychologically safe. But most students assess themselves incorrectly—either far too well (Dunning-Kruger effect) or far too weakly (low self-concept). Accurate self-assessment must be learned. If it's important to you, you need to make it an issue and practice it over and over again. Otherwise, don't do it.

Textbox 6.7 ACTIVITIES AND SUGGESTIONS

OBSERVE YOURSELF GIVING FEEDBACK, AND ASK OTHERS HOW YOUR FEEDBACK WORKS

In the earlier sections, you have already learned various activities and techniques to expand your repertoire when coaching students:

- Approach the topic of learning support by means of documentation, awareness, and self-observation.
- Explore your knowledge about students.
- Observe and listen using live observation, documents, and videos.
- Practice effective feedback to students, including using audios and videos.
- Improve explanations and modeling through domain expertise and observation.

Flip back and visualize these procedures and techniques. Use them now in two ways:

- Observe yourself giving feedback and pay attention to its effects.
- Get feedback from students.

Explore the Effect of Your Own Feedback

Choose a real situation and a promising technique (videos, audios, or live self-observation). Try to find out *how learners experience your feedback*. Be guided by the following questions:

- Does the feedback seem welcome from the learner's perspective?
- Is it helpful?
- Does it seem annoying?
- Does it confuse?
- Is it encouraging?
- If you put yourself in the learner's shoes, does the learner possibly have the feeling of not being able to do anything after the feedback?
- Is the learner encouraged to continue working?

Note your insights and seek exchange with peers.

What Do the Learners Think?

Feedback, as you know, can take place on four levels:

- Task
- Process

- Self-regulation
- Self

Now a fifth option is added:

- Deliberately not giving feedback at all

Missing the level of feedback does not help learners—the teacher is trying to help at a point where there is no problem at all, or at least where feedback does not address the main problem. Unfortunately, however, one often does not immediately notice that the level has been missed.

Suggestion 1: Classroom Discussion

Make giving feedback an issue in a classroom discussion. Announce it beforehand so that students are not caught off guard. Ask precise questions, as this will help you get more accurate answers. And pay attention to the principles of classroom discussion.

Suggestion 2: Survey

Do a small, simple survey with *open-ended* questions about the feedback culture in the classroom.

Suggestion 3: Resonance Group

Invite a few students to share about the feedback culture.

NOT THE TEACHER'S JOB ALONE: INVITE OTHERS TO PARTICIPATE

Learning is also teamwork. If the participation of everyone—students, teachers, student teachers, guests—is not harnessed, progress falls short of what would be possible.

It is clear that feedback and support cannot come from one teacher alone and that the teacher cannot provide it to the extent that it is needed. Therefore, everyone should participate in learning *and* teaching. The teacher creates a climate of shared responsibility for progress and involves everyone:

- *Students themselves* take responsibility for their own learning by actively thinking; by taking ownership of the goals; by being aware of

how they work, their skills, and their gaps; by checking in with themselves to see where they stand; by seeking support when needed.
- *Peers* take responsibility by noticing when classmates are not getting ahead, for whatever reason; by offering help if they themselves are doing better; by making sure that no one among the classmates is forgotten. If traffic light cups or cubes are used in class, peers can also see immediately if someone needs support. The point is, the teacher can expect learners to help each other. Cooperative learning can be learned, and it is up to the teacher to initiate and support it.
- *Student teachers, colleagues, lecturers, classroom assistants, and other guests* who linger idly or only observe in the classroom are wasted resources. The teacher in charge does not have a monopoly on feedback. On the contrary, it is absurd that, when necessary, capable and interested adults remain inactive when there are numerous opportunities for productive participation.

Participation and cooperative learning hold great potential to be exploited not only for cognitive and physical learning; they can also significantly support social development (Johnson & Johnson, 2016).

AND NOW?

All the aspects of learning support, diagnosis, and feedback are complex and multilayered. Just listing all the things that need to be taken into account can be overwhelming for any teacher. How to deal with it?

The solution is for student teachers or teachers to *gradually develop good practices of feedback*, enriching them with knowledge and experience, practicing and automating them, but also keeping them flexible by always leaving room for pause and change of mind.

Professional practices do not build themselves. Therefore, deliberate training and intensive exchange with peers are indispensable. The suggestions for activities in this workbook are certainly a good starting point.

Textbox 6.8 ACTIVITIES AND SUGGESTIONS

ERRORS IN FACTUAL FEEDBACK AND EXPLAINING

In texts on teaching and learning, there are numerous references to mistakes that can be made when explaining. They are fatal because the effort leads to no result and on the contrary confuses or frustrates.

Here is a suggestion for recapping the concepts of diagnosis and feedback that we discussed. Read the six common errors listed below. Comment on and interpret the errors in light of your knowledge and experience with diagnosis and feedback in this chapter. Translate the errors into the context and terminology of the feedback concept. Make notes about them here.

Error 1: Wrong Level

The teacher is mistaken on the level. For example, a student has trouble concentrating because she is tired, but the teacher reacts exclusively on the factual level and provides an explanation. Or the teacher explains again what the goal of this exercise is, whereas the student's main problem is organizing his workplace.

Interpretation of the error from the perspective of diagnosis and feedback:

Error 2: Question Not Understood

The teacher thinks she knows what the problem is, doesn't listen to the question, doesn't ask follow-up questions, and explains something the student doesn't want to know. At best, the student says that she actually wanted to ask something else.

Interpretation of the error from the perspective of diagnosis and feedback:

Error 3: Prior Knowledge Not Clarified

The teacher does not make clear, for example, where exactly this student stands with his knowledge. Either the teacher assumes things that are not available to the student or that have been forgotten or never learned or the teacher gets carried away and rambles on and explains things that have long since been clear to the student.

Interpretation of the error from the perspective of diagnosis and feedback:

Error 4: Not Understood Yourself

The teacher is not well versed in the subject. Thus, mistakes or half-truths creep in. Instead of clarifying, the teacher confuses. Or the teacher sticks to a single type of explanation because it's the only one he knows, even though it does not help the student.

Interpretation of the error from the perspective of diagnosis and feedback:

Error 5: Poorly Explained

The teacher explains incomprehensibly: with unfamiliar expressions, long-winded or fast, complicated or abstract, inflexible or rambling, and so on. The teacher obviously makes no effort to be clear and helpful. At times, one could get the impression that the teacher just blabbers whatever comes to his mind.

Interpretation of the error from the perspective of diagnosis and feedback:

Error 6: Bad Timing

The teacher explains at the wrong time. She continues to explain even though this is an unfavorable moment, such as when the student has long since stopped following and is increasingly frustrated, or when the teacher sees other waiting students and wants to finish explaining something much too quickly.

Interpretation of the error from the perspective of diagnosis and feedback:

Textbox 6.9 ACTIVITIES AND SUGGESTIONS

LOOKING BACK AND SUMMING UP

What Aspects of Learning Support Have You Worked On?

After you've worked through part II of the book, certainly you'll find a lot, if not all, of it familiar. Now see where you stand.

Take some colored pens and give them a meaning, such as green for "I know that well" or red for "important, I still have to practice it" or blue for "I want to know more about it" or purple for "I don't understand." Now color-code all the points in table 6.2.

When you have finished, lean back and ask yourself, What do I want to work on now?

How Have You Been Working with This Book So Far?

Part I explained in detail what this book is all about. It is more than just a textbook. If you don't remember, flip through the first pages again.

Now, how have you been using this book? There are many possibilities, as you can see below. For each point, make a brief note of how it applies or if you think it would be a good idea to follow it.

- Using the book as a source of knowledge about concepts important to teaching
- Engaging with the suggestions and activity proposals and recording your experiences with them
- Researching the topics in the book and consulting other sources
- Seeking and using opportunities to experience individual practices and analyzing experiences with them
- Taking systematic notes that can be bundled into a kind of handbook on practices
- Combining elements of the book, making cross connections and comparisons
- Rehearsing and reflecting on practices on an ongoing basis
- Sharing and cooperating with others who are working on the same thing or who can provide feedback
- Identifying well-founded critical points of view toward positions in this book

Table 6.2. Developing Practices of Effective Learning Support: A Checklist

What You Have Learned or What You Are About to Acquire

Pedagogical Content Knowledge	Communication and Relationship
– Knowledge of subject matter – Understanding the structure of learning tasks – Knowledge of the difficulties – Knowledge of the time required – Mastering multiple strategies of explaining – Mastering multiple strategies of problem-solving	– Psychological knowledge (development, learning, motivation) – Knowledge about successful feedback – Setting priorities – Finding the right tone – Knowledge and intuitions about resistance, obstacles to learning, potentials

How You Acquire Practices of Learning Support

Analyzing Your Learning Support	Training of the Learning Support
– Sharing observations with others – Analyzing audio or video recordings of learning support situations – Soliciting feedback from peers on your own learning support behaviors – Raising awareness of your own behavior while supporting – Comparing it with recommended behavior – Talking with students	– Seeking learning opportunities (school, peers, private settings) – Practicing learning support in real workplace situations – Practicing support in one-to-one conversations – Practicing support in simulations with peers – Using deliberately different procedures and techniques – Testing variations of your interventions

Practices of Support You Need to Learn

Diagnostic Abilities	Effective Learning Support
– Identifying the individual learning level and learning difficulties – Recognizing the need for support – Identifying the cause of the learning difficulties – Recognizing the learning potential – Developing empathy to better understand problems and resistance	– Setting appropriate, challenging, individual goals – Selecting suitable tasks und problems – Intervening adapted to situation – Giving correct feedback on tasks – Intervening appropriately in language and communication style – Assessing the effects of feedback

Part III

MANAGING INSTRUCTION

The following chapters of part III focus on the main activities of instruction. Teachers must inevitably consider how to structure lessons in terms of time, whether they are short units or longer blocks of up to half a day. The course of instruction may vary, but it is almost always based on a recurring pattern.

After introducing the common formal structure of lessons, phases are presented and discussed, and the related core practices and teacher activities are explored in depth.

Chapter Seven

Introduction

FOLLOW THE TEACHER THROUGH A LESSON AND LOOK OUT FOR ESSENTIAL PRACTICES

Of course, all lessons have a time structure; they begin and end, and in between people perform different activities in varying constellations. Everyone knows it; this is not really worth mentioning. And yet there is much more happening inside people: they are attentive or distracted or stressed, they change mood and motivation, they are excited or annoyed or desperate or bored, they want to move or be left alone, they want to laugh or talk or dream . . .

And it is usually the teacher who steers his or her "teaching ship" through this sea of constantly changing thoughts, needs, and emotions, from the first to the last minute. This means that the *teacher must manage instruction*. Whether at the end of instruction as many of the students as possible leave the class satisfied or at least not frustrated, whether they have learned something or at least do not have the feeling of having wasted time, a good teacher certainly wants to make sure of that.

In the following chapters, we will look at which points in the lesson the teacher passes by and, above all, with which practices he or she can be as successful as possible at these points. We will encounter numerous practices that have to do with managing instruction: arousing interest, setting goals, gathering prior knowledge, explaining a fact, introducing activities, checking progress, and so on.

What follows, then, is *not a planning scheme but a walk through the typical stages of most lessons* in order to identify and describe the practices required and to show how they can be learned.

MOST LESSONS HAVE A COMMON STRUCTURE

The vast majority of lessons are based on a phased scheme that can create the best possible space for learning and has proven itself in principle. Here we consider a single or double lesson or a thematic half-day—that is, a temporally defined unit in which the students have to tune in to something new in a particular subject.

Structuring teaching in phases is nothing new and originally results from the logic of a lesson. Herbart, a German pedagogue of the nineteenth century, who was also highly regarded in the Anglo-Saxon world (e.g., Dodd, 1898), had already advocated phases in teaching with his formal stage theory (cf. Compayré, 1908). Much fuss was made about such models of instructional design during the last century. In times when teacher-directed classroom instruction prevailed, much was invested in variations of artful staging, not least because it was associated with the expectation that the right phasing scheme would be essential to achieving goals. Learning was supposed to be optimally supported by the given sequence.

In the meantime, there is considerable skepticism with regard to such expectations, even if the advantages of certain teaching concepts continue to be eagerly promoted. Today, the dominant idea is rather that the progress of students does not depend so much on the external staging as on what happens inside the students and to what extent it is possible to set in motion these inner processes of thinking, feeling, and willing. We find that interest in the subtleties of structuring a lesson has generally waned. Nevertheless, teaching naturally has a temporal structure—but it has been shown that this is basically very simple when the focus is on enabling progress.

The merely formal framework of lessons is simple and enables innumerable variations of teaching, depending on the design of the phases. It is so open that it allows for learning progress in different ways and does not prejudge any particular form of teaching. The framework includes four sequences (figure 7.1):

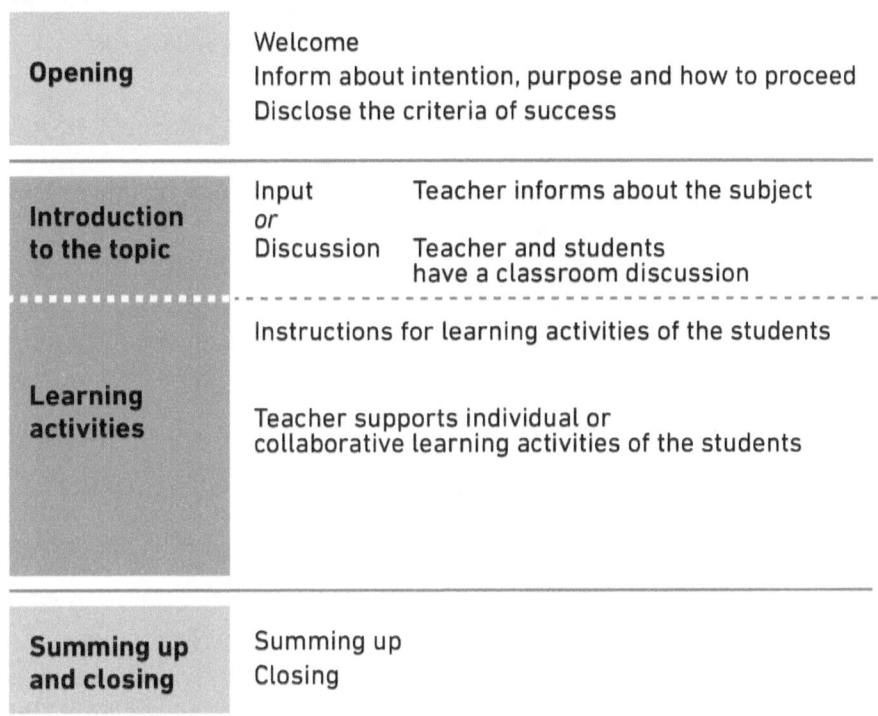

Figure 7.1. The basic structure of lessons. *Author created.*

- The opening and closing form the bracket, so to speak (lighter background).
- The ones in the middle focus on learning about the topic (darker background).

Does such a scheme unnecessarily restrict teachers and limit the variety of teaching options? This is not the case with this sequencing of teaching, and in fact, no one wants uniform teaching; no one wants to squeeze lessons into a rigid scheme. The general structure is simply a result of the logic of a lesson:

- The opening and closing are always necessary; they are a matter of course that belong to teaching, no matter how one wants to organize it.
- Each lesson needs a learning phase with some kind of input or stimulation and learning activities.

- Variety is created by offering meaningful variations in the sequences ("meaningful" in the sense of being helpful to achieve the goals).

And if the teacher has something in mind that lies outside of this structure, he or she certainly has good reasons for doing so. However, the teacher knows that instruction has a solid and well-founded basis with this formal scheme; one can fall back on it at any time.

The elements of lessons will now be discussed one by one: informing students about intention, purpose, and how to proceed; providing an input; guiding a classroom discussion; giving instructions for individual learning activities; and summing up and closing.

DRAWING ON RECENT AS WELL AS LONG-KNOWN CONCEPTS AND FINDINGS

Very little that follows is truly new. Since the nineteenth century, public schools have been established in the countries of the North, and since then, experts have thoroughly studied schools, teaching, and learning. Many insights and concepts have stood the test of time and are still valid today. For example, there has long been a broad body of knowledge about successful teaching, but it has not always found its way into teachers' daily practice. Also, the requirements changed over time (e.g., the competences of cooperation and self-organization of the learners), which required new teaching concepts.

Therefore, the whole breadth of knowledge is drawn on here. In addition to current findings and concepts, experts from longer ago are cited when they developed groundbreaking ideas or conducted fundamental research (e.g., Dewey, Bloom, or Gagné from the United States; Vygotski or Bakhtin from the then Soviet Union; Herbart or Alexander from Europe; Timperley or Hattie from New Zealand).

Textbox 7.1
UNIT, LESSON, CLASS: A CLARIFICATION OF TERMS

- *Unit (of work)*: A thematic unit that is worked on and deepened repeatedly over a period of several days or weeks.
- *Lesson*: Lessons are a part of a unit and usually last from thirty to ninety minutes, occasionally up to half a day or even longer. Their main characteristic is the thematic coherence with the focus on a few specific objectives. Lesson plans are typically created for lessons.
- *Class*: The terms "class" and "lesson" are quasi-synonymous and mostly interchangeable. To avoid misunderstandings, we use "class" here rarely and only in the sense of a time window and framework in which lessons take place. The term "period" is used only for a time slot.

Chapter Eight

The Transparent Opening of a Lesson

Many teachers think of the opening of the lesson as something motivating that will catch the students' attention. Of course, it is important that the students' interest and eagerness to learn are addressed, but the effect of superficial attempts to motivate usually fizzles out quickly. This is emphatically contrasted here with another very effective and central teaching element, the *transparent opening*, which in its own way also addresses interest and motivation. This idea is not new (e.g., Mager, 1962). In Europe, this approach has been particularly widely discussed (beginning with Grell & Grell, 1979).

Along with several other variants of starting lessons, the transparent opening takes a prominent position. It is, so to speak, the framework within which the teacher opens the lesson. It sets a tone that addresses the students as independent thinkers and feelers. Within this transparent opening, numerous variations and ideas are possible. What is special about it?

THE BASIC IDEA OF THE TRANSPARENT OPENING IS PARTNERSHIP

The opening informs students about what is to follow. The transparent opening is an expression of a partner-like relationship between the teacher and the learners. By providing transparent and clear information about what is to follow, the teacher shows that he or she takes the students seriously as people with whom a goal is to be achieved. The transparent opening is far from any staging. It does not use tricks, gimmicks, or manipulation, and it does not "motivate" in order to attract students to the lesson and the subject matter. It simply says what it is all about.

The unspoken message underlying this sort of opening is sober and honest. It might be something like, "We are gathered here so that you can learn something about a particular topic. I will try to explain to you why it is important and perhaps useful, and I will make an effort so that you will not have come to school for nothing and so that you will know and be able to do more afterward than you did before. And I'll do my part so that we can work in a cheerful and productive learning atmosphere."

Addressing students in this way treats them as partners in the common enterprise of learning and allows them to participate in what is happening. Students are given the opportunity to comment. For example, they report back that they did not fully understand the objectives or that the previous topic was not yet clear to them and they now suspect they are not getting the hang of it. Or they ask if they can work in groups, or they realize that they probably won't be able to complete the task in the time allotted. Such comments are insightful; the teacher will think briefly, respond, and adjust the objectives or schedule if necessary. When students think along in this way, they can share responsibility for the productive process from the beginning.

Of course, much is fixed in school. It is also clear to students that they cannot discuss things that are unchangeable at the start of class. On a superior level of regulation, there is a timetable, compulsory schooling, defined goals for each grade in each subject, but also agreements at the school level and in the classroom that are binding until further notice. Not that this should not be talked about, but the start of classes is not the right time.

The transparent opening usually takes only a few minutes and contains three elements. It follows a consistent logic by briefly and accurately informing students of the intentions, the context of the rationale, and the planned activities.

THE WELCOME SETS THE TONE

How do you shape the short transition from the moment students gradually arrive in class to the moment the lesson formally begins? This is highly individual, and there is no point in trying to formulate rules about it. But one thing is certain: the welcome, including the moments of informal contact before the actual start, sets the tone of the class. With the tone of the greeting, the teacher can also shape the atmosphere to a certain extent: serious, concentrated, dynamic, cheerful, relaxed, sober—or tense, fearful, irritable, paralyzing, and so on. Here is the recommendation: a teacher should *put himself or herself in the desired mood before the lesson*, because this also affects the atmosphere in the classroom.

INFORMING ABOUT INTENTION, PURPOSE, AND HOW TO PROCEED

First, a brief clarification of terms. What is the difference between intentions, purposes, goals, and objectives? Here, we are deliberately talking about "intentions" because students are not interested in what specific objectives the teachers (or preservice teachers) have noted for themselves but what they actually have in mind. Students have a claim and an interest in knowing what the subsequent lesson is about, what the *topic* is, and where the *learning focus* is—in other words, what exactly they have to learn within this topic. They want to know what the teacher has in mind and what needs to be done—basically, the big picture. The transparent opening takes this into account by having the teacher reveal what he or she plans to do, why, and how:

- Intention (What is it about? What am I planning to do?)
- Purpose (Why this? What's the use?)
- How to proceed (How are we going to get there?)

Basically, this is a given. Just compare it with adults who hold meetings. They know exactly these three things: (1) What is the point, or what is the intended outcome? (2) Why and for what are we meeting? (3) How do we proceed? When the purpose of a meeting is unclear and the participants do not quite know why or for what purpose they are sitting there, they sometimes show surprising reactions: they are visibly confused or annoyed; they withdraw and become lethargic; they occupy themselves with other things, answering mails, for example; they whisper with the neighbors; they regress and get into mischief; or they simply stay away.

And this is exactly how students can behave if they are kept in the dark about intentions.

The analogy with adults suggests that students should not be taken for fools. They readily take note of what the teacher's plan is and usually sense whether it is coherent. Students are capable of thinking about the planned lesson on a meta level, and they can comprehend intentions if they make sense and raise objections if necessary.

How do you present intention, purpose, and procedure? Following are some useful hints.

Choose Simple, Understandable Language

Do not use the formalistic jargon of operationalized objectives. Stay specific, for example, like this:

- "Today's topic is glue. You can make your own glue, and in doing so you'll see what's in it."
- "Today's topic is to identify trees that thrive in our climate zone and name them—we'll start with the trees next to our school."

Choose Goal 1: One Goal Describing Precisely the One Topic or Learning Focus

Communicate *only one clear subject matter goal* that describes the thematic learning focus. Don't enumerate in detail any cleverly constructed subobjectives.

Choose Goal 2: Add Exactly One Other Cross-Curricular Goal

Cross-curricular goals may have to do with activity during class, social processes, or strategies for self-organization. By providing a cross-curricular goal, you show students that learning always takes place on two levels (at least)—that is, not solely on the subject level. Examples:

- "You make sure everyone in your work group is on the same page."
- "You conduct all discussions with your neighbors in whispers."

- "You don't digress when researching on the Internet and focus solely on what you want answered."
- "You observe yourselves when your concentration wanes and report on it at the end."

And why exactly *one cross-curricular goal*? This is a pragmatic decision; learners are usually unable to pick up and focus on more than one thematic intent and one cross-curricular objective at a time. Anything beyond that is likely to be forgotten.

Do Not Anticipate What Learners Cannot Yet Know

Do not set learning goals in the following way: "You will be able to summarize the terms of the surrender at Appomattox on April 6, 1865." Students probably have no idea what this is about, and so the objective is meaningless.

Do Not Construct a Purpose and Meaning if It Is Not Obvious

It is sufficient if the teacher briefly explains why this topic or this learning focus is on the table today. If there is an everyday benefit for students, name it. Often the topics and goals are already predetermined by the curriculum; for example, students should understand Spanish phrases and words related to money and shopping, they should be able to catch a ball, or they should be able to calculate change. Even if the relevance is not immediately obvious to students, they will usually accept it if the teacher communicates transparently.

Visualize in Simple Bullet Points Your Content Goal and the Cross-Curricular Goal

Show the intention and the cross-curricular goal on the board, whiteboard, or flipchart so they remain visible throughout the lesson. Intentions need to be clear and remembered, and at any point learners and the teacher can refer to them to check if they are on track and getting closer to the goals. The specification of success criteria follows in the next step (in the section "Reveal Criteria of Success").

You Can Also Cut the Opening Short if Everything Is Clear

There are certainly situations in which the intention is clear, and everyone knows what needs to be done, for example, when working on a topic that has long since been introduced. Of course, the introduction is then kept to a minimum—and yet here, too, the students should have the opportunity to object or ask something about your plan.

REVEAL CRITERIA OF SUCCESS (BY REVEALING THE TEST TASKS)

By "success," it is meant that students have achieved the goals in whole or at least in part, and this has nothing to do with a summative and graded assessment but simply reflects learning progress. Learners are successful in this sense if they have made progress toward the goals. But how do learners know what their progress is like?

What certainly doesn't help them is a list of detailed learning goals and competency expectations, possibly copied verbatim from the curriculum or a textbook. No matter how detailed the descriptions of what needs to be done or the competencies that need to be built, students can't do anything with them. Will anyone seriously expect the students to read one of these objectives formulated in accordance with the rules, which—as is appropriate—use two verbs ("*can finish* in three minutes," "*can enumerate*," "*can draw*"), in order to check for themselves to what extent they have now achieved this goal? This is a completely unrealistic expectation that is therefore hardly ever seriously fulfilled.

What they do have in mind, however, is a summative test (exam, written test, class assignment, or other designations, depending on the region) that tells them exactly what is expected of them. *Test tasks are the currency by which students measure success.* They are used to the fact that the assessment of their performance is measured to a considerable extent by such test tasks. Accordingly, they are sensitized to it. The punch line: *test tasks that match the objectives replace the detailed learning objectives.* For the time being, however, the test tasks are only used as an orientation aid and purely formative.

With the tasks and test items, the students have exactly the right concrete criteria with which they can easily find out where they stand. Math is a good illustration of this, because the tasks play a central role and are usually very deliberately and ingeniously constructed, in a textbook, in a test database, or in learning software: countless tasks have been constructed for every subarea, every specific competence, and every level of difficulty in mathematics. By looking at the tasks that have already been successfully solved, students can see quite well to what extent they have achieved the objectives.

It becomes more difficult with topics that are less structured than mathematics. How can the learners recognize where they stand with regard to the topic "Mississippi navigation" or "domestic pig" or "exciting story" or "composing a catchy melody"? The teacher is especially challenged here to find or construct appropriate tasks that reflect exactly what the essence of the intention is.

How are the criteria of success revealed? It is very easy to reveal the criteria, and it is extremely useful for everyone.

1. *Find or construct tasks and test items that check exactly what you expect learners to do at the end.*
   Don't check something else that the items may be easier to construct or correct for but that don't get to the heart of the intended goal.
2. *From the start, give learners these tasks that you want them to use to check their competencies.*
   This way, learners can continuously check to what extent they have already achieved the objectives.
3. *Allow the students to check the correctness of the solutions and procedures.*
   This is easier with tasks that have a clear result than, for example, with self-written texts that need to be checked for their content, consistency, or formal coherence. Here, it helps if the teacher explains the criteria or reviews the work right away and gives feedback.

Some teachers may be hesitant to put on the table those test items that are usually reserved for summative assessment. Why not, really? If you present students with twenty items and announce that six of them will be used in a summative test, you create a win-win situation: learners know what they need to be able to do, can continually check their progress, and can learn in a more focused way; they are more motivated for learning, and the final performance of the class is likely to be better than if the teacher makes a secret of his or her assignments.

SUMMARY

The transparent opening again in brief:

- Welcome the students and create a warm atmosphere.
- Announce what you intend to do (the two goals), for what purpose, and how.
- Give learners unobstructed insight into the tasks, test items, and criteria that accurately reflect the goals for your lesson.

> Textbox 8.1 FURTHER INFORMATION AND RESOURCES
>
> **LEARNING OBJECTIVES: A FATAL MISUNDERSTANDING**
>
> The good intention of formulating learning objectives must be acknowledged; it should be clear to everyone what is to be learned. But what is well-intentioned is not necessarily good.
>
> Since Benjamin Bloom and colleagues (Bloom, Engelhart, Frust, Hill, & Krathwohl, 1956) presented their taxonomy of educational goals in the cognitive domain in 1956, there have been countless attempts to diversify and differentiate goals. Thus, extensive cascades of learning goals emerged. Similar goal hierarchies can be found today in competency or standard models.
>
> Having goals is of course a good thing; the problem arises when it becomes a formalized, almost ritualized practice whose meaning for actual learning is hardly apparent anymore. For student teachers, formulating goals is sometimes perceived as an additional task, largely of no consequence, and more likely to satisfy the demands of teacher educators. Teaching, it can be assumed, would not be much different without elaborated goals as long as goal definition remains a practice demanded by teacher education and does not reach the learners.

Ebel put his critique of formalistic goal setting as early as 1970 this way: "Little that is wrong with any teacher's educational efforts today can be cured by getting [the teacher] to define his objectives more fully and precisely. We ought not to ask teachers to spend much of their limited time in writing elaborate statements of their objectives" (Ebel, 1970, p. 173).

However, anyone who reads the original texts of Robert F. Mager (1962), who is considered a pioneer of specifying learning goals, may be surprised: his intentions are far different from the later formalisms. Mager was most emphatic that objectives must be understandable, accessible, comprehensible, and known to all learners, and that they should serve as a constant "guideline" for students while learning—in other words, that objectives are made at least as much for students as for teachers.

Sure, Mager wrote his book at a time when *behavioral objectives* were in focus. However, from today's perspective, his principles can as well be applied to all types of goals.

Here is an abridged excerpt from Mager's book *Preparing Instructional Objectives*:

> An objective is an *intent* communicated by a statement describing a proposed change in a learner—a statement of what the learner is to be like when he has successfully completed a learning experience. . . .
>
> When clearly defined goals are lacking, it is impossible to evaluate a course or program efficiently, and there is no sound basis for selecting appropriate materials, content, or instructional methods. After all, the machinist does not select a tool until he knows what operation he intends to perform. Neither does a composer orchestrate a score until he knows what effects he wishes to achieve. Similarly, a builder does not select his materials or specify a schedule for construction until he has his blueprints (objectives) before him. Too often, however, one hears teachers arguing the relative merits of textbooks or other aids of the classroom versus the laboratory, without ever specifying just what goal the aid or method is to assist in achieving. I cannot emphasize too strongly the point that an instructor will function in a fog of his own making until he knows just what he wants his students to be able to do at the end of the instruction.
>
> Another important reason for stating objectives sharply relates to the evaluation of the degree to which the learner is able to perform in the manner desired. . . . Unless goals are clearly and firmly fixed in the minds of both parties, tests are at best misleading; at worst, they are

irrelevant, unfair, or useless. To be useful they must *measure performance in terms of the goals*. Unless the programmer himself has a clear picture of his instructional intent, he will be unable to select test items that clearly reflect the student's ability to perform the desired skills, or that will reflect how well the student can demonstrate his acquisition of desired information.

An additional advantage of clearly defined objectives is that the student is provided the means to evaluate *his own* progress at any place along the route of instruction and is able to organize his efforts into relevant activities. With clear objectives in view, the student knows which activities on his part are relevant to his success, and it is no longer necessary for him to "psych out" the instructor. As you know too well, considerable time and effort are frequently spent by students in learning the idiosyncrasies of their teachers; and, unfortunately, this knowledge is often very useful to the student with insight. He may breeze through a course armed with no more than a bag full of tricks designed to rub the teacher the right way.

But how do you write the objective to maximize the probability of your achieving it? What are the characteristics of a meaningfully stated objective? . . . A meaningfully stated objective, then, is one that succeeds in communicating your intent; the best statement is the one that excludes the greatest number of possible alternatives to your goal. (Mager, 1962, pp. 3–10, abridged)

Mager's key messages in these sections can be summarized roughly as follows:

1. Without clear intentions, instructional design is characterized by arbitrariness; the teacher has no criteria for one course of action or another.
2. Review of learning becomes a farce when neither learner nor teacher knows what should have been learned.
3. Objectives must be formulated so clearly that there can be no misunderstanding of what is to be learned.
4. Learners must understand and internalize the objectives so that they can learn purposefully and monitor themselves.

Mager, on the other hand, says nothing about which goals to choose. In Mager's sense, however, goals should serve the learners so that they know exactly where the journey is going.

Textbox 8.2 ACTIVITIES AND SUGGESTIONS

TEST THE STRATEGY OF TRANSPARENT OPENING

The transparent opening is an ideal training ground for building a practice. You develop your own practices for classroom opening primarily by repeatedly testing and varying the proposed elements, observing the effects, learning to understand the opening better, developing it further, and dealing with it flexibly. Only in this way does a recipe become a flexible practice.

Atmosphere

Pay attention to the atmosphere before the actual start of the lesson. Try to influence the atmosphere favorably through your own informal behavior. Since this situation repeats itself several times a day, you may already be able to notice effects and adjust your behavior and make it more flexible. Work systematically on this aspect for a few days.

The Transparent Opening

Read again the suggestions for the transparent opening in this chapter.

Intention (Goals)

Follow the recommendation to consistently formulate the two goals in a way that is easy to understand: exactly one subject-based goal (topic) and exactly one cross-curricular goal. Resist the temptation to expand the goals, but stick to the one central point to be achieved. Write them down and communicate them at the beginning of each class. As Mager (1962) wrote, "A meaningfully stated objective is one that succeeds in communicating your intent" (p. 10).

Purpose

For each goal, briefly (!) explain why it seems important to you today. Stay concise and do not develop lengthy explanations.

Give students an opportunity to comment on the intentions and the purpose. Accept objections in a friendly manner; that way you show the whole class that you are willing to listen. If you can resolve an objection quickly, do so; otherwise, indicate when and how you will discuss the matter with the class.

How to Proceed

Outline in brief how the subsequent lesson is likely to proceed.

Review, Gain Experience, and Understand What Is Happening

It is important now that you practice the opening consistently, for example, for two weeks. Vary the elements and again pay attention to the effects. Also try to understand why something leads to better results or something else is poorly received or causes confusion.

For the time being, do not fundamentally question the transparent opening but rather try to optimize it.

Chapter Nine

Providing an Input

The days are gone when the teacher was the most important source of information for students. Yet professional practices of informing are still central, because only the teacher can optimally tailor information to learners.

Practices of informing are primarily about how a teacher communicates something to a group, "something" meaning facts, contexts, skills, and procedures. Depending on the topic, students' age, and circumstances, specifically tailored approaches are needed to get the point across. The goal of informing practices is always to help students better understand or be able to do something.

We always assume here that the input happens in the classroom. Indeed, that is almost always the case. But there are also approaches that move the input to the students' homes. One proven method is to have students read something at home. A newer approach is the so-called flipped classroom. This approach is occasionally mentioned here but not explored further (see textbox 9.1).

Textbox 9.1

THE FLIPPED CLASSROOM: INPUT FOR AT HOME

Flipped classroom is an instructional strategy that—as the word suggests—turns the typical classroom work upside down: input is shifted home, and homework belongs in school. Students work out the information on the topic on their own, now increasingly with videos and online rather than straight reading, and in the classroom the teacher is available to students if questions arise while solving problems or practicing.

Certainly, the flipped classroom requires an adjustment for everyone, Teachers prepare quite differently by providing input that students can work on themselves, and students must get used to the fact that their "homework" is now different; they must have already worked through the input before coming to school, because in the classroom basic information is no longer taught from scratch but is now reinforced.

Overall, the experience with the flipped classroom is mostly positive once it is implemented. The presence of the teacher while solving tasks and problems and practicing proves to be a key factor in improving student learning. According to a meta-analysis of research by Strelan, Osborn, and Palmer (2020), the flipped classroom has a positive effect on student performance and is beneficial regardless of discipline and education level. Research suggests that the key ingredient is the opportunity for structured, active learning.

"INPUT": NOT ONLY FACTS BUT AT TIMES ALSO INTRODUCING A TOPIC OR A CORE TASK

The term "input" doesn't just mean that something is "put into" the students—facts, information, procedures, connections—although that is indeed often the case. Sometimes also quite appropriately the term "mini lesson" is used.

Input can also introduce a new topic by delving into a significant question, problem, or challenge—not just any factual issue but something that is challenging and on which key aspects of a topic clearly emerge. Wiggins and McTighe (2006) call them "big ideas" or "core tasks"; other authors refer to them as "core ideas" or simply "problems." They are likely to open the door to larger contexts and important insights and are not to be understood as cheap motivational tricks to get students' attention. They unlock a new, perhaps even mysterious, field for students to explore on their own or in class. Such an input can provide the framework that gives meaning to isolated facts and skills and places them in a larger context.

Textbox 9.2
AN EXAMPLE OF INPUT WITH A CHALLENGING PROBLEM

The teacher might introduce the input in a quite conventional and not very motivating way:

> "Today we are talking about the buoyancy principle. I'm going to explain to you what forces act on a body in a liquid. You see here a basin of water, a cube of iron, and a spring balance to measure the forces."

Or the teacher might start somewhat like this:

> "Wooden ships float in water, which is not surprising, since wood floats, as we all know. But it's strange that ships made of steel usually don't sink, since everybody knows that steel sinks in water."

This input begins with the presentation of a problem that is challenging for the students so that a cognitive process is set in motion and students' interest in finding a solution to this problem increases.

SEVEN CHARACTERISTICS OF GOOD INPUT

The following seven characteristics are customized for an input in classroom instruction. Each of these seven characteristics for an input is crucial. If some characteristics are ignored, the likelihood that the input will be suboptimal or even counterproductive increases.

An input is clearly a monologue, and, in this case, that makes sense. As long as an input is short and precise, there is no reason to turn it into a dialogue in a contrived manner.

1. A Good Input Is Coherent in Terms of Facts and Well Prepared

If you have internalized good practices of providing information, you can sometimes give a professional impromptu input. However, this requires a lot of practice and just as much feedback from colleagues. A first basic requirement is again *the thorough understanding of the matter* (or the process, the technique, the context, etc.). This was mentioned earlier in the context of explaining.

In addition, professional input usually only succeeds *if it is also rehearsed*, especially in the case of less experienced teachers. Those who are not aware of the criteria of professional input may get used to the wrong thing. Experience alone is not enough; it does not necessarily lead to professionalism but only to untested routines that can be counterproductive and unprofessional.

2. A Good Input Is Limited to What Is Indispensable

The art lies in omission. Not everything the teacher knows about the topic needs to be shared. Input is an important (and often the first) building block in a longer learning process, to which much learner self-activity will be added later. Above all, students should get to know what will really help them in the learning activities that follow. Everything else tends to be a distraction at this stage.

You can just make a decision to avoid excessive chatter. But leaving out things that you think are important is more difficult and requires discipline. However, cutting things out is worthwhile, and those who have tried it will find that the inputs become more catchy, clearer, and more structured.

3. A Good Input Is Transparent and Says What the Content Is Meant For

Adults experience lectures as exhausting if the point and purpose are not clear. Students are not likely to feel any differently, even if they usually don't say so. Those who do not understand what exactly the lesson is all about soon drift off.

Learners have a right to know the purpose for which they are to listen attentively for the next few minutes. If it is clear to them that what is presented will help them better manage subsequent activities, they are likely to be more attentive.

What does it mean to communicate transparently?

- In all cases, *clearly state the topic*. For example, "I'm going to explain how we double and triple fractions. I'll also give you some examples. This will help you solve some problems and apply the procedure in

similar tasks." Students will not be more interested if you try to build suspense by not telling them exactly what the lesson is about, hoping for a stimulating surprise effect. This is hardly the way to get students interested in learning. On the contrary, such forced moments of suspense don't last long. There is a risk that students will turn away from the subject as soon as they realize it is nothing more than a flash in the pan.
- *Make it clear to learners to what extent it benefits them to pay attention.* It immediately makes sense to learners that it is useful to pay attention when they become aware that they understand things better afterward and can manage learning activities more easily.

4. Good Input Helps Students Make Connections to Their Prior Knowledge

It goes without saying that an input should connect to the learners' level of knowledge. A teacher might recall, "We looked at animal hibernation last week. Today we are talking about another way animals can survive the winter."

But it is not enough to connect to the material already covered; it is important to connect to the actual learning levels of all learners. For this, as we know, the diagnostic skills of the teacher are necessary. Particularly in the case of demanding topics in language and mathematics, students with gaps may no longer be able to find their way in and may drop out.

Earlier in the book, the zone of proximal development or learning zone was addressed. When the topic is outside the learning zone—too mundane or too difficult—students move into the comfort or panic zone. Both are problematic.

How to deal with it?

1. *Design the input so that it reaches as many students as possible.* This is easier said than done. It takes a lot of practice to design an input for multiple levels of ability so that no one drifts away. For those students who are struggling, you can sprinkle in a parenthetical explanation here and there, and for the more advanced, you can hint at another requirement in an aside without irritating the others. This fluency in bringing the whole class along requires practice, but it can be learned and is a result of constant training.

2. *Include short repetitions for consolidation in the input.* Even if the input is short and entertaining, students may miss something and lose the thread. Therefore, an input should not be strictly linear but should include short loops to bring along those who did not immediately understand or catch on. For example, "As I said, one of the five valley forms is clearly caused by glaciers; it's the U-shaped valley. Now the next form . . ."
3. *Make the level of difficulty transparent and offer alternatives for students with difficulties.* Again, the imperative of transparency applies. Say something like this: "I know that not everyone has mastered identifying verbs yet. If you are not sure, come to me later and we'll go over it again. But now I'll explain to you all how to recognize parts of speech."

5. A Good Input Is Simple, Structured, Precise, and Stimulating

An input should also be rhetorically brilliant. From their own experience, most people know bad presentations: they are complicated, unstructured, incomprehensible, unapparent, boring, long-winded, humorless. The opposite is true of a good lecture: it is simple, structured, precise, and stimulating. In the 1970s, the psychologists Langer, Schulz von Thun, and Tausch (2019) developed a manual on how to write and present texts in a comprehensible way. Exactly these four criteria (simple, structured, precise, and stimulating) made a good presentation according to the authors. One could add further adjectives: brisk, speedy, humorous, positive, interesting, trenchant, insightful.

Good input uses advance organizers and graphic organizers. The term "advance organizer" was introduced by Ausubel (1960) and means that at the beginning of a text or lecture an overview of the content is given so that the listeners can better understand what follows. In the 1960s and 1970s, the effect of advance organizers was extensively researched, and there was much evidence of their beneficial effects on comprehension, skill, and retention (Mayer, 1979).

The principle is plausible. If the teacher establishes context in a simple way, learners can fit in the explanations before the whole lecture is over. For example, "Today is about valleys as we all know them: wide or narrow valleys, those in the mountains, in hilly areas, or even in the middle

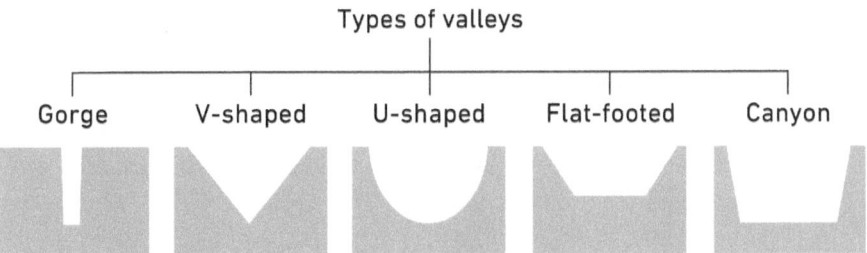

Figure 9.1. A graphic organizer to the focus "types of valleys." *Author created.*

of plains. I'll show you five different shapes of valleys, and we'll find out why they took this shape." In this case, learners know three things:

- We are talking about valleys as they are found all over the world.
- We learn about and distinguish between five shapes.
- We learn why they have this particular shape.

Everything the teacher is now presenting—through input, texts, media, models, and so on—revolves around these points, which are easy to understand and remember. Everything new fits into this "grid" and takes on meaning on an ongoing basis.

The beneficial effect can be enhanced by also using a *simple graphic organizer* (see figure 9.1). Among the best-known graphic organizers are tree diagrams, mind maps, concept maps, and Venn diagrams. The advantage of diagrams is that information can be structured, read, and retained with less effort (research review on text comprehension with graphic organizers: Robinson & Kiewra, 1995). Ideally, graphic organizers are simple and not cluttered so as to not cause confusion, especially when a topic is new to learners.

Good input uses models and illustrations with restraint. Sometimes too much is expected from showing and illustrating (see textbox 9.4). Illustration does not necessarily lead to understanding but can serve to *trigger a thinking process.*

6. A Good Input Is Short (That's Why It's Also Called a Mini Lesson)

There are three compelling reasons for short inputs:

1. *Too long inputs steal learning time.* That time is missing for the learners during the active consolidation.
2. *Attention span is limited.* There are different figures on this (Bradbury, 2016), but eight minutes for an input should be the upper limit in class.
3. *A short input prevents digression.* This way, students hardly miss anything they need for the next activity.

7. A Good Input Does Not Contain Questions

The obsessive asking of questions is a fad of teachers that is passed down from generation to generation. Sinclair and Coulthard (1975) analyzed this stereotypical question-answer game and identified the typical pattern of initiation–response–follow-up (IRF for short) that is exceedingly characteristic of many classroom conversations. Jay Lemke (1990) also coined the term "triadic dialogue" because it usually involves the same three-step process of question, answer, and evaluation. Grell and Grell (2005) sharply criticize this "egg hunt pedagogy" (the teacher knows where the eggs are but does not tell) and radically refute it with plausible arguments. They criticize teachers for wanting to "work out" content and reflexively turning information into questions for the learners. Instead of saying, "Valleys with this shape are called V-shaped," they ask, "What do you think these valleys could be called?"—a ridiculous question, since the term has already been established.

CONCLUSION: ENGAGE WITH THESE SEVEN CHARACTERISTICS

If you engage with these seven characteristics of good input and take on the exercise and processing suggestions, you will take a big step toward professional practices of informing. By doing and constantly optimizing, you will develop the input practice and use it quickly and flexibly.

Textbox 9.3 FURTHER INFORMATION AND RESOURCES
FINDINGS ABOUT ADVANCE ORGANIZERS

After Ausubel (1960) introduced the concept of advance organizers, other researchers soon took notice of it, used it, and intensively researched its effect. A review by Mayer (1979), one of the leading experts in educational psychology, showed the overall beneficial effects of advance organizers on learning and specified the criteria for good advance organizers:

> Twenty years of research on advance organizers has clearly shown that advance organizers can affect learning, and the conditions under which organizers are most likely to affect learning can be specified. Thus, it is now possible to suggest conditions for the use of advance organizers.
>
> As a general rule, advance organizers will result in broader learning outcomes in situations where the learner does not normally possess or use an assimilative context for incorporating the new material.
>
> In particular, advance organizers will result in broader learning
>
> - when the material is potentially conceptual but appears unorganized or unfamiliar to the learner,
> - when the learner lacks a rich set of related knowledge or abilities,
> - when the organizer provides a higher level context for learning, and
> - when the test measures the breadth of transfer ability. (Mayer, 1979, p. 161)

A good advance organizer provides an organized conceptual framework that is meaningful to the learner, and that allows the learner to relate concepts in the instructional material to elements of the framework.

In the present studies, good organizers have been

- concrete models or analogies or examples,
- sets of general higher order rules, and
- discussions of the main themes in familiar terms.
- In the present studies, poor organizers have been
- specific factual prequestions,
- summaries, outlines,
- directions to pay attention to specific key facts or terms."
(Mayer, 1979, p. 162)

Textbox 9.4 FURTHER INFORMATION AND RESOURCES

MEDIA OF VISUALIZATION

Perception as a Basic Principle of Learning . . . but Is That Enough?

Many teachers think that using as many visualizations and real encounters with objects as possible is definitely conducive to learning. But is it true in this way?

Today there is no lack of concrete things in the classroom: objects, animals, plants, household items, blackboard, projector, musical instruments, models—much of course also available digitally. The children should see, hear, if possible feel and touch, with the expectation that this will facilitate access to the material and that they will better understand what it is about. It is only about two hundred years since this then-revolutionary principle of direct access to things found its way into schools.

The Swiss educator Heinrich Pestalozzi (1801/1894) coined the term *Anschauung*, which literally means the act of looking at something. The German term was subsequently also used in English. One of the most ardent advocates of the importance of *Anschauung* was the German educator Wilhelm Rein, whose works were also published in English. He was convinced that all learning must start from "perception" (that is, in English, what he called *Anschauung*). He described the essence of his method this way:

> If the aim of the lesson has been rightly put, it produces a flood of thoughts in the pupil at once. This is above all essential, if one expects to produce clear percepts from which to deduce accurate notions. In fact, the process of learning may be summed up in these two activities. From the percept to the concept or notion. (Rein, 1895, p. 171)

Later, Takaya (2003) summarized it this way:

> One of the major inventions of modern education is an instructional use of *Anschauung*. . . . This German term essentially means the direct knowledge of the object without intermediary processes such as reasoning. . . . It implies the primacy of the direct experience of the individual, as opposed, for example, to such secondhand experience as

reading books or listening to explanations of others. . . . An appeal to Anschauung is a part of the broader scheme of education which trusts the individual's capacity for obtaining knowledge and rationality by using his or her own innate ability, primarily, by means of the five senses. The assumption that every individual is, at least in principle, able to achieve knowledge and rationality using his or her own senses meant the rejection of the old assumption which underlay the authoritarian, speculative, and deductive method of education. (pp. 77–78)

"An Ox Goes Out to Pasture for Twenty Years and Yet Does Not Become a Botanist"

This popular saying about the ox (quoted from Neuweg, 2016, p. 31) expresses a plausible insight: one does not learn by looking at things alone. The naïve belief in the power of mere observation was increasingly criticized by psychologists in the twentieth century. Many visualizations and mindless actions—even in class—do not trigger thinking and understanding; they remain at the level of thoughtless execution (e.g., coloring pictures and maps or schematically carrying out chemistry experiments).

The cognitive psychology of the twentieth century overcame this naïve notion and showed that it takes an *active mental effort* of one's own to understand a thing. For example, the psychologist Jean Piaget showed in his famous experiments that the mental development and thinking of children develops according to certain regularities. Depending on age and circumstances, they "see" the same thing differently. Although Piaget's findings were later partially relativized in some respects, the understanding of an inner structure and regularity of cognition and thinking was a groundbreaking discovery (e.g., Wadsworth, 1989).

Pairing Visualization with Activation

The hoped-for short-circuit from visualization to insight has been disproved; what is needed, therefore, is *an active mental effort on the part of the students*. Therefore, the presentation of objects, visualizations, and so on is *always only a means to an end* in order to initiate a mental process that the children must actively bring about.

Textbox 9.5 ACTIVITIES AND SUGGESTIONS

REHEARSE PROVIDING GOOD INPUT—IT'S IMPORTANT

It is tempting to skip the following exercise because it takes time and concentration. But rest assured, it's worth the effort.

Once you have worked through an input very thoroughly a few times, you will internalize the criteria and learn something for your entire professional future. The next time you talk in an unfocused, long-winded manner, the criteria will come back to you, and chances are you will adjust your style.

Your teaching will become more concise, and both the students and you will be highly satisfied with the results.

1. **Plan and Record an Input**
   - Choose a topic that you will introduce in your next class.
   - Review the seven criteria of a good input.
   - Outline your input, taking into account the criteria for good input.
   - Write it down (type it or use the dictate feature of the computer) on a maximum of two pages, which corresponds to about eight minutes of speaking time.
   - Recite the input to yourself and record yourself doing it (audio or video).
2. **Check the Input**
   Now check the recorded input according to the above criteria:
   - *Factual accuracy:* Eliminate vagueness and errors.
   - *Limit to what is indispensable:* Omit anything superfluous unless it contributes decisively to the quality of the input.
   - *Transparent communication of benefits:* Rephrase or rethink if the benefit is not immediately obvious.
   - *Connectivity for learners:* If there is the slightest suspicion that the listeners might not follow at some point, rewrite and rephrase.
   - *Comprehensible, structured, stimulating presentation:* If the input does not come across well, identify parts that are difficult to understand or tedious and long-winded, rethink the dramaturgy, and work with organizers and illustrations if necessary.
   - *Shortness:* If necessary, shorten to eight minutes or less.
   - *Refrain from questions:* As a matter of principle, do not ask questions; however, no rule is without exception: if a question is really necessary, you certainly have your good reasons.

3. **Determine the Consequences**
   - Note what you should improve.
   - Record the input one more time and subject it to another rigorous review.
   - Keep going until you've got the input sorted!

Use Your Own Training Videos of an Input in the Flipped Classroom

If you have recorded some videos for practice purposes, you already have a small stock of elaborated inputs. Why not use these to try out the flipped classroom (if you don't have experience with it) or produce more videos that would be suitable for it?

1. Reread textbox 9.1. Do further research on the flipped classroom if needed. You will find many references on the Internet.
2. Choose a sequence of a few lessons where you would normally give an input.
3. Inform the students about the experiment with the flipped classroom.
4. Make your video of the input available on a platform and give the students the link.
5. Set a deadline by which the video should be studied.
   Encourage students who do not have a smartphone or other access to the Internet to watch the video with peers, or give them a time slot after school to watch it.
6. Consider how to proceed with students who have not watched the video.
7. In the next lesson, start right away with the activities to deepen the topic.

Chapter Ten

Guiding Discussions

If a matter can be presented and explored in depth to the best advantage with good input, there would be little reason to replace it with whole-class discussion, but there are situations where discussion adds real value, and so it can be useful to explore a topic with the whole class. That is what this section is about.

THE ADDED VALUE OF CONVERSATION

Working out pure facts in conversation is unproductive and even confusing. Reinventing or discovering things under the tight guidance of the teacher cannot be the point of conversations. However, having a *genuine conversation on an issue and involving all participants* has potential benefits that no lecture or reading can replace:

- It forces one to use and *sharpen language*.
- It requires *listening, understanding, and critically examining* what others have said.
- It pushes students to be *cognitively engaged* (otherwise everything said goes in one ear and out the other, as we know).
- It requires *searching for answers together* (i.e., exploring an unsolved problem).
- It encourages *reflection* and the presentation and consideration of *arguments*.
- It helps to *clarify a significant issue* (i.e., to deepen it together, to understand it better, and to arrive at solutions).

Genuine conversations not only help with understanding; more importantly, they *develop the generic skills* of argumentation and respectful dialogue ("argument literacy"; Reznitskaya & Wilkinson, 2015). But, of course, only genuine, fear-free, and respectful conversations about a meaningful open question lead students to develop and use these qualities. This is what we are going to talk about next.

CRITIQUE OF THE TRADITIONAL RECITATION PATTERN

A characteristic of the so-called recitation is that the teacher repeatedly asks students questions to which he or she expects a specific answer. This has already been addressed in relation to the initiation–response–follow-up (IRF) template. Rightly, this pattern, which only pretends that students are participating, has been questioned. It is basically a monological style of discourse. Since the 1970s, much research and observation has confirmed this critical view, starting with Sinclair and Coulthard (1975). The teacher maintains control in this sham dialogue style of discourse, which makes it difficult, if not impossible, for students to engage in genuine, thoughtful participation.

The IRF pattern (or triadic dialogue, according to Lemke, 1990) is often used to query knowledge that students should know, for example:

"Where do penguins live?"
"Where it's cold . . . Antarctis?"
"Yes, good!"

The IRF pattern is particularly aberrant when it is used to elaborate on a new subject that is unknown to the students. Since the students are still completely lacking the relevant information (or they only know something about it by chance), the lesson often becomes a time-consuming guessing game. The dialogue goes something like this:

"What do you know about Hawaii?"
"That's where the Ironman race takes place every year."
"Mhm. What do the others think?"

The answer is not wrong, but the teacher wants to hear something else. As Young (1991) puts it, the first example is of the WDPK type ("What Do Pupils Know"), the second of the GWTT type ("Guess What Teacher Thinks").

Textbox 10.1

> In a traditionally run classroom discussion, do students learn much from one another? Do they learn to like or respect one another? Do they tend to remember what was talked about? Do they listen to each other? Do large percentages of them speak? Are they unafraid to speak? In addition, do physically handicapped or learning-disabled children feel comfortable speaking or otherwise participating in the large group setting of the discussion? Since these are important questions and the answer to them is *no* for large numbers of students, is there an alternative discussion strategy to the teacher-question/one-student-respond-at-a-time format? (Lyman, 1981, pp. 109–110)

According to Cazden (2001, p. 30), this was still the most common pattern of classroom discussion at the turn of the millennium. Hage et al. (1985) cite a 49 percent share of guided instructional talk in total instructional time (p. 61), and similar findings are described by Alexander (2001) and Lyle (2008). According to a more recent study by Bauer, Reinartz, and Gehrmann (2017), students even *planned to introduce* a topic in a teacher-led questioning manner in 56 percent of cases. The points of criticism are manifold (e.g., Cazden, 2001; Lyle, 2008):

- It is—soberly considered—a perverse way of communication that the teacher asks things she or he already knows, while students are supposed to give answers about something they mostly do not know yet.
- Lessons are perceived as a ritual that has little to do with real life; recitation is a form of conversation virtually nonexistent outside the classroom.
- The students learn indirectly that school consists to some extent of reproducing knowledge on order.
- Most of the students' cognitive activity is directed toward guessing what the teacher wants to hear.

- As the teacher has an idea of the outcome of such an elaborative conversation, independent and genuine answers to the teacher's questions are only desired and positively reinforced if they correspond to the teacher's (secret) plan.
- How do you make sense of the fragmented and tentative responses of students? The knowledge acquired in this way is composed of piecemeal answers from the students and rarely forms a consistent whole. A jigsaw puzzle of isolated contributions in no way ensures learning and understanding for *all* students.
- Do teachers' questions stimulate learners to think? This claim, sometimes made, is one that has long since been disproven (summarized by Lyle, 2008).

Today, one can hardly argue that any benefits can be gained from *this* kind of talk.

Many efforts and recommendations have focused on perfecting the teacher's questioning technique within the traditional IRF pattern (e.g., Ecroyd, 1960). There have also been many practical suggestions to create more symmetrical and democratic communication between teachers and learners (for a conceptual overview, see Howe, Hennessy, Mercer, Vrikki, & Wheatley, 2019; see also Schultz, 2009; Young, 1991). Classroom discussion has a place in a contemporary teaching culture when it goes beyond the ritualized mode of guiding through mostly closed questions.

THE ALTERNATIVE APPROACH OF THE SOCRATIC DIALOGUE

The opposite of the teacher's incessant questioning is the open classroom discussion, which is sometimes also referred to as the Socratic method. Through the writings of Plato, the dialogues of Socrates have been handed down to us. In ancient Athens, Socrates practiced philosophy by asking challenging questions that were intended to force the interlocutors to think. This method has been taken up again and again. For example, all major works of Galileo Galilei are written in dialogue form, in which a fictitious person named Salviati moderates the Socratic dialogue and leads the other participants to fundamental insights by asking subtle questions (e.g., Galilei, 1632/1997, 1638/1914). Even twentieth-century philosophers still proceeded in this way (e.g., Feyerabend, 1991).

In teaching concepts of the twentieth and twenty-first centuries, too, we repeatedly find echoes of Socratic dialogue and suggestions of how it could be usefully employed in the classroom. It is striking that the historical approach via the examples of Socrates, Galileo, and others lead to similar conclusions and demands for the classroom conversation as more recent research-based concepts by Alexander, Resnick, and others that will be presented here.

Martin Wagenschein: A Representative of the Socratic Tradition

First, however, an author will be introduced here who is not known in the English-speaking world but who has received a great deal of attention in Europe and has strongly influenced the teaching of mathematics and physics in particular, even if his approach was often met with skepticism and incomprehension at first.

The most central concern of Martin Wagenschein (1896–1988) was for students to understand things truly and deeply, which he believed could only happen through patient and persistent dialogue. He was convinced and demonstrated with countless examples that students can explore many remarkable concepts and facts on their own, and even track down errors and thinking mistakes themselves (with smooth guidance from the teacher) and understand things through reflection and discussion. The teacher should only create the appropriate framework so that the inquiry as well as thinking and exchange can get going (for the example based on the law of free fall, see Wagenschein, 2015).

Research-Based Approaches of Recent Times

Even if some concepts seem quite plausible, there is a justified demand today to check their effects and implications before they go out as recommendations. Therefore, approaches to classroom discussions that have emerged from larger development and research programs are presented below. The programs of Resnick and Alexander, which are presented next, have proven successful in this sense.

Textbox 10.2 ACTIVITIES AND SUGGESTIONS

YOUR INVENTORY OF CURRENT PRACTICE

Here's How You Can Quickly Learn What Your Discourse Habits Are

In a limited period of time (class period, double period, or half day), encourage yourself to survey your own practices of talk. Ask either peers or selected students to collaborate by doing the following surveys (this works very well live and without videos):

1. If the teacher provides input: How long does the input last?
   Ideal result: maximum eight minutes
   Real result: .... Minutes
2. How many questions in total does the teacher ask during an input?
   Ideal result: none
   Real result: ....
3. If a whole-class discussion is conducted: What is the ratio of teacher to student talk time during this phase?
   Ideal result: Students talk more than teacher
   Real result: Students.......... Minutes
   Teacher.......... Minutes
4. How many closed questions (mostly factual questions with a clear solution) does the teacher ask during the whole-class discussion?
   Ideal result: as few as possible (unless it was deliberately agreed)
   Real result: ....
5. How many open questions (i.e., questions that activate thinking and stimulate reflection) does the teacher ask during the class discussion?
   Ideal result: as many as possible
   Real result: ....

Consequences from the Inventory

Analyze the results and compare them with the desired values.

- To what extent do your class conversations have the character of genuine and authentic conversations?
- To what extent do you follow the teacher-centered interaction–response–feedback pattern?
- Where do you see a need for action?
- What will you do differently next time?
- What concrete training opportunities do you see?
- With whom would you like to discuss the outcome (e.g., peers, students, friends, lecturers)?

Textbox 10.3 FURTHER INFORMATION AND RESOURCES

CLASSROOM COMMUNICATION AND CONVERSATION IN FOCUS

Since the 1970s and 1980s, there has been increased analysis, description, and research into the ways in which communication and conversation take place in classrooms. The following texts by two prominent scholars who have decisively shaped the debates of the last decades provide a first insight into the problem.

Courtney Cazden, Professor Emeritus at the Harvard Graduate School of Education

In typical classrooms, the most important asymmetry in the rights and obligations of teacher and students is over control of the right to speak. To describe the difference in the bluntest terms, teachers have the right to speak at any time and to any person; they can fill any silence or interrupt any speaker; they can speak to a student anywhere in the room and in any volume or tone of voice. And no one has any right to object. But not all teachers assume such rights or live by such rules all the time. . . .

Changes in speaking rights and in the functions of the teacher's own utterances are aspects of classroom discourse to which the teacher has to give focal attention. Another feature of discussions is a shift in speech style. In the words of British educator Douglas Barnes, it will be more "exploratory" and less "final draft." In the words of linguist Elinor Ochs, it will be more "unplanned" than "planned," as ideas are thought out in the course of their expression. (Cazden, 1988, pp. 54, 61, slightly abridged)

Lauren B. Resnick, Professor of Psychology at the University of Pittsburgh

When we think about talk in the classroom, most of us picture the same thing. The teacher stands at the front of the room, posing questions, asking students for brief answers, and evaluating their responses. This form of classroom dialogue, known as recitation, allows teachers to transmit facts and effectively manage large groups of learners. The assumption underlying recitation is that school is where children learn to repeat what others have deemed to be important knowledge.

However, we can and should set higher goals for all students. We can use the opportunity of classroom talk to teach students to think—to make knowledge. The time now devoted to the recall of facts can instead be devoted to helping students grapple with complicated questions, puzzle through new kinds of problems, and interpret complex texts. Rather than passively absorbing the small body of knowledge the teacher is able to transmit, students can learn reasoning skills by talking and arguing their way through problems to conclusions and solutions. (Resnick, Asterhan, & Clarke, 2018, p. 14)

RECENT APPROACHES TO RESPONSIVE CLASSROOM DISCUSSIONS

The term "responsive classroom discussion" was coined by Frank Lyman (1981), who also was one of the first to publish research on the well-known strategy of "think-pair-share." He called for a type of talk that activates students and encourages them to exchange and share thoughts with others.

To the present day, there has been repeated consternation that the IRF pattern is a dominant form of classroom talk. Nonetheless, there have been numerous serious and respected efforts to transform classroom discussions into a more participatory and cognitively sophisticated mode, both from the theoretical side and with proposals for concrete alternative courses of action. This is especially the case for mathematics, where the discursive approach has not been very common until recently (e.g., Barwell, 2016; Webb et al., 2019; Whitin & Whitin, 2000).

First Step: Simply Avoid It!

A first step that leads out of the trap of small-step IRF conversations is simply the teacher's conscious effort to avoid such whole-class conversations, which also comes with an increased sensitivity to conversational forms. A common and long-standing recommendation is to increase the waiting time after *open-ended* questions (e.g., Tobin, 1987).

The problem, however, lies deeper: Who is *responsible for the flow of the conversation*? If the teacher wants to push the conversation in a certain direction of elaboration, insight, and understanding, a certain impatience is inherent; the teacher's intention is, after all, to lead the class to a result in the foreseeable future, and with this comes the tendency to monopolize the discussion, to hold the strings, and to try to direct it in a more or less subtle and time-efficient way. In other words, How does a de facto teacher monologue become a genuine dialogue?

Engaging Students in Challenging and Accountable Conversations

The strategy of deliberate avoidance does not solve the fundamental problem of narrowly directed talk. If you want to overcome classroom talk of the conventional kind, consider the following strategies:

1. Set and reframe the goals of classroom talk more ambitiously.
2. Share responsibility for meaningful and productive conversations with learners or engage the latter.
3. Have concrete strategies and procedures for opening up conversations toward more challenging goals and shared responsibility.

Anyone expecting to achieve more substantive classroom conversations just with some practical advice is bound to be disappointed. Real dialogues can only be achieved with a culture of talk and teaching that engages learners in the responsibility of having meaningful conversations but also gives them a voice in all aspects of learning and teaching.

Since about 2000, more and more concepts have been developed and researched that work toward more meaningful dialogue in the classroom. Although the rationale for some of the concepts varies, they ultimately converge when it comes to classroom implementation. Two concepts that are currently prominent internationally are very briefly presented here as representative examples: Lauren Resnick's "accountable talk" (Resnick et al., 2018) and "dialogic teaching" by Robin Alexander (2018). It is recommended to continue reading in the original texts. Several texts by both authors are freely available online.

Accountable Talk

Resnick and colleagues' concept is very well summarized in their publication "Accountable Talk: Instructional Dialogue that Builds the Mind" (2018, free download). The following summary briefly outlines the key points of the concept and draws on quotes from this booklet:

> The goal of Accountable Talk is to develop students' ability to think. By practicing the skills and habits of argumentation through social interaction, students learn to reason. . . .
> In Accountable Talk classrooms, the teacher models the norms of argumentation (ways of behaving that further a discussion) and encourages students to take them up. Eventually, students become more sophisticated, self-directed, and flexible arguers. (pp. 17–18)

Resnick and colleagues emphasize that there are clear standards for what constitutes a good discussion. They identify "three responsibilities" that are constituent: accountability to knowledge (getting the facts right even if it is a struggle to find the right wording), accountability to reasoning (providing a rational justification for a claim), and accountability to community (showing respect for the ideas and feelings of classmates).

The three accountabilities can be summarized as follows.

Accountability to Community

- The right to speak: Positioning all students as valid and valued contributors in building collective understanding supports motivation and participation in accountable talk.

Accountability to Reasoning

- Elicit students' explanations: Making student ideas and student thinking public allows for the identification of errors and misconceptions and improves learning.
- Engaging differences: Through participation in accountable talk, students practice, refine, and develop their reasoning competencies.

Accountability to Knowledge

- Working with and toward knowledge: Students hold themselves responsible for grounding their claims in knowledge.
- Disciplinary knowledge: Students learn to argue in ways that are unique to each discipline.

Resnick and colleagues (2018) conclude:

> The process of understanding is seen as a collaborative endeavor. The discussion space can and does contain errors, disagreements, incomplete statements, and ideas expressed in students' informal languages. These are all seen as contributions to the learning process.
>
> The talk searches for truth; its purpose is not merely to allow everyone to be heard, or to identify a debate winner. Because the goal is a fully developed solution, conclusion, or explanation for the problem at hand, participants must back up their statements with facts and evidence. Resources, including a teacher knowledgeable about the subject, are available in the

classroom. Talk is about genuine questions and problems that ask students to look beyond surface explanations. (p. 31)

Dialogic Teaching

Dialogic teaching is closely associated with the name of Robin A. Alexander, who has been tirelessly researching, publishing, developing concepts, and advocating for their implementation for decades. From his extensive work, only a few elements are picked out here so that one can get an idea of how dialogic teaching appears in his view.

Essentially, according to Alexander (2018), dialogic teaching is based on *five principles*, and to make these principles effective in the classroom, teachers need a *repertoire* of strategies and techniques.

First, about the *five principles*: Alexander's principles are independent of the organizational form of the conversations and instruction—that is, they apply to all dialogues in the instructional context, although he notes that discussions in smaller groups might make better use of the potential of dialogic teaching. The five principles are summarized below (Alexander, 2018, p. 6):

Collective	The classroom is a site of joint learning and enquiry.
Reciprocal	Participants listen to each other, share ideas, and consider alternative viewpoints.
Supportive	Participants feel able to express ideas freely, without risk of embarrassment over "wrong" answers, and they help each other to reach common understandings.
Cumulative	Participants build on their own and each other's contributions and chain them into coherent lines of thinking and understanding.
Purposeful	Classroom talk, though open and dialogic, is structured with specific learning goals in view.

Alexander makes two comments: (1) Seemingly "dialogic" patterns of talk are not intrinsically productive; if its impact is not primarily cognitive, then the prospects for learning are greatly diminished. (2) He refers to an imperative shift in the center of discursive gravity from what the teacher asks, instructs, or tells to what the pupil says and, especially, what the teacher *does* with what the pupil says (p. 11).

Dialogic teaching is not a single, circumscribed method but an interlocking set of permissive repertoires through which, steered by principles of procedure, teachers energize their own and their students' talk. The repertoire of tools and strategies is extensive and is to be used flexibly by teachers; rigorous application of techniques does not guarantee success. Table 10.1 is an abbreviated overview of this repertoire, which requires further explanation. That would take us too far here, so please refer to Alexander's texts, in particular Alexander (2018).

The crucial point is that Alexander does not take a quasi-moralistic stand and *does not want to condemn certain elements of the repertoire* at all, as is often done. Rather, he appeals to the conscientious consideration of teachers to employ those procedures that will best serve learners in making the desired progress.

Nevertheless, he takes a clear position and says that, in principle, those procedures should be preferred that promote students' thinking and their ability to engage in dialogue. As Nystrand and colleagues (1997) state, "What ultimately counts is the extent to which instruction requires students to think, not just report someone else's thinking" (p. 72).

Table 10.1. Repertoire of Tools and Strategies for Dialogic Teaching (Alexander, 2018, p. 564)

Interactive settings	*From whole class to one-to-one*
	Whole class; group work (teacher-led); group work (student-led); one-to-one (teacher–student); one-to-one (student–student)
Everyday talk	*From transactional to evaluative*
	Transactional; expository; interrogatory; exploratory; expressive; evaluative
Learning talk	a. *Eleven categories of student talk*: narrate; explain; speculate; imagine; explore; analyze; evaluate; question; justify; discuss; argue
	b. *Coupled with four student capacities:* listen; think about what we hear; give others time to think; respect others' views
Teaching talk	*From rote to dialogue*
	Rote; recitation; instruction; exposition; discussion; dialogue
Questioning	Character of the question (test of authenticity); response cue; participation cue; wait/thinking time; feedback; purpose; structure
Extending	Time to think; say more; revoice; rephrase/repeat; evidence of reasoning; challenge or counterexample; agree/disagree; add on; explain what someone else means

CLASSROOM TALK: WHAT DOES IT MEAN IN PRACTICE?

Alexander (2017) and Resnick and colleagues (Michaels, O'Connor, Williams, & Resnick, 2016) developed programs to help teachers learn how to lead conversations.

As a core practice of teaching, classroom talk has a legitimate and important place in teachers' repertoire, and it would be misguided and unrealistic to seek to minimize or even eliminate it. On the contrary, the outdated patterns and habits must now be countered by more professional, developmental practices that recognize and develop the potential of conversations and understand them as learning opportunities. In textbox 10.5, a brief training program for classroom conversations is outlined on these bases.

Textbox 10.4 ACTIVITIES AND SUGGESTIONS

CAN WE SUCCEED IN BANISHING PHONY AND PHRASAL TALK FROM THE CLASSROOM?

One can ask which of the five principles of Alexander (see page 141) the recitation or IRF pattern is consistent with. Probably you will conclude that the recitation violates all of them. That is enough reason to do everything possible to overcome these ritual forms. Here is an introduction.

Become Aware of Conversation Rituals that Are Out of Touch with Reality

First of all, take notice of the classroom conversational rituals you use or observe. The first step is to simply pay attention and listen to yourself (and others). Here's a second suggestion, but be careful: this experiment may not endear you to colleagues.

- Use common classroom conversation forms (IRF pattern) in your circle of friends, peers, or family.
- Pay attention to the reactions and then disclose your intention for this little experiment.
- Then share about the experience.

Raise Awareness of a "Different" Culture of Conversation in the Classroom

Take the opposite approach:
- In a class, *imagine* you are discussing an interesting topic with familiar people, and you are somewhere else in the "real world" with your conversation partners, not in the classroom.
- Use only conversational forms, questions, tone of voice, and so on that you would use among adults.
- If you need to give instructions or intervene or speak up, do so as if you were moderating a round of adults.
- Pay attention to the reactions in yourself and in the students when you do so.
- Discuss the experience with peers, in courses, in private, or even with the students.

This can make you more aware of the problem of ritualized versus genuine conversation, but it does not yet mean that authentic conversations will occur. Therefore, the following third step is necessary.

Training of Accountable Dialogic Teaching

In order to make the stilted conversational style that is deeply rooted in the teaching profession more authentic, good intentions are not enough; it takes a lot of training and concrete tools. Therefore, consider the following recommendations:

- Practice the truly dialogic conversation culture intensively. Since classroom discussions are an integral part of teaching, there is no lack of opportunities to practice.
- The basis for the training is in textbox 10.5. Numerous tips are compiled there.
- Take one aspect to focus on for a day (e.g., arranging group discussions, establishing conversation rules, using some moves)
- Make conversation culture the focus of training during a longer period, such as a few weeks or months.
- Acknowledge your own progress and that of the class, and talk about it with students as well.

Textbox 10.5 FURTHER INFORMATION AND RESOURCES

A SHORT TRAINING PROGRAM ON PRODUCTIVE (WHOLE-CLASS) TALK

The following advice and training opportunities rely on numerous sources. They also draw on ideas from Michaels et al. (2016), Alexander (2017), Reznitskaya and Wilkinson (2015), and Reichmuth-Sprenger (2017). This program can be applied not only to class or group conversations but also to one-on-one conversations, such as in learning support.

Ideally, when working on improving your talk, always imagine it from a real-life planned lesson or topic that you are currently dealing with.

The Topic

You and your students need a meaningful and stimulating topic for a meaningful conversation. Themes with open-ended outcomes and multiple solutions or solution strategies are particularly suitable.

- Look for such challenges with potential for exploring a question collaboratively in the subjects and grade levels you currently teach.
- What you address should be of interest to you, and you should understand it yourself.
- Make a list of several such "core ideas" (Mitchell, Keast, Panizzon, & Mitchell, 2017; Windschitl, Thompson, Braaten, & Stroupe, 2012), also called "core tasks" or "big ideas."
- Check your topics with the question, "Would this have challenged me as a student?"
- Consider whether, in principle, all students can contribute to a deeper understanding of the topic.

Do You Need a Class Discussion at All?

Consider whether you are really aiming for deeper collaborative thinking about a topic. If not, perhaps input is more appropriate, or maybe it makes more sense for learners to follow other learning activities. Without good reasons for a class discussion, it is better to leave it aside.

Planning a Whole-Class Discussion

Unsuccessful whole-class discussions are frustrating for everyone. Problems can include no one wanting to talk, hardly any interest, irritable mood, or the teacher struggling through the lesson with questions. Therefore, prepare the whole-class discussion well, preferably in co-planning, along the following points. Sharing with peers who have similar experiences will give you new ideas (Reznitskaya & Wilkinson, 2015).

The Impetus That Gets the Conversation Started

You've chosen an issue and have an idea of what needs to be figured out. But how do you get the problem across to students so they start thinking?

- From your list of appropriate topics, choose a specific problem that is just inside the learning zone (the zone of proximal development) and that seems somehow challenging or interesting. Simple phenomena or problems of everyday life that can cause irritation on closer inspection have proved particularly useful (e.g., when washing up, the water that does not "want" to flow out of the upturned glass). Why?
- It is important that the problem is open-ended. "Why" questions are particularly suitable, or "How does it work?" or "Can we find a way to . . ." or "How can we achieve . . ." This way you can develop a shared interest in wanting to figure something out.

The Form of the Conversation: Moderated, Self-Organized, One-on-One, Think-Pair-Share

In addition to the whole-class conversation, there are other forms:

- Conversation moderated by the teacher in a smaller group while the class devotes itself to other activities.
- Self-organized conversations in groups, if necessary with role assignments (e.g., conversation leader)
- Conferences of the teacher with one or two students
- Whispered discussions with neighbors inserted into a class conversation (think-pair-share, Lyman, 1981)

Make a conscious decision before class about which forms of conversation to use.

Challenging and Accountable Conversations as a Matter of Course

Such conversations take some getting used to for students. Initially, they may feel uncomfortable and hesitant to express their thoughts freely. So, it takes time for the class to find an authentic culture of conversation. Therefore,

- You should always frame conversations *deliberately*. That will make it easier to get started. Routines and rules become established over time.
- Use a format *repeatedly or even daily*. That way, challenging conversations become second nature.
- Make some rules explicit (see below).

The culture of conversation will gradually develop, and particularly visitors to the classroom will find that conscientious and engaging conversations are taking place.

Principles and Rules

Consider how you will establish rules and routines: explicitly or by modeling them and having students implicitly learn how such a conversation goes.

As you know, Alexander (2018) has articulated five clear principles: collective, reciprocal, supportive, cumulative, and purposeful. In a first step you can reduce them to two absolutely basic and universal principles:

- All students can speak and be heard, and vice versa: No one is excluded, no matter what their situation, abilities, or prior knowledge.
- What is discussed should always contribute to learning, and vice versa: We leave aside for the time being what does not contribute to progress in the subject.

Depending on the subject and age level, the rules can also be more differentiated and explicit.

The Right to Speak

Who speaks? Rules are only the first step. The goal is respectful interaction, as among adults. As a rule, anyone who wants to speak can do so without moderation. Options range from closed to open:

1. The teacher actively gives the floor—to those who speak up, or even to those who remain silent.
2. The teacher moderates discreetly (e.g., with gestures) and returns questions to the class.
3. Those who speak pass the floor to a person of choice.
4. The conversation proceeds largely without moderation. The teacher participates in the conversation like everyone else. She or he only steers the flow of the conversation to ensure it continues or intervenes to switch to the meta-level.

Language

When someone approaches a new area, the correct technical terms are usually not yet familiar, so sentences are often incomplete and tentative. This may be allowed and can even be enriching. In a further, explicit step, a valid formulation can be sought together.

This means, don't reprimand someone for lack of technical language, but look for the best expression together at the appropriate time.

Patience, Tonality, Climate

Learners are asked to figure out an unfamiliar issue in an incredibly short period of time—but in human history, it may have taken centuries to clarify the issue. Keep in mind that high expectations are placed on students. The common interest is focused on a challenging question that needs to be answered, and the attempted solutions are usually not linear, not textbook. Be patient, stay calm, as long as the attention is focused on the matter.

Wait Time and (the Stress of) Silence

Numerous studies have demonstrated the beneficial effects of longer wait time (Tobin, 1987).

- Increase the wait time after an *open-ended* question.
- Do not build tension or waiting will be counterproductive.
- Don't stare at students but think for yourself, with them; keep the atmosphere calm.
- Every extra second counts.

But let's face it, silent students create stress for teachers who expect a response. One inevitably wonders why the students are silent: Cluelessness? Active reflection and search for solutions? Or self-protection? Resistance? Power games? Pressure is not the way to get students to talk. Try the moves listed below. If silence becomes a problem, try to find out the causes in a nonconfrontational conversation (if you want to deepen the topic of silent voices, see Schultz, 2009).

Rigor in Thinking and Arguing, Progressing on the Matter

Again, keep in mind Alexander's five principles for productive dialogic teaching mentioned earlier. Before (whole-class) conversations, take note of one or two principles to which you want to pay particular attention.

Collective	The classroom is a site of joint learning and enquiry.
Reciprocal	Participants listen to each other, share ideas, and consider alternative viewpoints.
Supportive	Participants feel able to express ideas freely, without risk of embarrassment over "wrong" answers, and they help each other to reach common understandings.
Cumulative	Participants build on their own and each other's contributions and chain them into coherent lines of thinking and understanding.
Purposeful	Classroom talk, though open and dialogic, is structured with specific learning goals in view.

Impulses from the Teacher (Moves) to Support Challenging Discourse

If the teacher wants to get a conversation going or keep it flowing, he or she can work with impulses that do not primarily refer to the matter at hand but rather to the way of talking to each other (i.e., to the course of the conversation, the participation, and the culture of the conversation). The impulses, or moves, always aim at continuing and deepening the joint reflection on the matter. Some are more subject-specific (e.g., summarized for math by Webb et al., 2019), while others are applicable across a variety of situations and grade levels. The following table summarizes moves suggested by Michaels et al. (2016).

Table 10.2. Summary of Moves as Proposed by Michaels et al. (2016, pp. 21–25)

Functions of Moves and Practices	Specific Moves	Suggestions for Wording of the Moves
Teacher moves in **group discussion**	• Marking	"That's an important point." "Did you hear what . . . said? That's interesting."
	• Challenging students	"What do *you* think?" "What does the class think?"
	• Modeling	"Here's how mathematicians do it."
	• Recapping	"What have we discovered?"
Moves and practices that support **accountability to the learning community**	• Keeping the channels open	"Did everyone hear that?"
	• Keeping everyone together	"Who can repeat . . . ?" "Was that what you were trying to say?"
	• Linking contributions	"Who wants to add on?" "Does everyone agree?" "Who disagrees?"
	• Verifying and clarifying	"So, are you saying . . . ?" "Did I understand properly that you . . . ?"
Moves and practices that support **accountability to accurate knowledge**	• Pressing for accuracy	"Where can we find that?" "That could be right. How could we get more evidence for that?"
	• Building on prior knowledge	"How does this connect?" "Didn't we find out something similar before?"
Moves and practices that support **accountability to rigorous thinking**	• Pressing for reasoning	"Why do you think that?" "So you're trying to tell us that we can't decide that until we . . . ?" "How do you explain that?"
	• Expanding reasoning	"Take your time; say more." "Just keep talking." "Try again. I get the impression you're on a good path."

Dealing with Difficulties During Whole-Class Discussion

How should we deal with conversations that are not progressing, in which no one wants to speak, in which people are constantly digressing and giggling, in which there is no concentration and no substantive exchange is possible? What do you do when a student monopolizes the conversation and others don't get a chance to speak? When someone hastily presents ready-made solutions that were not developed together?

Option 1: Address on a Meta-Level

If the discussion doesn't get off the ground, address it in a friendly way: "It's not going well today," "You seem very tired," "I have the impression you don't like to say anything on this topic. Why is that?"

Conversations must not turn into spitefulness, impatience, or accusations. If students are open about why they think the conversation is stagnating, it is an indication of a good conversation culture.

Option 2: Take Statements Seriously and Examine Them Together

Even seemingly disruptive or cheeky statements can be taken seriously—without embarrassment—and made the subject of inquiry: "X presents a ready-made solution. Let's see together if that's true."

Option 3: End It

It is also possible to exit from a tough conversation: "I suggest we do something else first."

Textbox 10.6 ACTIVITIES AND SUGGESTIONS

CHECK HOW YOU SEE YOURSELF REGARDING CLASSROOM CONVERSATIONS: BE HONEST WITH YOURSELF

Changing habits that have been so long and deeply rooted in your profession is not easy, even if you are willing to do so. Certainly, you are about to change some of your patterns. It is good to know at what point you are currently at.

- For each question, you will find two extreme statements.
- Tick on the scale where you would place yourself now—not where you would like to be but where you are now.
- You don't have to show the result to anyone; it's just a matter of being realistic and honest about where you stand.

Evaluation

As you can guess, the further to the right you tick, the more likely you are to have embraced dialogic teaching (or "accountable talk" or "responsive classroom discussion"). So, what does this mean?

It Is Nowadays Indispensable to Have Challenging Conversations in the Classroom: Learn to Make It Happen

No matter how often and intensively you are going to use dialogic teaching, it is something your students need in order to acquire the competencies and skills expected of children and adolescents today, and to learn to participate in challenging discourses that a responsible citizen must be able to engage in ("argument literacy").

Make a Plan

- Look self-critically at your evaluation above and other aspects previously addressed.
- Make a plan to rehearse and improve these practices until they become part of your professional habit.

1. Imagine that you are about to begin a whole-class discussion on a prepared topic. What is your expectation?					
	☐	☐	☐	☐	☐
I am tense. I am worried about whether it will succeed. I think that an unfavorable course of the classroom conversation is quite possible.					I am relaxed. I am confident that an interesting and productive conversation will develop.
2. To what extent do you feel that you tend to ask closed questions in class and expect certain answers (IRF pattern)?					
	☐	☐	☐	☐	☐
Very much so. Unless I consciously avoid it, I "automatically" fall back into the IRF pattern.					Hardly. I have gotten into the habit of asking genuine and often open-ended questions as much as possible.
3. How do you deal with waiting time?					
	☐	☐	☐	☐	☐
I usually expect students to answer quickly, otherwise I get impatient or unsure if the question is asked correctly.					I have no problem giving students time to think, especially with open-ended questions.
4. How would you rate your repertoire of facilitation techniques to ensure the flow of the conversation?					
	☐	☐	☐	☐	☐
My main tool is questions, with the effect that the conversation mostly flows through me and rarely between students.					I have no problem giving students time to think, especially with open-ended questions.
5. Open, dialogic teaching is less strictly predictable because authentic conversations can take unexpected courses and sometimes lead to creative ideas and outcomes. How do you deal with this?					
	☐	☐	☐	☐	☐
It's important to me that lessons go as planned; I don't want to take risks, so I'd rather tightly steer conversations.					I feel prepared for lessons to take unexpected turns, depending on student contributions.
6. How do you deal with the dilemma that open conversations usually take more time, which means that less of the material required by the curriculum can be covered?					
	☐	☐	☐	☐	☐
The curriculum is mandatory, so I think I often don't have time for dialogic teaching.					I accept the fact that I occasionally have to cut back on the material and therefore can go much deeper into specific topics.

Figure 10.1. Check yourself regarding classroom conversations. *Author created.*

Chapter Eleven

Guidelines for Learning Activities

Teachers have the duty to guide students to activities that are effective for learning. Instructing activities fits well into the practices of opening, input, and classroom talk discussed earlier. In all cases, partnership is the best foundation. The three components of transparent opening also apply to activity guidance:

- Intention (What is it about? What am I planning to do?)
- Purpose (Why this? What's the use?)
- How to proceed (How are we going to get there?)

This practice is a seemingly small matter, but if not mastered, planned activities can go in an unfavorable direction and miss their purpose. Therefore, here are some hints.

IF NECESSARY, GET ATTENTION

Anyone who interrupts an activity phase should be aware that this will disrupt or interrupt some ongoing work and thinking. It has been known for a long time that when people are *interrupted while working on tasks*, it has effects on memory and can trigger frustration and aggression (Ovsiankina, 1928; Zeigarnik, 1927).

The manner of interrupting work in progress is therefore consequential for further activity, which suggests a careful approach, for example, by announcing the interruption shortly beforehand or by the teacher going through the class and drawing attention to the upcoming phase change.

Since attention-getting is one of the everyday tasks of teachers, they usually have a lot of practice at it and have also developed some creative ideas for bringing about calm and attention, from staring motionlessly into the classroom to hitting a gong or turning on a red light. Every teacher can and should use the appropriate means (which, from a psychological point of view, usually correspond to classical conditioning). What is decisive, however, is what the teacher says afterward.

EXPLAIN THE GOAL AND THE PURPOSE OF THE ACTIVITY

As with the opening of the lesson, the purpose here is to let the learners know what the activity is now about, what the intention is, and why or what it is for. Again, the message is that the learning activity is a joint enterprise of learner and teacher, about which the students may have something to say.

Usually there is no need for detailed explanations, especially if it is obvious what the activity is useful for, for example, exercises on the current topic in a foreign language class. Nevertheless, there is often a need to explain *why this particular activity should be done*. If the teacher has good reasons for suggesting group work, the students are likely to accept it without further ado, or at least to come to terms with it, and if it could be done differently, the teacher can withdraw from the planned procedure and allow alternatives.

Ultimately, the goal at this point is to quickly reach agreement on how to proceed so that everyone can work without distraction or irritation as much as possible.

BALANCE ORAL AND WRITTEN INSTRUCTIONS

With the flood of materials for individualized and self-organized learning, learners increasingly find themselves having to read their assignments and tasks themselves. Teachers then tend to limit themselves to organizing what happens in class, for example, how students rotate from task to task, and forgo oral and contextual explanations of the activities ahead.

The written nature of the assignment may sometimes be appropriate and necessary, and yet it is strange when teachers communicate with students primarily in writing. Especially with open-ended and challenging problems, the written word can hardly substitute for the person who plausibly states his or her intent. Watch out: Some students have difficulty understanding texts and instructions even though they could follow the actual material well. It is not fair to let them fail just because they do not understand the written assignment correctly.

Ideally, teachers should strike a thoughtful balance between oral contact with students and appropriate writing. More complex challenges in particular should be introduced and contextualized by the teacher.

INSTRUCT PRECISELY, OR MODEL

It goes without saying that instructions should be *precise and comprehensible*. How tasks and assignments can be phrased can be seen from numerous good examples in teaching materials, which have been worded with great care by the authors. For less experienced teachers, it helps a lot to write down the most important points of an instruction in the correct order on a small notepad. Logically, the call to action should only come at the end (e.g., "Fetch a ball each," "Now form groups," "Fill the test tube with water") so that the rest of the instructions do not get lost in the ensuing activity. Experienced teachers know it, but even they had to learn it first.

Modeling, a crucial tool of explanation, has already come up in the context of feedback. Basically, modeling is a very detailed way of showing how a problem can be solved, provided with comments on the particular steps ("thinking aloud"). Modeling is appropriate when introducing new procedures that learners have difficulty working out or discovering on their own. Modeling shows what other people have thought about the problem and how they proceeded to arrive at a solution. Of course, modeling is always followed by the learners' own activity.

Textbox 11.1 FURTHER INFORMATION AND RESOURCES

LEARNING FROM WORKED EXAMPLES: A FORM OF MODELING

Especially in mathematics and in scientific-technical areas, countless tasks are solved in school, and most of the time the students have to find the solution themselves or the solutions are worked out together bit by bit. Rarely, however, do students receive ready-made solutions that they can use as a guide. Why not?

This has been studied in detail, especially in the 1990s (summarized by Atkinson, Derry, Renkl, & Wortham, 2000). According to a video study by Renkl, Schworm, and Hilbert (2004), fewer than 10 percent of the tasks are worked examples, although their beneficial effect on learning has long been proven (Atkinson et al., 2000; Paas & Van Merrienboer, 1994) According to Renkl and colleagues, teachers are reluctant to provide ready-made exemplary solutions because they mistakenly believe that only superficial knowledge is acquired as a result. While worked examples may limit creative processes, this could be corrected with varying examples of solutions or with incorrect or multiple solutions. According to the findings of their study, the principles of example-based learning can also be applied to complex problems (see the second and third examples in figure 11.1). Thus, learning from worked examples is a promising complement to traditional tasks and problem solving.

When it comes to acquiring cognitive skills, learning from worked examples is an effective method that is preferred by learners. However, the extent to which learners benefit from examples depends strongly on how well they can explain to themselves the principle behind the example solutions ("self-explanation effect"). Unfortunately, the self-explanation style of many learners is passive. By being passive in self-explanation, learners are forfeiting an opportunity. If self-explanation is to be encouraged, it needs appropriate cognitive activation and support.

The following example illustrates the difference between classical task solving and example-based learning, as well as a task that follows a worked solution. It is taken from the study by Paas and Van Merrienboer (1994, p. 125).

Conventional problem without solution

Given:
P_1 (15/60)
P_2 (−50/20)
Calculate the length of line P_1P_2.

Answer:
$P_1P_2 =$

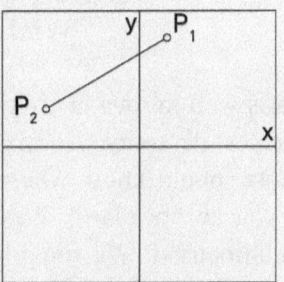

Worked problem with solution

Given:
P_1 (15/60)
P_2 (−50/20)
Calculate the length of line P_1P_2.

Solution:
1. Design right-angled triangle abc by drawing lines from P_1 and P_2 parallel to x- and y-axis
2. Length of a: difference of the x-coordinates
length of b: difference of the y-coordinates
a = 15 − (−50) = 65
b = 60 − 20 = 40.
3. Using the Phytagoras theory, the length of the line P_1P_2 (= c) can be calculated:
$c^2 = a^2 + b^2$
$c = \sqrt{5825}$
$P_1P_2 \approx 76.3$

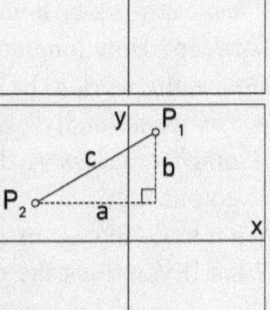

Varied problem after the worked problem with solution

Given:
P_1 (−15/−15)
P_2 (x /−55)
Length of P_1P_2 = 68

Determine the x-coordinate of P_2.

Answer:
x-coordinate of $P_2 =$

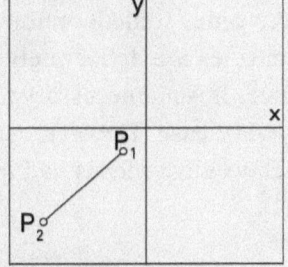

Figure 11.1. A conventional problem and the worked problem with solution, followed by a varied problem. *Based on Paas & Van Merrienboer, 1994, p. 125.*

WHAT DO STUDENTS HAVE TO DO? WHERE IS THEIR LEEWAY?

As is well known, activity phases can range from strict uniformity to the greatest diversity. No matter how the activity phases are organized, students should know where their scope of action and decision-making is. If you do not clarify these issues, you risk students becoming confused or unfocused. We roughly follow the familiar questions: What? When? How? With what? Where? And then? The questions below are not a checklist but something you need to automate as quickly as possible:

- *What exactly* are they supposed to or allowed to do? Can they choose the tasks or activities? Is there a performance goal (e.g., the number of correct tasks)?
- *When* can work be done? Is the order given? Can other things be done in between? How long does the phase last, and when exactly does it end?
- *How* is the work to be done? Alone, in pairs, in groups? Can one whisper or speak loudly?
- *With what and where* do you work? With a smartphone? Is one allowed to go outside?
- What to do in case of *questions and ambiguities*?
- What if you think the *goals have been achieved*?
- How to *check the progress*? What are the solutions? Who can be shown the product? Who can check the results?
- *What happens afterward*, when one is finished?

Over time, students know how things work in a classroom. Sometimes firm rules are deliberately set or decided on; sometimes habits are established. It is not necessary to explain the entire setting of the activity period in every case. However, students should always know how free they are to choose the means and procedures.

MAKING TRANSITIONS SMOOTH: DISCOVER A SMALL BUT IMPORTANT PRACTICE

As you know, good practices are developed in the constant interplay of experience, reflection, and enrichment with scientific knowledge. Managing transitions is a good example of how you can rehearse a practice and learn it step by step.

What Is It About?

Introduction, input, classroom discussion, instructions, learning activities, summing up: each phase is organized differently, and students are expected to do different things in each. Transitions are to be made in a compatible, respectful manner, yet at a brisk pace. Bumpy and slow transitions are a waste of time ("time thieves") and worsen the classroom atmosphere. For example, if you reduce transitions from 10 percent to 5 percent of class time, in one year you gain more than a whole week of class time that would otherwise be wasted. Therefore, design transitions consciously and develop them further.

Two Transitions at Once

Moving from one phase to the next involves *two transitions*: (1) to a different classroom organization and (2) to different expectations for learners. Transition is therefore not only a matter of classroom management but also a mental challenge. Learners must, at the teacher's direction, immediately focus on something new, even though what has preceded may not yet be completed and processed.

Textbox 11.2
TIPS AND TRICKS: PROFESSIONALLY PROCESSED

If you search the Internet, you will find masses of advice on all kinds of topics related to teaching. The sheer volume is staggering, and "what works" advice is known to be transferable only to a limited extent; the advice may fail at another time in a different school and context with other people. Moreover, even good advice is often forgotten again because it is not understood and rehearsed (like practices).

    Nevertheless, other people's practices can be inspiring. For example, some websites contain video-enriched resources for teachers, usually far from theory. The TeachingChannel (https://www.teachingchannel.org) and edutopia by the George Lucas Foundation (https://www.edutopia.org) are worth mentioning. If you are looking for videos on issues of transitions, you can find them with the search term "transition."

Thinking from the Learner's Perspective

There are obvious reasons for a phase change, but the transition should also be thought about from the learners' perspective. Is the change coming too soon for learners, or is it high time? Is everyone ready for it? Can I get them ready for something new now?

There Are No Rigid Rules: Develop Your Own Practice

Transitions are a really good opportunity to develop your own practices. There is no such thing as an underlying theory, nor are there any foolproof rules that can be established.

Textbox 11.3 ACTIVITIES AND SUGGESTIONS

HERE'S HOW YOU CAN EXPAND YOUR PRACTICES OF TRANSITIONS

1. **Collect your own and other people's experiences.**
   Since every teacher is confronted with transitions every hour, the amount of experience is enormous.
   - Ask peers, teachers (and yourself) how they proceed, what they look for, what tricks they use, and so on.
   - Compile a list of approaches and considerations and group them: similar things together, different things separately.
2. **Classify your approaches.**
   - Which procedures and considerations convince you spontaneously the most, which the least?
   - Which approaches and considerations remain on the surface (i.e., on a purely organizational level)?
   - Which procedures and considerations include social and psychological aspects?
   - Which procedures and considerations take special account of the students' learning?
   - Make a "ranking" for yourself.
3. **Consider what you already know about the design of transitions.**
   Transitions are not a weighty subject of theory and research. Therefore, this practice is based primarily on experiential knowledge.
   - Do some research on the topic (see textbox 11.2).
   - Ask experts: lecturers, educational scientists, experienced teachers.

- Tally the new aspects and ideas that your investigation has yielded.
- Which of these would you like to integrate into your practice?
4. **Try out your preferred methods.**
    - Based on your expanded knowledge, intentionally redesign transitions.
    - Set a period of time (a week, for example) in which you focus entirely on these transitions.
    - Take a piece of paper and write down your experiences in bullet points each time.
    - There will always be unforeseen events, or a previously successful procedure will suddenly no longer work. Try to figure out why.
    - As always, you only learn by repetition and even better by "overlearning" (i.e., continuing to learn even when you think you already know how). Therefore, continue to vary and flex your transitions.

Chapter Twelve

Summing Up and Closing

It is often the case that teachers summarize their lessons. The review deliberately concludes working and learning and is usually scheduled to end at the same time as the lesson. Those who think in terms of larger units of time may also prefer to simply let a lesson end, knowing that a review will take place the following day, for example, or they may choose to review repeatedly in shorter segments. Summing up is not necessarily about the end of the current class but about the *conclusion of a learning unit*.

SUMMING UP: WHAT IS MEANT?

Summing Up: Recap Based on the Intentions at the Beginning of the Lesson

As a rule, the intentions and expectations have been stated at the beginning of the lesson, preferably in a simple and plausible form: a thematic goal, a cross-curricular goal, and the performance expectations.

Connecting again to these expectations is important because it lets students know that the teacher is serious about the intentions. Therefore, summing up is connected with the genuine and open-ended question with which the teacher shows his or her real interest: "Now, where do we stand in terms of expected progress regarding subject matter, learning focus, and specific performance?"

Preliminary Saving of Fragile Learning Results

All learning is fleeting if it is not retained. The momentary insight, the fact once heard, the successful movement, the information read, the context recognized is usually all forgotten again. Everyone has experienced learning something but forgetting it again in the next moment. We know from learning psychology that learning and retention increase with the number of repetitions for both declarative and procedural knowledge ("knowing what" and "knowing how," or remembering and doing). If multiple completions are not possible and implemented during the learning phase, what has been learned may not last in the memory.

Furthermore, it is important that everything new is linked to existing knowledge or existing competencies—that is, there should be a connection between what is known and what is new.

Thus, summing up serves, among other things, to record the still-fleeting learning results in order to increase the probability that the things learned will be placed in a context and better understood or remembered. However, summing up alone does not ensure that content is permanently and solidly internalized and can be used or recalled fluently on other occasions. As a rule, this requires several accomplishments over a longer period of time. This process is called consolidation.

Textbox 12.1

AGAIN, WHAT MAKES LEARNING SUCCESSFUL?

How is what is learned processed and retained? These are central questions in the psychology of learning. In this context, here are four basic principles of successful intentional knowledge acquisition:

1. The learner must pay sufficient *attention* to the new information.
2. A certain amount of *repetition* or practice is required.
3. It requires *alignment*: new information must be aligned and connected with previously available knowledge.
4. There must be some form of *consolidation* of the new knowledge.

Merging Distributed Results (if They Are Important for Everyone)

Not all students have dealt with exactly the same thing. Suppose a teacher has had students work in groups. As a result, the newly acquired knowledge is manifold and, moreover, distributed among several learning groups. Or the learners have worked individually. As we know, not all of them are at the same point; they have different results or have not worked at the same speed. Certainly, it is not possible that all students have learned exactly the same thing; therefore, when summing up, it is only about those points that are considered so significant that they are addressed together in class.

Clarify Questions Only if They Are Really of General Interest

It is usually a dead end if the teacher wants to quickly clarify questions in the class that have arisen after the activity phase. These questions do not concern all students. When working through such questions quickly, the concentration in the class can quickly drop. The teacher must therefore decide *which unanswered points are really of general interest* and which should be left open for the time being.

Align Results with a Larger Context

Making connections is challenging. Reviewing is also an occasion when everyone, learner and teacher, can put into a *larger context* what they have learned. They link it to other knowledge and what they have learned earlier, they structure it, and they look at things again from other perspectives and perhaps also consider their significance.

This aspect of summing up can be *cognitively very demanding*:

- *On the content level*, prior knowledge of the topic must be (re)activated, links between elements must be established, and contradictions and questions must be identified. Certain insights arise only in the overall view of the matter.

- The whole topic can also be looked at on the *meta level* (strategies, self-regulation). Choose one or two of the following questions and answer them from the meta level:
  - "What exactly did we do?"
  - "Have we achieved what was intended?"
  - "Were you guided by the objectives or tasks that showed what was to be learned?"
  - "Was the approach helpful?"
  - "How were you able to break the deadlock if you didn't move forward?"
  - "What should we do differently next time?"

Where Do We Stand Now (with Regard to the Intentions)?

Summing up is the phase for firmly establishing where we are now. Preferably, this is done together. Again, some questions will help connect intentions and achievements:

- "These were the intentions and expectations. What have we achieved?"
- "What is still unfinished? What still needs to be done?"
- "Who should work on what further?"
- "How and when will we be assessed summatively on what has been accomplished?"
- "What are the next steps?"

FORMS OF SUMMARIZING

Take Sufficient Time . . .

Serious summing up is demanding and usually not something that can be done quickly, no matter what form it takes. Only in rare cases will a few minutes be enough. You need time to reflect again, and yet concentration and energy should not drop. So, a balance has to be found between providing enough time to get involved again and ensuring the summary is concise and gets to the heart of the matter.

... Or Invite Everyone to Make a Very Short Statement ("Flashlight")

If there is not enough time or a proper summary is not planned, the teacher can still get a brief overview of learning and students' mood by having everyone make a statement (e.g., "I learned . . ." "I didn't finish . . ." "I had difficulty with . . . " "It was fun"). Of course, this is not about processing the content but only about providing a short feedback to the teacher, which helps him or her with further planning.

Whole-Class Discussions: Have Only if They Are Challenging and with Enough Time

Classroom talk for summing up only makes sense if a *cognitively challenging exchange* is possible, and that takes more time than a few minutes at the end of the lesson. In this case, it is clearly the teacher who leads the conversation.

Use Visualizations

Summarizing and deepening class discussions are greatly supported by visualizations. Teachers are using the blackboard less to develop an overview simultaneously to the summary, but other analogous forms (whiteboard, flipchart, visualizer) serve the same purpose. Sketching a comprehensive synopsis step by step is a technique that teachers will probably also use in the future as a means of making contexts visible ("chalk and talk").

Group and Project Presentations Must Be Connectable

Group and project presentations are pointless if the other students can't do anything with them. The same applies as for any other learning: the presentation should be *connectable for the other participants*. What does that mean?

There are *two good ways* to avoid presentations that are meaningless to others:

1. *New perspectives only on a familiar topic*: the other participants have enough prior knowledge to be able to follow the presentation, for example, if the same task was to be solved in different ways. Everyone else has delved into the same thing but may have come to different conclusions. It only works if there is a genuine interest in the other solutions or contributions and if the other solutions can contribute something to one's own considerations (e.g., "Aha, that's how you did it!" "Did you also think about that . . .").

    For example, in foreign language classes, different conversations can be presented and compared that have been worked out for a given situation; or for a geometry task, groups present their solutions, which are then discussed.

2. *Presentation as input*: Presentations can even be connectable if they present something completely new, but they have to *introduce that topic from scratch* to the other participants. The presentation has the character of any input, which displays something new in an understandable way. Thus, the students learn, in addition to the factual discussion, the skills of a good presentation that must be understandable, interesting, and fruitful for the listeners.

If this connectivity is not given, presentations are without benefit and even counterproductive.

Write It Down

Writing down the essential contents or learning outcomes, especially in the cognitively demanding subjects, has its fixed place in schools.

Formal and handwritten notes during lessons have probably lost some of their importance, especially since the core statements on learning subjects are usually summarized in the teaching materials. The time can be better used. Nevertheless, making one's own (!) written summaries helps enormously in processing the learning content; the best example is the secret cheat sheet on which many students skillfully condense their memory aids in a minimum of space.

Textbox 12.2

HANDWRITING OR TYPING?

Handwriting experience can have significant effects on the ability of young children to recognize letters. Early handwriting practice affects visual symbol recognition because it results in the production of variable visual forms that aid in symbol understanding. Handwriting serves to link visual processing with motor experience, facilitating subsequent letter recognition skills. (James, 2017)

Numerous forms are available for meaningful, learning-promoting writing, some of which are also used in adult education.

Learning Journals (Learning Diaries, "Travel Journals" of Learning, Blogs)

They are used by some teachers as a means to encourage students to reflect on their learning and their learning outcomes. They create writing prompts, make learning achievements visible, and encourage developing cognitive and metacognitive learning strategies.

Portfolio

The (analog) portfolio, as a collection of students' own documents, was used primarily in the 1990s as a tool for documenting learning and learning outcomes but also for formative and summative assessment. This form of analog documentation has recently receded somewhat into the background, while digital forms (blogs, social media, e-portfolio) are receiving more attention. However, the basic idea that students produce their own texts and documents to show what they are learning or have already learned is still recommended. The teacher will find the most appropriate form depending on the students' previous experience, subject, age, and class.

Collectively Written Texts

All learners have blind spots: things they overlook, don't understand, or simply pass over but are pretty sure another learner understood. When all learners' thoughts and ideas are available as notes, one learner can benefit from the input of others. The class as a whole has the knowledge it needs, which is now shared with everyone. When it comes down to a collaboratively written text, learners or the teacher synthesize the collected notes or journal entries, in which students can also recognize in the end their own contribution. Such forms of collective knowledge-building may well take on the character of so-called collective intelligence (see also textbox 12.3).

Poster

As is often done in adult education and workshops, learners produce posters or flipcharts that capture the essence of the work or findings. One advantage is that they can remain visible in the classroom for longer periods of time.

Textbox 12.3 FURTHER INFORMATION AND RESOURCES

NOTES

Writing Down Evolving Thoughts

In all subjects and at all levels, taking notes is an important methodological tool. Notes on a piece of paper, in a journal, in a portfolio, or in a blog are utility texts and always have a preliminary character; they are first thoughts, impressions, questions, tentative reflections. And they are also unfinished in form. Such notes have a variety of functions, only a few of which are mentioned here:

- Bringing memories and previous knowledge into consciousness: Often, while writing, you realize that you have more knowledge and thoughts about a topic than expected (you activate your tacit knowledge).
- Notes against forgetting: Observations, impressions, ideas are quickly recorded.
- Support for structuring while thinking: Those who write can better organize their thoughts.
- Preparation for speaking and sharing: Notes can facilitate subsequent speaking and sharing with others; they provide confidence.

- Building blocks for a collaborative work: The individual notes are compiled, and from the many short texts (or excerpts from them) a rich overall picture is created.

Notes in a Cognitively Activating Lesson

Short notes help capture unfinished thoughts, ideas, or questions. Often their potential remains underutilized in the classroom. Here a procedure is suggested:

Each student writes *one sentence* on a postcard-sized piece of paper about an issue, such as a video they have just seen, a process in nature, a social process, or a physical phenomenon. Then choose or vary one of the following options:

- You hand over all the pieces of paper to a group of two to four students. They read the sentences and try to arrange them so that they form a coherent text. They do not have to use all the slips of paper.
- You form groups and each group has to write a coherent, factually correct, and understandable text with the help of the slips of paper.
- You collect all the sentences and use as many sentences as possible for a summary, off the cuff, if you feel confident, or for later. It is important that students recognize their own sentences. Justify (or have them justify) why some sentences were not used.

Textbox 12.4 FURTHER INFORMATION AND RESOURCES

CONSOLIDATING KNOWLEDGE WITH SOCIAL MEDIA AND INTERNET: SOME RESEARCH FINDINGS

Here, some key findings from a research review (Reinhardt, 2019) focusing on virtual learning environments in foreign language learning are briefly presented.

Blogs
- Blogs can be beneficially used in foreign language acquisition for culture learning and intercultural exchange, for reflection and self-presentation.
- Blogs can enhance the development and expression of deep knowledge and expertise on topics in which the learner has had some say.
- As blogging becomes a niche practice (like wikis) it may require more explicit instruction.

Wikis

- As group learning tools, wikis may afford cooperation and shared authorship but not necessarily true collaboration.
- Students need to be aware of how and why to use wikis.
- Wiki-enhanced instruction may help develop audience awareness if learners believe their collective expertise is worth sharing.
- As with blogs, formal wiki tasks may be more effective if they are authentic and are similar to naturalistic, informal wiki authoring activities.

Social Network–Enhanced Commercial Computer-Assisted Language Learning Sites and Services

- Poor site design not grounded in best practices ultimately leads to frustration and abandonment.
- Studies of some particular site features and affordances have shown less than encouraging results.
- Customers may find the status, ranking, and gamified rewards systems motivating, but poorly designed, decontextualized memorization drills may not lead to long-term learning gains.

Some Conclusions

- Because social media is increasingly commonplace, it should be used by learners and teachers as a tool for experiential, situated learning, and as social practices deserving of critical attention.
- Not researched in any of the surveyed literature is mobility and the impact of anytime, anywhere access on learning and how this truly blurs the lines between formal and informal learning.
- It should not be overlooked in either research or practice that all vernacular social media, and most educational social media, are commercial enterprises.
- There is no question that social media literacies, as they continue to be researched and defined, will be key to modern language proficiency in the future.

The above statements, which originally concern second language learning, can also be applied analogously to other subjects and contexts.

PROBLEMATIC FORMS OF RECAPPING AND SUMMARIZING

Some types of recapping and summarizing are of little use, inefficient, demotivating, or counterproductive. They should not be an integral part of the practices of summing up. If they do come into use, there would have to be really good reasons. Following are some examples of methods to question.

Problematic Form 1: Pure Copying of Texts, Illustrations, and Diagrams

Pure copying is senseless. The texts and sketches must be connected with one's own cognitive effort; otherwise it makes no sense. The assignment of mere copying can hardly be justified, because writing alone does not lead to understanding. Moreover, valuable time is wasted on unproductive activities.

Problematic Form 2: Correcting Tasks from the Activity Phase Together

Correcting together is a waste of time. If students can check the solutions for correctness themselves, they should do so, for example, for easy-to-correct tasks in math or language classes. This allows them to continue working on the assignments without delay and improve them, or they can get help to do so.

However, if a genuine exchange about the students' results or suggestions is needed, this is done in a whole-class discussion, and the teacher should make every effort to ensure that this takes place as a *genuine dialogue* between all parties involved.

Problematic Form 3: Joint Filling in of Cloze Texts and Worksheets

Joint filling in devalues the preliminary work and is demotivating. What is the point of collecting results or proposed solutions and then filling in the unified and "correct" solution in a cloze text or worksheet? One wonders for what purpose the learners should have engaged in the previous phase. Presumably, next time they will simply wait for the teacher to announce the correct solutions. Such phases have little in common with meaningful summing up that seeks to establish coherence. They have a tendency to be tedious and are unproductive from a learning outcome perspective.

Problematic Form 4: Having Individual Students Show Off

This setting can soon lead to embarrassment of the student. But apart from that, such a demonstration is usually unsuitable to support the necessary synthesis after an activity phase. Not yet fully elaborated or incoherent contributions of learners are important for their own learning process but unsuitable to be presented to the class as a summary. Why not? The contributions are usually not optimally elaborated; the listeners have to search for meaning in mostly half-baked statements, check for accuracy, fill in missing parts themselves, and uncover misunderstandings. This is very demanding and can be better managed in a well-conducted dialogic whole-class discussion or in a written form.

But no rule without exceptions: demonstration by students is okay if they show something that has the quality of a good presentation. It is also okay if students show different solution variants of the same problem and put them up for discussion, which can be cognitively stimulating for the whole class.

WHERE DO STUDENTS STAND NOW? DON'T NECESSARILY TAKE A TEST

Some teachers think they have to routinely end lessons with a small test to know what the students have learned. This should be questioned. Tests, even the most low-threshold ones, cause stress, and testing doesn't teach students anything. You don't fatten the pig by weighing it, as the saying goes. Moreover, we know that such quick tests are unreliable and that especially the weaker students tend to systematically overestimate themselves (Brown, Andrade, & Chen, 2015).

Wouldn't it be better to spend the time on deepening learning and understanding, and keep the number of formal tests to a minimum? In the previous part of the book, after all, many ways of informal diagnosing were addressed. This is often more informative than a written test and even less work for the teacher.

However, if you want to know from the class in writing where we stand now, you will probably get some useful information for further planning. This information is in fact feedback to the teacher and shows the extent to which learning has been successfully facilitated. But remember that often no consolidation has taken place; things are still volatile. Therefore, find "gentle" ways of exploring that don't stress students and still allow the teacher to know where students stand. These types of assessments, designed to determine how students are doing and where they are struggling, are called classroom assessment techniques. Many of them are quick and easy to conduct and provide good insight into successful or unsuccessful learning, as well as problems that may be preventing students from learning successfully. Some classroom assessment techniques are summarized in textbox 12.6.

SUMMING UP AND SUMMATIVE ASSESSMENT ARE TWO DIFFERENT THINGS

As presented so far, summing up emphasizes bringing together, completing, and clarifying learning outcomes that are still fragile. It also has a formative function in that learners receive feedback on learning to date and learning that is still needed.

To avoid any misunderstandings:

- *Teaching is in principle formative* ("forming" in the sense of "educating"), and assessments are also in principle formative.
- But in fact, *summative assessment* is a kind of accounting to determine where learners currently are in relation to the desired level of learning. The result is a comprehensible outcome (e.g., seven out of ten tasks solved correctly). However, this does not have to be accompanied by a grade at all.
- *Grading is an entirely different matter*. It can be based on summative assessments, but it does not have to be. Grading operates on a different level. It often has serious consequences and can affect careers. Grades

in the form of a number or a letter are the currency in most educational systems. They have taken on a life of their own and have become partially disconnected from real learning and competencies.

In today's use of language, summative assessment is usually equated with grading. However, this is not coherent, which can be made clear with an example: A teacher administers a summative test under strictly controlled conditions with no possibility of cheating, checks the results, and reports back to the students where they stand, but without giving grades. This is a perfectly realistic scenario.

Again, when learning and summing up is done in class, it has nothing to do with grades for the time being. If graded assessment is needed in due course, it is a different setting apart from "normal" teaching. It is pure convention that grading is often tied to ritual examinations (performance tests, exams, essays, or whatever they are called). Today, teachers have many options for arriving at a fair overall assessment of competencies beyond the usual summative tests.

CLOSING

We have now gone through all the phases of a lesson, discussing what practices the teacher needs in each case. When summing up is also finished, everything concerning teaching and learning has been said. The lesson can be ended. How?

On Time

- Now the most important rule: end the lesson on time, and do not steal the students' break (if you don't respect that, you will have to learn it the hard way).
- Anything shouted into the classroom after the lesson is over will be without any effect.

Plan Time for Organizational Things

- Think ahead about what organizational things you still want to communicate.

As in the Beginning, So Now: Make Sure the Atmosphere Is Friendly

- Sure, a lesson can end without fuss when everything is clear to everyone. But as is the rule in human encounters, you say goodbye.

Textbox 12.5 ACTIVITIES AND SUGGESTIONS

INTENSIVELY TRAIN THE NEGLECTED PRACTICE OF SUMMING UP

Teachers usually prepare less well for summing up than, for example, for input or learning activities. Summing up is often done unprepared and therefore rather unprofessionally. Why is that so? Summing up is to a large extent related to the actual course of the lesson and is therefore more difficult to plan than the introductory parts.

It is all the more advisable to train summing up. Therefore, consider the following recommendations:

1. For the next fifteen lessons, for example (or for longer periods of time), make a conscious effort to professionally sum up.
2. Read the section "Summing Up" again carefully, or at least skim it if you have already worked through it thoroughly.
3. Before a lesson begins, think about the type of summing up that would be most appropriate for this topic, class, or level of learning, and try to imagine how summing up would need to be done.
4. Reserve enough time at the end of the lesson—at least five minutes more than you would spontaneously spend on it.
5. Inform the students about your focus on summing up.
6. After summing up, try to find out what effect this form of summing up had on the students (e.g., with a few oral questions).
7. Be sure to end the unit on time and do not overdo it.
8. After the end of each lesson, review the summing-up period and think about what you want to avoid, reinforce, or do differently next time.

Textbox 12.6 FURTHER INFORMATION AND RESOURCES

TECHNIQUES FOR OBTAINING FEEDBACK (CLASSROOM ASSESSMENT TECHNIQUES)

For decades, the body of suggestions for simple ways to elicit students' knowledge, interests, difficulties, suggestions, and opinions has been growing. Many of the ideas in Angelo and Cross's (1993) extensive summary have been expanded and varied over the years. While many of the suggestions in the following compilation derive from Angelo and Cross's *Classroom Assessment Techniques*, they are found in many sources in varying forms. For some, the original source can no longer be determined, or they are simply part of the profession's commonly known body of techniques.

Formative Evaluation and Anonymity

For all of the following techniques, student feedback is usually anonymous unless there would be an important reason for the teacher to know the names. The point, after all, is not to evaluate individual students but to get an overall picture of how successful learning has been and where there are deficiencies. It must be made clear to all students that these are formative evaluations and feedback that will not be used for performance evaluation.

Always Communicate the Time Frame and Have the Material Ready

In many cases, these techniques are used at the end of an activity or lesson. To avoid stress, a reasonable amount of time should be allotted, and students should know how much time they have. The materials (notes, questionnaires, etc.) should always be at hand.

Use Digital Tools as Well

Digital tools and media can also be used for many of the following suggestions if they are already established in the classroom: chat groups, feedback apps, email, forums, blogs, and so on.

Vary!

All suggestions can be varied depending on the subject, level, and circumstances so that they are as informative as possible for the teacher and answer the question at hand as well as possible.

A DOZEN SUGGESTIONS

1. **What Prior Knowledge Do Students Bring Along?**

   Elicit Prior Knowledge and Attitudes Technique
   What It Is About
   For effective teaching, the teacher needs to know what students already know and can do. Sometimes the teacher may already be aware of it. But sometimes a short survey is the most effective way to find out. The teacher will learn where to start and at what level the majority of the students are, and where there are problems or potential. And it becomes transparent how far apart the learning levels of the students are.

   What to Pay Attention To
   - Do the survey the day before. If the survey is conducted right at the beginning of the lesson, it is difficult or even impossible to adapt the lesson to the previous knowledge.
   - Explain the purpose of the survey.
   - What exactly should be asked? Prior knowledge of the lesson? Attitudes? Interest?
   - Question type: yes-no questions, scale from 1 to 5, or open-ended questions.

2. **Where Do the Students Stand After This Learning Phase?**

   Postcard Technique
   What It Is About
   This technique is simple and self-evident. Instead of asking the class and expecting verbal feedback, the teacher asks students to provide brief written feedback about their learning, usually near the end of a lesson. The length is limited, such as half a sheet of paper or just a postcard. The teacher asks short and simple questions (e.g., "What do you remember most about this lesson?" or "What do you continue to struggle with?" or "Of what you learned, what is most important?"). Students write down their answers and hand them in.

   What to Pay Attention To
   - Communicate whether a particular form is desired (complete sentences, keywords, etc.).
   - Prepare questions ahead of time, and maybe even write them down for all to see.
   - Inform students at what point you will comment on the notes.

3. **Was the Teaching Understandable and Comprehensible?**

   Muddiest Point Technique
   What It Is About
   This technique is simple and efficient. The teacher learns where problems exist in a very short time. Angelo and Cross call the technique "muddiest point," meaning something that was unclear or incomprehensible. Students briefly respond in writing to the question, "What was the muddiest point in this lesson (this input, this text, this discussion, etc.)?"

   What to Pay Attention To
   - Decide on what feedback is desired.
   - Schedule when the teacher will give feedback.

4. **How Well Can Students Argue?**

   Pros and Cons Technique
   What It Is About
   Students outline a list of pros and cons on an issue that might require an opinion or decision. This classroom assessment technique provides the teacher with information about students' ability to consider different points of view.

   What to Pay Attention To
   - The teacher presents a situation in which a position must be taken—a dilemma or a problem that is relevant in the context of the subject matter (e.g., "Transporting goods by air is sometimes controversial. What are the reasons for it, and what are the reasons against it?").
   - The teacher can also present a pointed position for discussion, for which arguments for and against are to be noted.
   - If necessary, specify the minimum number of arguments and a structure (e.g., two columns on a sheet).

5. **Do Students Know What Matters?**

   Student-Generated Test Questions Technique
   What It Is About
   The benefits of this activity are immense. It allows the teacher to learn what the students consider to be the most important concepts in the unit and to receive, virtually as a by-product, formulated tasks and test items about them, at least in a raw version.

   What to Pay Attention To
   Step 1. Create questions and have them tested.
   - Students are given ample time to write their own test questions. The questions should allow to show the essence of the learning unit.

- The assignment must be clear: it is about this learning unit and about the essential competencies (e.g., not just questions that recall factual knowledge).
- Students should be free to use a variety of question formats.
- Students test each other's questions and assess them for comprehensibility, difficulty, and relevance.

Step 2. Discuss congruence of questions with the core intentions of the unit.
- A class discussion is recommended on what the key learning expectations of this unit were.
- Students should discuss the extent to which the questions really make visible whether someone understood the core of the learning unit.
- The teacher raises the prospect that some of the questions will be used for formative or summative evaluation.

6. **Did the Students Really Understand the Issue?**

Mail to Laypeople Technique
What It Is About
Have students explain a fact they have just worked on in their own words in a short letter, email, or blog post aimed at people with little prior knowledge. This technique is particularly useful when a deeper understanding of a context or issue is needed.

What to Pay Attention To
- The teacher describes to the students exactly what issue they should present in a simple way.
- The text is framed in an appropriate way, for example:
  - Addressee: "Explain to your grandmother / your friend / your WhatsApp group . . . "
  - Issue: ". . . how X works / what you have learned about X / what you now understand about X."
- Students should use simple language and only those technical terms that they are sure the addressees are familiar with.
- Students are given a realistic time frame.
- The teacher reads the texts to see what the students have understood and will inform the students to what extent the texts will affect the future lessons.
- If appropriate, the teacher can use a few of the students' examples for subsequent lessons.

7. Are the Goals Appropriate and Achievable for the Students?

Mutual Alignment of Intentions or Goals Technique

What It Is About

The point here is for learners and teachers to agree on realistic goals. It is ideal if both are pulling together. The teacher announces the goals, but are they the students' goals? The goals of teacher and students may be too far apart (e.g., students want repetitive practice, the teacher wants deeper mathematical understanding). Thus, the interest of the learners decreases and with it the learning progress. With a short survey, the teacher may get more authentic answers than in a class discussion, and the students learn to think about their goals. This is the basis for adjusting the goals together.

This technique is challenging, but if you can find common goals that teachers and students fully accept, your class will have taken a very big step toward becoming a productive learning community.

What to Pay Attention To
- The teacher first clarifies for him- or herself the intentions and considers to what extent they can be adapted depending on the reaction of the students (if the goals are not adaptable, this assessment technique makes no sense).
- The teacher informs the class in a relatively general way about the topic of the unit or lesson and asks the students what they would like to achieve on this topic.

Now there are two possibilities.

Option 1: You simply have a class discussion on this question if the learners have learned to talk openly and to the point about such matters and the teacher is willing to listen to their objections and arguments.

Option 2: Students write down on a piece of paper two or three things that they think they would like to accomplish or can accomplish in this unit (at least one content goal and one cross-curricular goal each). Then have students rank them in order of importance (numbers 1, 2, 3, etc.). To quickly keep track, colored slips of paper can also be used, with each color having a meaning (e.g., importance). Then all slips of paper are laid out and the class gets an overview. Divergent and concordant goals are identified. Together, the need for action is determined (e.g., "This clearly seems too difficult," "Many are more interested in . . ." "Some would first like to consolidate what they have learned so far before we continue," "I, as the teacher, will be especially available for those who find the goals too challenging," etc.).

8. How Do Students Proceed While Working?

Process Analysis Technique

What It Is About

This suggestion takes a little more time, but you don't need a separate time slot for this activity; it goes like this: in parallel to the usual work on a task, students write down *how* they solve the task.

With this analysis the teacher learns what thinking processes and strategies the students use, and at the same time the students learn to think about their own strategies and thinking ("metacognition"). It is not about solving a task "correctly" but about becoming aware of the steps. An analysis can be good and enlightening, even if the task is solved incorrectly.

What to Pay Attention To
- It is important that students not only solve the (interesting and solvable) task but also write down what steps and missteps they chose.
- Students should not be praised for finding the correct solution but for accurately visualizing the process.
- Do not impose rigid formal requirements but allow everyday language.
- Do not judge the process or the solution too quickly; sometimes strange, unexpected, and original ways also lead to the goal.

You can vary the analysis of the process in many ways:
- Students write down all the steps; you, in turn, analyze the process and report back or present your findings for discussion.
- Students use their notes to report what they thought about and how they proceeded.
- The class compares and discusses the different approaches.

9. Where Is the Shoe Pinching?

Mailbox Technique

What It Is About

A mailbox by the classroom door allows students to anonymously post notes, suggestions, and criticisms about class or subject matter.

What to Pay Attention To
- The mailbox is placed so that students can post their feedback unobserved.
- If necessary, formulate rules about the tone of the feedback (no insults, no sweeping judgments, etc.).

The teacher empties the mailbox periodically and informs the class about the feedback and how the teacher deals with it.

10. **How Do Students Work Together?**

    Evaluation of Group Work Technique
    What It Is About
    Group work is sometimes opaque: it remains unclear what each has contributed and learned. A simple evaluation can help here and also raise awareness of group collaboration in the medium term. The teacher will know which group the student was in, but otherwise the feedback can remain anonymous.

    What to Pay Attention To
    - Prepare a short questionnaire to be filled out by all students who have participated in group work, something like the example shown in textbox 12.7.
    - The teacher reviews the questionnaires and presents the observations for discussion at the next opportunity.
    or:
    - The groups exchange ideas after completing the questionnaires and make suggestions for more efficient work.

11. **How Do Students Experience a Summative Assessment?**

    Students Give Feedback After Summative Tests Technique
    What It Is About
    This suggestion is easy to implement, very effective, and much appreciated by students. After all, during tests, most students are under stress and pressure to perform, and they care about fair assessment. Therefore, the teacher gives students time and opportunity at the end of the test to provide meta-level feedback on summative assessments (tests, classwork, etc.). Informal feedback at the end of the test can provide the teacher with useful background information, and students have an opportunity to explain themselves and their performance.

    What to Pay Attention To
    - Allow some time at the end of each exam for students to respond in writing.
    - The teacher may leave it open to what is commented on and how or suggest questions like these:
      "How well were you able to demonstrate your skills in this test?"
      "If you are not satisfied with your performance, why could that be?"
      "Is there anything that made it difficult for you to perform at your best today?"
      "What grade do you think is appropriate for your performance?"
      "If you don't think the test was fair, why not?"

Textbox 12.7

EVALUATION OF GROUP WORK: EXAMPLE OF A QUESTIONNAIRE

Your Group:
 Group no.:
 Number of members:
Overall, how effectively did you work together?
 ☐ *not effective at all*   ☐ *somewhat ineffective*
 ☐ *somewhat effective*   ☐ *very effective*
How many group members actively participated most of the time?
 Number:
How many of you were fully prepared for the group work most of the time?
 Number:
Give an example of something you learned from the group that you probably would not have learned on your own.

Give an example of something the other group members learned from you that they probably would not have learned otherwise.

What could the group do to improve collaboration and performance?

---

12. How Can We Improve Working, Climate, and Learning?

Feedback Group Technique
What It Is About
The teacher meets with a small group of students on a regular basis to share ideas about instruction, progress, opportunities for improvement, climate, and so on.

What to Pay Attention To
- Once implemented, the feedback group contributes greatly to good teaching, well-being, and learning.
- This form of feedback is comparatively time-consuming.
- Participation in such a group must be voluntary for the students.
- And, of course, the teacher must be able to keep an open mind and listen without defending or justifying him- or herself.

Textbox 12.8 ACTIVITIES AND SUGGESTIONS

AGAIN, ACCORDING TO JOHN HATTIE, WHAT MAKES A GOOD TEACHER?

In the context of diagnostics, a box called "Plea for the Dedicated Teacher" (textbox 4.3) cited five key points that John Hattie believes are part of the profile of the committed teacher:

1. Teachers are among the most powerful influences in learning.
2. Teachers need to be directive, influential, caring, and actively engaged in the passion of teaching and learning.
3. Teachers need to be aware of what each and every student is thinking and knowing, to construct meaning and meaningful experiences in light of this knowledge and have proficient knowledge and understanding of their content to provide meaningful and appropriate feedback such that each student moves progressively through the curriculum levels.
4. Teachers need to know the learning intentions and success criteria of their lessons, know how well they are attaining these criteria for all students, and know where to go next in light of the gap between students' current knowledge and understanding and the success criteria.
5. Teachers need to relate and then extend multiple ideas such that learners construct and reconstruct knowledge and ideas. It is not the knowledge or ideas but the learner's construction of this knowledge and these ideas that is critical.

You were then asked for your opinion of the five points. Now check your point of view again.

- Do you agree with the first three points? If not, why not?
- In particular, consider the second point. Has your position changed after working through this chapter? In what way exactly?
- For the third, fourth, and fifth points, reassess the extent to which you match the description (on a scale of one to ten).

You might now check to what extent your opinion has changed in the meantime, after you have worked through some more chapters.

Chapter Thirteen

Some Variations of the Basic Lesson Structure

LOOKING BACK AT THE PREVIOUS CHAPTERS

The scheme presented at the beginning of part III is purely formal. It reflects the almost inevitable flow of a lesson of any length, prescribing nothing except what is obvious—namely, that the lesson begins and ends, that the teacher addresses the students, and that there are activities:

- Opening
- Introduction to the topic
- Learning activities
- Summing up and closing

This scheme is a kind of stable container that allows the teacher to design productive lessons and the best possible learning. Thus, the teacher remains free to design the content and instructional setting of the lesson in such a way that students can make progress.

Again, the presented scheme provides an enabling framework. However, a structure as such does not guarantee good teaching.

Now What Does All This Have to Do with Practices?

These phases are, in a sense, the backbone of every lesson, but the practices used in the phases are the real mainstays of every lesson. The teacher must be able to rely on them. Teaching is unlikely to be better than the teacher's practices, or vice versa: teaching is likely to be as bad as the practices are unprofessional. Certainly, no one can perform effective and flexible practices from day one, and therefore student teachers and those entering the profession are well advised to work on their initially clumsy practices as early as possible, while they still have a support system of teacher education professionals around them.

Practices may be "good" and recommended because they are based on thorough research. At the end of the day, the real criterion for good, professional practices is their positive impact on climate and learning. They make teaching more appreciative, productive, interesting, and instructive. And they increase the likelihood that learners and teachers will enjoy learning.

VARIATIONS OF PRESTRUCTURED LESSONS

As mentioned earlier, there are many other recommendations for how to structure lessons. Some lesson structures try to pack a certain understanding of teaching into them. The teacher follows a predefined sequence and trusts that the fixed procedures and enactments will serve their purpose. The teacher rightly says to himself or herself, "Why should I reinvent everything? Why shouldn't I use what others have worked out and tested with a lot of effort? Why shouldn't I trust that proven patterns will work for me?"

Prepared teaching structures are not self-propelled enactments, even if at times the belief prevailed that choosing the "right" conception of a lesson could automatically guarantee teaching success. Today we know that they are at best a tool to trigger the learning we hope for. This always requires a cognitive and motivational activation of the learners; otherwise nothing much happens.

If the staging contributes to this purpose, all the better; but it is not a guarantee. The narrower and more determinant a structure or a staging is, the more it also takes over the decisions about the intentions and the topics of the lesson. An inattentive teacher could, to some extent, become a blind executor of foreign ideas.

Two forms of prestructured lessons can be distinguished:

- *Content-based lesson plans*: Fortunately, these do exist, because without the preparatory work of other professionals, teachers would be completely overwhelmed. After all, they only have about twenty minutes on average to plan and prepare a lesson (Richter & Pant, 2016). Those looking for such ready-made lessons will find them on many platforms, in courses on subject-specific teaching and learning, and in teaching materials.
- *Cross-thematic (generic), tried-and-tested approaches* that are applicable to different intentions and topics. Often, such forms aim to implement certain principles of teaching and learning and to influence learning and motivation in a favorable way.

There are numerous examples of these two variants, of which some particularly significant ones are briefly described below.

In this book, no organizational form of school and teaching is preferred or excluded. Traditional forms, defined staging, open forms with varying spatial and temporal structure, use of digital media: everything is possible, nothing is "forbidden," *as long as* the progress and growth of the students are the focus, and *as long as* they rely on flexible and elaborate practices that ensure effective instruction. In other words, staging should not just get it "right" on the surface level, but the teacher should use professional practices to support deeper learning and understanding.

Textbox 13.1

All of the following approaches are inherently driven by the desire to improve teaching and learning and are to be appreciated from this perspective. However, they are all more or less dependent on having teachers with professional practices who implement and manage these approaches in ways that optimally help students achieve learning success.

The following lesson structures, staging patterns, or concepts comprise only a small selection and cannot be presented in depth, nor is this the goal. As you review the concepts, also focus on the following aspects:

- Ask yourself which of your acquired practices this conception of teaching requires in order to succeed.
- Do research if you want to know more about a concept.

SCRIPTED LESSONS

An extreme form of external control through elaborated patterns are the so-called scripted lessons, in which they instruct almost word for word how a lesson should proceed. This is not only about defining the content but also about controlling the teacher's methodological approach and influencing the students' learning and thinking. "The intention of a teacher using a scripted lesson is to follow the sequence indicated in the lesson, relying on the resources provided in the lesson, with minimal deviation from the sequence outlined" (Winch & Winch, 2019, p. 183).

Scripted lessons are therefore often seen as a disenfranchisement of the teacher, whose only task is to serve up ready-made lessons. In contrast, defenders of this approach argue that for most teachers, such guidelines are a great help and provide students with some assurance that minimum standards of instruction will be met (Hiebert & Morris, 2012). For more on this debate, see textbox 13.2.

One might argue that in this scenario, teachers' practices are not as important. Considerable doubts are raised against this argument, because if the teacher has to deviate from the predefined script, he or she has to rely on skills that cannot be foreseen in the script. In fact, it is their professional practices that help teachers along in these situations.

TEXTBOOKS

Probably the most common form of elaborated content offered to teachers is the textbook, which is used to structure the lesson. Around three-quarters of all math teachers worldwide use a textbook; in Germany, the figure is as high as 86 percent (Mullis, Martin, Foy, & Arora, 2012; van den Ham & Heinze, 2018). The use of textbooks is also intensive in foreign languages. In many cases, they are accompanied by extensive supplementary materials (guidelines and instructions for the teacher, worksheets, software, task collections, etc.). In some places, the teaching materials for certain subjects and levels are prescribed by the authorities, which always gives rise to controversy, especially in the subjects of history and geography.

Some teachers rely on textbooks to be curriculum-compliant and to incorporate the required standards. So, teachers are tempted to just follow the textbook's ready-made steps to meet the requirements "from above." Note that many textbooks focus heavily on factual knowledge. But sometimes there are more demanding goals to be achieved, for example, making connections or solving more complex problems. Therefore, teachers should consider which goals they can achieve with the textbooks and to what extent they should add additional challenges.

Beyond that, there is no doubt that textbooks can be a powerful pedagogical tool and not simply a teaching script in the hands of poorly qualified teachers, as is often said. With the necessary knowledge und practices, teachers may intend to use the textbook with great benefit within the structure of the lessons they have themselves prepared (Winch & Winch, 2019).

Textbox 13.2 FURTHER INFORMATION AND RESOURCES

CONTROVERSY: UNCERTAINTY VERSUS INSTRUCTIONAL PRODUCTS THAT GUIDE TEACHING

Yes, there are always unplannable situations in the classroom where the teacher has to make quick decisions. This uncertainty (or rather, unplannability) may unsettle many teachers, but it is something that is actually normal and occurs in one form or another in virtually every profession.

For less experienced teachers, making ad hoc decisions seems particularly challenging, which is why it has been a recurring focus of experts: for example, Herbart's "pedagogical tact" (1802) or "reflection-in-action" (Schön, 1983) or "instructional engineering" (Stylianides & Stylianides, 2014). The latter trenchantly ask, "Is ambitious teaching some sort of mystical practice that can only be enacted by expert teachers who are able to manage some of its uncertainties in real time?"

Hiebert and Morris (2012) take a very clear position. With regard to teacher education, they argue that the full backpack of teachers' university knowledge requires an enormous transfer effort into everyday teaching, which can hardly be accomplished under real-life conditions. Therefore, teachers have to work on specific teaching situations right from the start instead of dealing primarily with general and overarching problems. Hiebert and Morris also criticize the confusing talk about the unpredictability of all teaching situations; in contrast, they argue, it is precisely the elaboration of options for action and materials that helps teachers to deal with everyday challenges. The following quotation clarifies their point of view:

> A common belief about teaching is that teaching is so complex and requires so many spontaneous decisions that it is inherently uncertain. This belief calls into question the goal of creating instructional products that could be implemented by different teachers in different classrooms with predictable results. . . . As Ball and Forzani (2009) acknowledge, "a second problem in identifying the core tasks of teaching rests with the dominant contemporary view of teaching as highly improvisational and wholly context dependent" (p. 503).
>
> The consequences of believing that teaching is uncertain gain strength when combined with the negative reaction to previous attempts to "script" teaching. Scripting teaching has become interpreted as taking away teachers' intellectual and pedagogical capabilities and turning them into robots. It has become an incendiary phrase associated with de-professionalizing and de-skilling teachers.
>
> In contrast, we believe, with others, that asking teachers to design, study, and improve detailed annotated lesson plans that can be shared with other teachers and taught as scripts (appropriately interpreted) is one way of professionalizing teaching (Hiebert, Gallimore, & Stigler, 2002; Morris & Hiebert, 2011; Stigler & Hiebert, 1999). It places teachers in the position of working in the domain they know best—teaching students content—and it allows them to take ownership of improving their profession's performance. . . .
>
> We do believe that working directly on improving teaching is a more productive approach because as parts of this problem get solved, teaching necessarily improves. We believe that the . . . approach of training teachers to acquire the core practices of teaching would benefit significantly from placing the training directly into the context of studying and improving instructional products. The easiest way to do this would be to situate teacher education in the context of learning to teach a particular curriculum designed to help students achieve learning goals valued by the stakeholders. (Hiebert & Morris, 2012, pp. 98–99)

Indeed, teachers' active use of the exceedingly numerous materials seems to indicate that structuring materials meet a need and that teachers feel better prepared as a result, especially in complex situations.

The issue of so-called uncertainty and certainty is the subject of continuing debate. While it is undisputed that lessons are not predictable in detail, the extent of uncertainty and how to deal with it are interpreted and weighted very differently (e.g., Dotger, 2015).

LESSON STUDIES

So-called lesson studies have received increasing attention since the turn of the millennium. Like textbooks, they are also oriented toward specific lesson content. The basic idea developed by Japanese teachers has remained unchanged: teachers do not adopt other people's lesson plans unchecked but rather analyze, improve, and comment on jointly selected plans of specific lessons that they will later teach themselves and then add further cycles of analyzing and improving (Stigler & Hiebert, 1999). Each teacher involved contributes his or her knowledge, ideas, and experiences, and together they arrive at a deeper understanding of content and methods (e.g., Lampert & Graziani, 2009; Lewis, Perry, Friedkin, & Roth, 2012). Teachers learn in the very context in which the new knowledge will then be used; what they learn will be useful to them. Thus, teachers are motivated to learn from the thoughts and experiences of others and to do their part. There are actually no problems of transfer and adaptation to their own teaching.

Here, teachers do not see themselves as executors of a plan that others have developed for them but bring in their own experiences, knowledge, and practices. Creative ideas, interesting experiments, understandable reasoning, appropriate procedures: everything that the teachers have already developed or picked up themselves can be brought in, discussed and tested by the team, and, if successful, incorporated into the joint product.

Thus, this approach can be understood as a kind of bridge: on the one hand, a ready-made and elaborated plan, and on the other hand, the teachers' own practices (Murata & Kim-Eng Lee, 2021).

PROBLEM-BASED LEARNING

The terms "problem-based teaching" and "problem-based learning" cover a wide range of similar approaches that describe the visible "surface" of teaching. At its core, it is always about approaching content in a problem-solving way. The approach is strongly related to the philosophy and pedagogy of John Dewey (1916). The expectations of problem-based learning are effects in deeper learning and understanding; it can promote motivation and autonomy and be cognitively activating. Introduced into

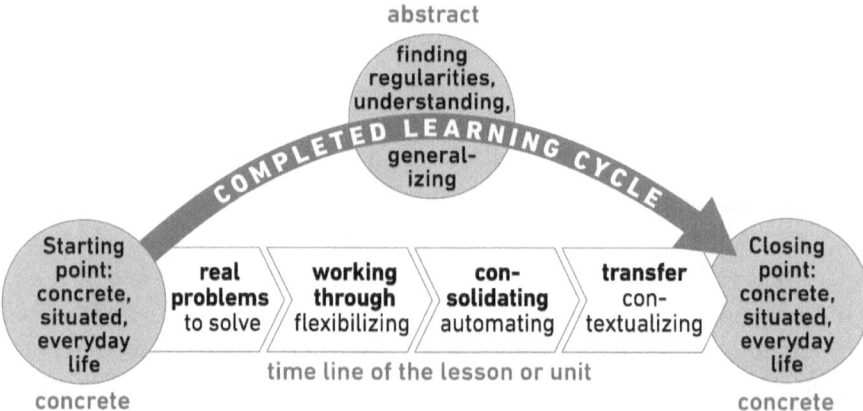

Figure 13.1. The completed learning cycle and the associated activities. *Based on Aebli (1983).*

medical education by Barrows and Tamblyn (1980), it is now found in all educational settings. However, the beneficial effects of this approach on motivation, cooperation, and learning are controversial (Schmidt, Rotgans, & Yew, 2011).

A model to translate the approach of problem-based learning into a lesson structure comes from Hans Aebli (1983), who suggests that learning should be triggered with an initial problem that learners work on. By doing so, they can better understand the content and acquire knowledge and solution patterns that they can apply in analogous situations. Thus, a completed learning cycle is created (see figure 13.1). Conversely, it is suboptimal, sometimes even disastrous for learning, if the teacher omits or severely shortens one or more stages of this cycle.

PROJECT-BASED LEARNING

Another example of a generic (subject-independent) concept is project-based learning. This approach focuses on students working together in projects with the goal of both producing an outcome and having students acquire generic skills in the process. The beginnings of the project method can be found in the United States in the nineteenth century (Dewey, 1931; Kilpatrick, 1918).

The pragmatic idea in the project method lies in joint execution und collective problem-solving. Exactly as much theory, knowledge, and advice as is necessary is incorporated to make progress in the project; when progress falters, resources are again drawn upon through reflection, discussion, research, calculation, and so on (see textbox 13.3).

The project method has often enough been trivialized in "project weeks" or in teacher-imposed activities, which are perceived by the students as externally determined. Projects do not tolerate over-planning; if the project is not about problems that students consider meaningful and are willing to work to solve, it is more of a prescribed activity than a project.

Grossman and colleagues (2021) describe in their book *Core Practices for Project-Based Learning* the goals of problem-based learning thus: supporting subject-area learning; engaging students in authentic work; encouraging student collaboration and agency; and building an iterative culture where students are always prototyping, reflecting, and trying again. What makes this work special is that the authors address core practices that are important to the implementation and successful execution of projects, such as methods to elicit higher-order thinking, engage students in disciplinary and interdisciplinary practice, or mentor student decision-making.

Textbox 13.3 FURTHER INFORMATION AND RESOURCES

CHARACTERISTICS OF THE PROJECT METHOD, ACCORDING TO JOHN DEWEY

John Dewey, one of the prominent promoters of the project method, briefly lists here some key characteristics that are still valid:

- A problem setting that connects to the learners' range of experience and abilities
- A problem that raises new questions and encourages them to investigate, undertake, and research
- Sufficient time
- The need of intellectual activity of teacher and student, the condemnation of passive receptivity
- Obtaining knowledge and resources only when needed.

Here is a longer quote from John Dewey (1931) on the project method:

> There cannot be a problem that is not a problem of *something*, nor a project that does not involve doing something in a way which demands

inquiry into fresh fields of subject-matter. Many so-called projects are of such a short time-span and are entered upon for such casual reasons, that extension of acquaintance with facts and principles is at a minimum. In short, they are too trivial to be educative. But the defect is not inherent. It only indicates the need that educators should assume their educational responsibility. It is possible to find problems and projects that come within the scope and capacities of the experience of the learner and which have a sufficiently long span so that they raise new questions, introduce new and related undertakings, and create a demand for fresh knowledge. The difference between this procedure and the traditional one is not that the latter involves acquisition of new knowledge and the former does not. It is that in one a relatively fixed and isolated body of knowledge is assumed in advance; while in the other, material is drawn from any field as it is needed to carry on an intellectual enterprise.

Material may be drawn from a variety of fields, number and measure from mathematics when they are needed, from historical, geographical, biological facts when they carry forward the undertaking, and so on. But the central question acts as a magnet to draw them together. Organization [of knowledge] in one case consists in formal relations within a particular field as they present themselves to an expert who has mastered the subject. In the other case, it consists in noting the bearing and function of things acquired. The latter course has at least the advantage of being of the kind followed in study and learning outside of school walls, where data and principles do not offer themselves in isolated segments with labels already affixed.

Another feature of the problem method is that activity is exacted. I suppose that if there is one principle which is not a monopoly of any school of educational thought, it is the need of intellectual activity on the part of teacher and student, the condemnation of passive receptivity. But in practice there persist methods in which the pupil . . . stands at the end of a pipe line receiving material conducted from a distant reservoir of learning. How is this split between theory and practice to be explained? Does not the presentation in doses and chunks of a ready-made subject-matter inevitably conduce to passivity? The mentally active scholar will acknowledge, I think, that his mind roams far and wide. All is grist that comes to his mill, and he does not limit his supply of grain to any one fenced-off field. Yet the mind does not merely roam abroad. It returns with what is found, and there is constant exercise of judgment to detect relations, relevancies, bearings upon the central theme. The outcome is a continuously growing intellectual integration. There is absorption; but it is eager and willing, not reluctant and forced. There is digestion, assimilation, not merely the carrying of a load by memory, a load to be cast off as soon as the day comes when it is safe to throw it off. Within the limits set by capacity and experience this kind of seeking and using, of amassing and organizing, is the process of learning everywhere and at any age.

While the student with a proper project is intellectually active, he is also overtly active; he applies, he constructs, he expresses himself in new ways. He puts his knowledge to the test of operation. Naturally, he does something with what he learns. Because of this feature the separation between the practical and the liberal does not even arise. It does not have to be done away with, because it is not there. (pp. 86–87).

DIRECT INSTRUCTION (OR EXPLICIT INSTRUCTION)

In contrast to the previous examples, so-called direct instruction is independent of specific content. The term "direct instruction" stands for *highly effective, tightly guided, teacher-centered whole-class instruction with high student activity*. The direct instruction approach fits into the larger movement of effective teaching, according to which teachers instruct in a way that students learn the content of the curriculum quickly, effectively, thoroughly, and sustainably.

Textbox 13.4

Siegfried "Zig" Engelmann (2004):
　"If the learner hasn't learned, the teacher hasn't taught"

Grell (1999):
　"Your job as a teacher is to teach the students. Take that job seriously and do it as effectively as you can."

Rosenshine and Stevens (1986):
　"All teachers use some of these behaviors [of direct instruction] some of the time, but the most effective teachers use most of them almost all the time."

"Direct instruction" suggests a specific lesson structure, which is described here. It should be noted that this structure does not conflict with the formal structure discussed in previous chapters. However, the reverse conclusion must not be made: not all lessons that follow such a structure are based on the principles of direct instruction.

One might notice that some elements of direct instruction, for example, guiding student practice, providing scaffolds for difficult tasks, or independent practice, have already been mentioned in other contexts. In fact, some elements belong to the basic repertoire of routines and practices of teachers; they are, in a sense, universal and not only specific to direct instruction.

Context

Direct Instruction (with an uppercase *D* and *I*) in the *original* sense was developed by Siegfried Engelmann and his collaborators beginning in the 1960s. The central idea of Direct Instruction is to guide students closely through highly elaborate materials that allow the teacher to move students quickly to better performance without going astray. Over the past half a century, the corpus of Direct Instruction curricular materials has grown, as has the literature evaluating its effectiveness (e.g., Engelmann, 2007; Muijs & Reynolds, 2011; Stockard, Wood, Coughlin, & Khoury, 2018).

In a broader sense, "direct instruction" (with a lowercase *d* and *i*) stands for educational programs that incorporate elements of systematic and explicit instruction. In particular, Barak Rosenshine (2008, 2010, 2012; Rosenshine & Stevens, 1986) has been committed to compiling research findings and presenting the concept in its broader sense over the past several decades.

Direct instruction is used in many situations where structured learning is required. It is based on an immense body of research from different perspectives on the effectiveness of classroom instruction. In describing the most effective elements of direct instruction, the question has always been what factors are beneficial to the *acquisition of defined and highly structured content*.

The objection that direct instruction is less suitable for open problems and discursive lessons is somewhat justified and has led to critical positions toward this approach. Today, direct instruction is hardly seen as a one-size-fits-all approach, and teachers must be very deliberate in deciding where to use specific elements of it appropriately. Where academic content needs to be learned with a high degree of structure, the direct instruction approach can be used to great effect.

Since about 2000, the term "explicit instruction" has been increasingly used. For Hughes and colleagues (2017), however, "it is clear that the roots of explicit instruction come directly from Direct Instruction and direct instruction, both of which have a history of effectiveness" (p. 145).

Some key points about the concept of direct instruction are summarized in textbox 13.5.

Textbox 13.5 FURTHER INFORMATION AND RESOURCES

DIRECT INSTRUCTION: A SUMMARY

Barak Rosenshine prefaces his booklet "Principles of Instruction" (2010) as follows:

> This pamphlet presents ten research-based principles of instruction, and suggestions for classroom practice. These principles come from three sources: (a) research on how our brain acquires and uses new information; (b) research on the classroom practices of those teachers whose students show the highest gains; and (c) findings from studies that taught learning strategies to students. . . . The fact that the instructional ideas from three different sources supplement and complement each other gives us faith in the validity of these findings. (Rosenshine, 2010, p. 6)

Below each of the ten principles are research-based practices that are typical of effective teachers; this is much abridged summary of the booklet mentioned above. Reading the original text, which is not very long, gives a more complete picture (downloadable for free).

Again, keep in mind, these recommendations refer to a specific type of closely guided instruction that is highly structured and focused on the efficient acquisition of knowledge and skills.

1. **Provide a Daily Review**
   Daily review can strengthen previous learning and can lead to fluent recall.
   Effective teachers . . .
   - begin lessons with a five-to-eight-minute review of previously covered material.
   - include reviewing the concepts and skills that were necessary to do the homework.

- review the knowledge and concepts that are relevant for that day's lesson.
- review material that needs overlearning.

2. **Present New Material Using Small Steps**
Only present small amounts of new material at any time, then assist students as they practice this material.
Effective teachers . . .
   - do not overwhelm their students by presenting too much new material at once.
   - only present small amounts of new material at one time.
   - teach in such a way that each step is mastered before the next step is introduced.

3. **Ask Questions**
Questions help students practice new information and connect new material to their prior learning.
Effective teachers . . .
   - find ways to involve all students in answering questions to quickly consolidate what has been introduced.
   - reteach some material when it is considered necessary.
   - may use choral responses to provide sufficient practice.

4. **Provide Models**
Providing students with models and worked examples can help students learn to solve problems faster.
Effective teachers . . .
   - teach skills in classrooms by providing prompts, modeling the use of the prompt, and then guiding students as they develop independence.
   - present worked-out examples by modeling and explaining the steps that can be taken to solve a specific problem.

5. **Guide Student Practice**
Successful teachers spend more time guiding the students' practice of new material.
Effective teachers . . .
   - can help the rehearsal process by asking questions, because good questions require the students to process and rehearse the material.
   - present only small amounts of material at a time, then guide student practice.
   - spend more time in guided practice, more time asking questions, more time checking for understanding, more time correcting errors, and more time having students work out problems with teacher guidance.

6. **Check for Student Understanding**
   Checking for student understanding at each point can help students learn the material with fewer errors.
   Effective teachers . . .
   - stop to check for student understanding by asking questions.
   - ask students to summarize or to repeat directions or procedures.
   - ask students whether they agree or disagree with other students' answers.
   - ask students to think aloud as they work to solve mathematical problems, to plan an essay, or to identify the main idea in a paragraph.
   - ask students to explain or defend their position to others.

7. **Obtain a High Success Rate**
   It is important for students to achieve a high success rate during classroom instruction.
   Effective teachers obtain this success level . . .
   - by "teaching in small steps."
   - by combining short presentations with supervised student practice.
   - by giving sufficient practice on each part before proceeding to the next step.

   Effective teachers . . .
   - limit the development of misconceptions by providing guided practice after teaching small amounts of new material and by checking for student understanding.
   - provide tutoring to help students master each unit ("mastery learning" is a form of instruction where lessons are organized into short units and all students are required to master one set before they proceed to the next set).

8. **Provide Scaffolds for Difficult Tasks**
   The teacher provides students with temporary supports and scaffolds to assist them when they learn difficult tasks.
   Effective teachers use forms of scaffolding . . .
   - by giving students prompts for steps they might use.
   - by thinking aloud themselves.
   - by asking students to think aloud during their problem-solving processes.

   Effective teachers . . .
   - anticipate students' errors and warn them about possible errors that some of them are likely to make.
   - provide students with expert models to which they can compare their work.

9. **Allow for Independent Practice**
   Provide for successful independent practice.
   Effective teachers . . .
   - provide for extensive and successful practice, both in the classroom and after class.
   - prepare students for their independent practice.
   - circulate around the room and monitor and supervise seatwork.

10. **Review on a Weekly and Monthly Basis**
    Students need to be involved in extensive practice in order to develop well-connected and automatic knowledge.
    - Effective teachers provide for frequent or extensive review and sometimes tests after these reviews.

COOPERATIVE LEARNING

Cooperative learning is both a general principle that can be applied to any learning opportunity and an approach that also suggests specific classroom practices. Here we briefly examine both aspects.

Many student activities are done alone. Not least for the pragmatic reason that it creates more quiet in the classroom, many teachers prefer the organizational form of individual seatwork. But cooperative work can be very effective on several levels.

Numerous forms of cooperation with room for decision-making by the learners are taken for granted nowadays. Cooperative learning is linked to increased autonomy of the learners and the learning group. When learners cooperate, they inherently take some control over how and what they work on. But it doesn't always work the way teachers want it to. Whether the students take responsibility for the social processes and for learning depends largely on whether they are capable of productive cooperation.

To make cooperative learning successful, there are a few things to keep in mind, some of which are discussed here. These things should also gradually become part of teachers' professional practices. However, many of the very basic insights and research results have not yet passed into the collective knowledge of teachers everywhere. For example:

- Forming random groups is more effective for learning than self-selecting groups.
- Roles in groups should not be assigned from the outset (e.g., "Who will present?") with the exception of moderating the group.
- Learning in groups is particularly effective if *at the same time* (!)good cooperation is rewarded *and* the success of the group also depends on the learning success of *each* individual group member.

Research and dissemination of cooperative learning are strongly associated with brothers David and Roger Johnson (2008), and Robert Slavin (1995). Textbox 13.7 goes into more depth on some fundamental aspects of this topic.

Textbox 13.6 ACTIVITIES AND SUGGESTIONS

COOPERATIVE LEARNING AND PRACTICES YOU ALREADY KNOW

Johnson and Johnson rightly note that the cooperative learning approach has gained recognition over the years and has now been integrated into many other approaches to teaching.

Here's a simple task: What practices do you recognize in cooperative learning? Read the following pages about cooperative learning and note what teacher practices you already know are in them. Make connections ("Oh, I already know this from . . ."), preferably in table form. Do you also find new practices that you think you should acquire and engage in?

Textbox 13.7 FURTHER INFORMATION AND RESOURCES

COOPERATIVE LEARNING

Johnson and Johnson: The Basic Elements of Cooperative Learning

The two American professors and brothers David W. and Roger T. Johnson have not only distinguished themselves as leading researchers in this field since the 1970s but have also repeatedly presented cooperative learning in an understandable and accessible way for teachers. The following excerpt from an essay provides a look at the practical implementation of cooperative learning in a formal setting.

Beforehand, a brief explanation of the concept of social interdependence that appears in the text below: Social interdependence theory is based on the idea that individuals' performances are influenced by the actions of others. There are two types: positive interdependence, in which the actions of individuals promote the achievement of common goals, and negative interdependence, in which the actions of individuals hinder the achievement of common goals.

Teacher training should emphasize conceptual understanding of the nature of cooperative learning and the basic elements that make it work. Although many teachers like take-and-use sessions, developing a mental model of the cause-and-effect relationships inherent in the use of cooperative learning increases retention of what is learned, improves transfer to the classroom, and supports long-term maintenance of the use of cooperative learning. Conceptual understanding provides teachers with a framework to organize what they know about cooperative learning, to guide their practices, and to integrate their new knowledge. Seeing the internal cohesion of cooperative learning procedures, where each step in conducting a cooperative lesson cues the next, increases the likelihood of teachers using it with high fidelity year after year. Operational procedures were formulated for three types of cooperative learning: formal, informal, and base groups.

Formal cooperative learning consists of students working together, for one class period to several weeks, to achieve shared learning goals and complete jointly specific tasks and assignments (such as problem solving, completing a curriculum unit, writing a report, conducting an experiment, or having a dialogue about assigned text material). Any course requirement or assignment may be structured to be cooperative. In formal cooperative learning, teachers do the following:

1. *Make a number of preinstructional decisions.* A teacher has to decide on the objectives of the lesson (both academic and social skills objectives), the size of groups, the method of assigning students to groups, the roles students will be assigned, the materials needed to conduct the lesson, and the way the room will be arranged.
2. *Explain the task and positive interdependence.* A teacher clearly defines the assignment, teaches the required concepts and strategies, specifies the positive interdependence and individual accountability, gives the criteria for success, and explains the expected social skills in which to be engaged.
3. *Monitor students' learning and intervene* in the groups to provide task assistance or to increase students' interpersonal and group skills.

A teacher systematically observes and collects data on each group as it works. When needed, the teacher intervenes to assist students in completing the task accurately and in working together effectively.
4. *Evaluate students' learning and help students process how well their groups functioned.* Students' learning is carefully assessed, and their performances are evaluated. Members of the learning groups then process how effectively they have been working together.

Informal cooperative learning consists of having students work together to achieve a joint learning goal in temporary, ad hoc groups that last from a few minutes to one class period. Students engage in quick dialogues or activities in temporary, ad hoc groups in response to a limited number of questions about what is being learned. The brief dialogues or activities may be used to focus student attention on the material to be learned, set a mood conducive to learning, help set expectations as to what will be covered in a class session, ensure that students cognitively process the material being taught, and provide closure to an instructional session. Informal cooperative learning groups are often organized so that students engage in 3- to 5-minute *focused discussions* before and after a lecture and 2- to 3-minute *turn-to-your-partner* discussions interspersed every 10 to 15 minutes throughout a lecture.

Cooperative base groups are long-term, heterogeneous cooperative learning groups with stable membership whose primary responsibilities are to provide support, encouragement, and assistance to make academic progress and develop cognitively and socially in healthy ways as well as holding each other accountable for striving to learn. Typically, cooperative base groups (a) are heterogeneous in membership, (b) meet regularly (e.g., daily or biweekly), and (c) last for the duration of the semester, year, or until all members are graduated. Students are assigned to base groups of three to four members and meet at the beginning and end of each class session (or week) to complete academic tasks such as checking each member's homework, doing routine tasks such as taking attendance, and engaging in personal support tasks such as listening sympathetically to personal problems or providing guidance for writing a paper. (Johnson & Johnson, 2009, pp. 373–374; see also http://www.cooperation.org/what-is-cooperative-learning)

The Role of the Teacher in Cooperative Learning

On the question of the role of the teacher in cooperative learning, Pauli and Reusser decisively state

> that the teacher plays a more important role in cooperative learning than previous research literature would suggest. As a designer of learning

situations and developer of additional learning aids or supports, as a behavioral model for subject-specific problem solving, for constructive cooperation and discussion, as an organizer and facilitator of cooperative learning activities, and as an expert in the subject discipline, the teacher can actively influence the success of group and partner work at different levels, at different times, and by different means. (Pauli & Reusser, 2000, p. 434)

Further, they emphasize that teacher intervention in group and partner work is not taboo:

> Results of some studies indicate that the promotion of independence on the one hand and controlling intervention on the other hand do not necessarily have to contradict each other. It has been shown that well-dosed, adaptive interventions by teachers can intensify students' cognitive activities, that students find such interventions helpful, and that the interventions do not lead to increased dependence of students on their teachers. Interventions can, in some circumstances, be in the service of independence by specifically modeling or working on learning and collaboration skills, for example, when teachers use the small group constellation to work with students on adequate patterns of reasoning and forms of collaboration. From this perspective, engagement with the subject matter and collaboration with the teacher need not be mutually exclusive; all the less so if it is possible to build a learning culture in which a class or learning group sees itself as a "knowledge-building community" in which it is experienced as "normal" for individuals with different levels of knowledge to work together in different situations and to support each other. (p. 436)

Slavin and Cooper: Cooperative Learning Groups in Order to Promote More Cross-Race Relationships

> Cooperative learning appears to facilitate the development of positive cross-race peer relations, whether at the level of weak friendship ties or close, reciprocated friendship choices. The implications of such research results are encouraging. These findings suggest that positive social relations among students of differing racial and ethnic backgrounds help students to transcend and transform shared cultural norms and attitudes that can prohibit meaningful cross-cultural interactions. Such transformation does not require students to ignore or eliminate

the differences that exist among their classmates, in their histories, communities, and families, but rather to understand them using a different cultural paradigm. The positive social relations that are built between students of different racial and ethnic backgrounds as they work collaboratively to solve complex problems or to complete meaningful tasks are not simply a matter of students' liking each other or having positive thoughts about each other. These cross-cultural interactions are about broadening the cultural frames of reference that define the social worlds and dictate social network patterns for these students. (Slavin & Cooper, 1999, p. 658)

Johnson and Johnson: Cooperative Learning and Teaching Citizenship in Democracies

In order to ensure future generations of citizens in a democracy understand their rights and are committed to their responsibilities, schools must involve them in the processes of democracy on a day-to-day basis. The two steps for doing so are using cooperative learning the majority of the school day to engage students in the basic processes of democracy and utilizing constructive controversy procedures to engage students in the processes of political discourse.

When working cooperatively with classmates becomes a way of life within a school, learning how to be a citizen in a democracy inherently takes place. There are a number of important parallels between being an effective member of a cooperative learning group and being an effective citizen in a democracy.

The overall goal of education in a democracy is to ensure citizens understand their rights as a citizen and be committed to fulfilling their responsibilities as a citizen. This requires the internalization of the values, attitudes, and patterns of behavior necessary to fulfill the responsibilities of citizens in a democracy. While most instruction is aimed at promoting mastery of information and conceptual frameworks, citizenship education in addition focuses on value and attitude acquisition and behavioral change, as well as continuing motivation to add to one's knowledge about citizenship in a democracy. The achievement of these goals depends on utilizing cooperative learning.

In essence, a cooperative learning group is a microcosm of a democracy: . . .

Cooperative Learning	Democracy
Work with others to achieve mutual goals (e.g., members are expected to learn and to help groupmates learn)	Work with others to achieve mutual goals (i.e., the flourishing of the democratic society in a way that benefits oneself and all other citizens)
Each member is responsible for participating in the group, doing his or her fair share of the work, and maintaining good working relationships among members.	Each citizen is responsible for participating in democratic processes, doing his or her fair share in achieving their society's goals, and maintaining good working relationships among citizens.
All members are considered to be equal regardless of gender, ethnicity, or religion. Equality does not mean doing the same things or making equal contributions to the group; it means having the same value and being given equal consideration and opportunities.	All citizens are considered to be equal regardless of gender, ethnicity, or religion. Equality does not mean doing the same things or making equal contributions to society; it means having the same value and being given equal consideration and opportunities.
All members have the right and obligation to express their ideas, conclusions, and opinions (including opposition to others' ideas) and to be listened to with respect and consideration.	All citizens have the right and obligation to express their ideas, conclusions, and opinions (including opposition to others' ideas) and to be listened to with respect and consideration.
All members are expected to provide leadership, communicate effectively, build trust among members, ensure effective decisions are made, ensure conflicts are resolved constructively, and ensure agreed-upon tasks and decisions are carried to completion.	All citizens are expected to provide leadership (including running for office), communicate effectively, build trust among citizens, ensure effective decisions are made, ensure conflicts are resolved constructively, and ensure agreed-upon tasks and decisions are carried to completion.
Decisions are made by a combination of consensus and majority rule after a thorough discussion considering the merits of all points of view and focusing on the quality of the reasoning and information.	Decisions are made by majority rule with safeguards for minority opinions after a thorough discussion considering the merits of all points of view and focusing on the quality of the reasoning and information.
Members value contributing to the well-being of groupmates and the common good.	Citizens value contributing to the well-being of fellow citizens and the common good.

Textbox 13.8 ACTIVITIES AND SUGGESTIONS

DESCRIBE YOUR PREFERRED PATTERN OF LESSONS: ANALYZE AND COMPARE

Many teachers have their preferred patterns of lessons that help "do" or "deliver" instruction. They hope for a manageable amount of work and automatism in terms of learning. The focus often tends to be on the visible, external flow of the lesson—that is, on the surface level. But what does it do? Is it educational? Is it learning?

Do You Have a Preferred Lesson Pattern? What Are Its Characteristics?

Perhaps you, too, have your favorite pattern that gives you confidence in teaching. But the question is, Is it an enabling pattern that allows flexibility and gives you freedom to allow students to move forward, or is it a pattern that makes some things impossible and constricts both you and the students?

1. Describe off the cuff and in a few words what your most used lesson staging looks like, (i.e., a lesson in which you would feel quite confident and comfortable).
2. What elements are most important to you? Is there a preferred order?
3. What should never be missing?
4. What will you pay special attention to (e.g., because you feel particularly insecure here, or because this element is particularly difficult)?

Compare

You have briefly learned about some lesson structures that suggest and justify a particular sequence, some of which deviate from the basic pattern (opening, input/discussion, activities, closing). Try to form a first opinion. For each, write down

- at least one positive point—that is, what you find interesting or attractive about that approach specifically.
- at least one caveat that you would raise about that approach specifically, based on your current knowledge.

Scripted Lessons

positive:
caveat:

Following Textbooks

positive:
caveat:

Lesson Studies

>positive:
>caveat:

Problem-Based Learning

>positive:
>caveat:

Project-Based Learning

>positive:
>caveat:

Direct Instruction

>positive:
>caveat:

Cooperative Learning

>positive:
>caveat:

Last Point: Dig Deeper

Research and read about those points that particularly concern you (that attract you, that annoy you, that make you insecure, that you want to understand better, that you want to practice).

Part IV

WHERE DO WE STAND NOW?

This final part encourages a review of what has been achieved so far. It does not introduce new practices but delves deeper into what they actually mean.

The impact of this book increases when, on the one hand, the concepts presented are understood and contextualized, and on the other hand, of course, the reader actively engages, for example, by immediately trying out new practices.

Finally, the reader can get an overview from his or her point of view which practices have been addressed and deepened.

Chapter Fourteen

A Closer Look at the Concept of (Core) Practices

So far, this book has focused primarily on specific practices that are likely to be important to prospective and in-service teachers. Let us now take a step back and look more closely at where the concept of core practices comes from and how it is framed.

CORE PRACTICES

Beginnings and Clarifications

The idea of focusing on practices and learning them in practice is the core idea of this book. However, the idea is not new. Almost two hundred years ago, the German educator Diesterweg, addressing teachers, wrote, "Practice is learned only in practice" (Diesterweg, 1838, p. 37).

Since then, teacher education around the world has undergone numerous developments that have led overall to more professional preparation for the field. But Diesterweg's thought remains undisputed and has taken on renewed relevance in more recent times, since rooting in practice has increasingly become the guiding principle of teacher education.

Since about 2000, voices have been growing in the United States advocating a fundamentally different approach to teacher education. This current is now often referred to as the "practice turn" (Ball & Cohen, 1999). It is not a unified movement, but the common central concerns are clearly evident. One focus is the development of professional teaching practices with a twofold purpose:

1. To initiate the adoption of such practices in undergraduate education
2. To develop procedures for how these practices are learned, flexed, elaborated, and made habitual, and how to work habitually to develop them further

Proponents of this approach describe this process as shifting the focus away from bodies of knowledge and toward bodies of depictions of practice (Kennedy, 2016). The intent is to show student teachers ways in which they can support student learning (Zeichner, 2012). It requires those involved in teacher education to be willing to organize education around a set of core practices. They should help student teachers develop knowledge and professional activities as well as a professional identity based on these practices (Grossman, Hammerness, & McDonald, 2009).

This approach describes the essential requirements for teachers in the classroom with a degree of concreteness that is more manageable for student teachers and lecturers than lists of hundreds of competencies and standards (Gamson, Eckert, & Anderson, 2019; Zeichner, 2012). This approach claims to closely link the theoretical and practical elements of teacher training and to arrange all study content around the goal of professional agency.

The aim is not to build up competence in a linear step-by-step manner but rather to try out, develop, and contextualize practices (Forzani, 2014, pp. 364–365). The representatives of this approach reject the accusation that only techniques for immediate application are aimed at. Rather, they argue, practices are particularly effective with an underlying conceptual understanding, the ability to think, analyze, argue, and critique in a disciplined manner with reference to professional challenges. The goals of teacher education would also include, according to the authors, critical and creative thinking and the ability to solve problems in relation to local, national, and global issues (Ball & Forzani, 2011, pp. 19–20). They assume that core practices can be identified along essential professional requirements and that their learning should be situated as early as the undergraduate years. Grossman et al. (2009, p. 277) recommend focusing first on those core practices that most clearly serve student teachers as well as students.

In the understanding of the core practices approach, core practices are formed from *clusters of specific activities*. Since the word "activity" is used with very different meanings, let us briefly explain what is meant in this context. Sometimes "activities" refers to a segment of the lesson in which students are active. Here, however, we are talking about teacher activities: small and concise units of the teacher's action, sometimes routines, sometimes conscious actions. Thus, core practices are not isolated teacher activities (such as "designing a worksheet") but rather, for the most part, a whole cluster of activities that serve to master a challenge of the profession with confidence (e.g., "incorporating students' ideas in a meaningful way during a discussion"). They are built up, expanded, and practiced while consciously linking them to related scientific knowledge and one's own stock of experience. "Candidates will blend practitioner knowledge with academic knowledge as they learn by doing. They will refine their practice in the light of new knowledge acquired and data gathered about whether their students are learning" (NCATE, 2010, p. ii).

Search for a Precise Description of Practices— and for Their Individual Shaping

Again and again, the question arises as to which are the most important core practices. For some experts, the priority is for teachers to have a repertoire of routines that they can use as the situation demands. Many of these routines, they say, can be easily described and trained, and they are almost universally applicable. In this view, the core practice would tend to be the ability to use these tools in ways that benefit student learning. They argue that practices should be teachable to student teachers, and that would inevitably involve some standardization. Undoubtedly, this work of scrupulous analysis and description of practices is very important work that helps prospective and in-service teachers as a resource.

However, other experts tend to refrain from drawing up an exhaustive list of characteristics of defined and meticulously described core practices. From their point of view, the indispensable criterion of practices is precisely that they become concrete in specific circumstances and meet the real needs of the teacher in this cultural context, and thus cannot be rigid. From this point of view, which also underlies this book, it is the teacher who goes on shaping his or her own practices (in dialogue with others, with the actual situation, with professional and scholarly sources, and with knowledge about practices). The teacher, building on knowledge about practices, creates something distinctive that is both important to himself or herself and improves the quality of teaching. In other words, it is precisely the identification and construction of a practice and the constant engagement with it that are considered constitutive. It is in this way that a practice is most likely to be internalized and to become part of the teacher's identity.

An essential characteristic of practices, then, is that they are *individually shaped*. Nevertheless, how practices are selected and shaped is *not arbitrary*. When teachers work on their practices, they should listen to voices from three directions:

1. The knowledge about practices and, more generally, the established knowledge of the profession, which is accessible to the teacher in a variety of forms
2. The friendly critical view of others: colleagues, peers, professionals, students
3. Actual success in the teacher's professional activities

The individual shaping of practices makes it difficult to answer the question of how exactly to define practices as they appear to us in the end. Due to the personal touch, they elude a precise determination of content. Nevertheless, there is, of course, a desire among student teachers and in-service teachers to "learn" practices (i.e., to acquire defined practices).

Specifications and Inventories of Core Practices

Certain authors name and describe a set of practices that they consider significant. Indeed, some core practices can be identified that are fundamentally important to the teaching profession; this book has also addressed some practices that are pretty much indispensable for teachers. But an approach that merely describes practices and adds some more material to the plethora of learning content in teacher education would rather undermine the intent of *achieving sustained adoption* and flexible use of professional practices. Student teachers need *opportunities to practice practices*. For this reason, elaborate training settings in on-campus courses for learning core practices are developed and implemented in many teacher education programs (Grossman, 2018).

Undoubtedly, different practices are at the forefront from case to case, depending on the teacher, subject, level, and cultural context, as Grossman and Pupik Dean (2019) point out. One example of a cross-disciplinary core practices framework called "TeachingWorks" comes from a University of Michigan program led by Deborah Ball (see textbox 14.2). Various core practices concepts have since been put forward, including subject-specific ones (e.g., for teaching mathematics, history, science, and English language arts), but they are not discussed further here (Fogo, 2014; Kavanagh & Rainey, 2017; Kazemi, Ghousseini, Cunard, & Chan Turrou, 2016; Windschitl & Calabrese Barton, 2016; Windschitl et al., 2012).

Textbox 14.1 FURTHER INFORMATION AND RESOURCES

THE CORE PRACTICE APPROACH AS A CHALLENGE TO TEACHER EDUCATION

The scholars who have studied core practices in depth since the first decade of the twenty-first century have also developed a rich body of research and publications. Some of them have joined together in the Core Practices Consortium. The following excerpt from a publication by Grossman and Pupik Dean (2019) briefly summarizes the challenges teacher education faces with regard to teaching practice.

> A growing body of evidence illustrates the critical role that teaching quality plays in fostering significant and meaningful student learning. At the same time, the ability of teacher education programs to prepare teachers to take on this challenging work is under scrutiny. University teacher education programs, in particular, have been critiqued for over-valuing knowledge for teaching at the cost of cultivating teaching practices. In this atmosphere, the field of teacher education is in the midst of a major shift—a turn away from an intense focus on the knowledge needed for teaching to a focus on the use of that knowledge in practice (Grossman et al., 2009; Zeichner, 2012). The fundamental goal of this turn is to better support novice teachers in learning how to skillfully enact core teaching practices (Ball & Forzani, 2009; Grossman et al., 2009; Lampert, 2010; Zeichner, 2012).
>
> The focus on core practice grows out of what has been learned through past efforts to reform teacher education. Reforms in the 1960's and 1970's focused on providing novice teachers with opportunities to practice discrete skills, while efforts in the 1980's encouraged teacher educators' use of case-based methods to build teachers' knowledge

for making the complex, moment-to-moment decisions required for teaching (McDonald, Kazemi, & Kavanagh, 2013). Both efforts failed to successfully address the problem of enactment (Kennedy, 1999). Attending to practice links the focus on skill with the focus on knowledge required for the complexity of teaching, leading to a view of teaching practice as the application of knowledge in action. Core practices in teaching, then, are identifiable components fundamental to teaching and grounded in disciplinary goals that teachers enact to support learning. Core practices consist of the enactment of knowledge, beliefs, and dispositions through strategies, routines, and moves that can be unpacked and learned by teachers. They are distinguished from other efforts to focus on teaching practice (e.g., Lemov, 2010) in that core practices recognize the highly intersubjective and complex nature of teaching and are deeply connected to the goals of disciplinary learning (McDonald et al., 2013). This goal of improving disciplinary learning is particularly necessary in poverty-impacted schools where students are seldom invited to participate in authentic disciplinary inquiry and too often are offered only rote and remedial instruction. Another feature of this work is an acknowledgement that teacher educators must both identify core practices, but also study and improve the pedagogies used to develop teachers' capacities to enact these practices (e.g., Lampert et al., 2013). (p. 158)

Textbox 14.2 FURTHER INFORMATION AND RESOURCES

THE TEACHINGWORKS PROGRAM

The TeachingWorks program, founded by Deborah Ball, is often cited in the context of Core Practices. The Core Practices articulated by TeachingWorks are largely cross-curricular and were originally developed for primary teachers (www.teachingsworks.org).

The TeachingWorks strategy is designed to ensure that all teachers have the necessary foundations for accountable teaching. Deborah Ball calls it the heart of the whole endeavor. She says it's about focusing on a set of foundational skills called "high-leverage practices."

According to Ball, it is these high-leverage practices that form the foundations of teaching; they are used all the time and are critical to helping students learn the things that matter. The website states, "These practices are used constantly and are critical to helping students learn important content. The high-leverage practices are also central to supporting students' social and emotional development. They are used across subject areas, grade levels, and contexts. They are 'high-leverage' not only because they matter to student learning but because they are basic for advancing skill in teaching."

Whether the core or high-leverage practices can be precisely named, and whether there is an exhaustive list to do so, is debatable. The following nineteen practices from TeachingWorks is one such attempt to name an indispensable core of practices. Each practice is then described in more detail in about one hundred words each; only the titles are reproduced here. With good reason, one could group these practices differently, put some together, or omit some, depending on the context. Either way, the TeachingWorks approach should be commended as a bold step, and it explicitly consists of defining a set of practices that should be acquired in practice-based teacher education.

Here are the nineteen high-leverage practices of TeachingWorks:

1. Leading a group discussion
2. Explaining and modeling content
3. Eliciting and interpreting individual students' thinking
4. Attending to patterns of student thinking
5. Implementing norms and routines for discourse
6. Coordinating and adjusting instruction
7. Establishing and maintaining community expectations
8. Implementing organizational routines
9. Setting up and managing small group work
10. Building respectful relationships
11. Communicating with families
12. Learning about students
13. Setting learning goals
14. Designing single lessons and sequences of lessons
15. Checking student understanding
16. Selecting and designing assessments
17. Interpreting student work
18. Providing feedback to students
19. Analyzing instruction for the purpose of improving it

Source and detailed descriptions of the practices: https://www.teachingworks.org/high-leverage-practices (retrieved December 28, 2022).

> A study by Martin-Raugh and colleagues (2016) surveyed more than six hundred teachers and teacher education professionals in the United States to determine which of these practices they considered important. Not surprisingly, all seemed important to them (on a six-point scale, all mean scores ranged from 4.8 to 5.7). Although the TeachingWorks concept was originally developed for teaching mathematics (Ball & Forzani, 2009), it seems to find approval in other subjects as well.

Some Open Issues

Everyone can agree on the basic intent: train teachers to use practices that best support student progress. But when it comes to specific questions, things get tricky. Many researchers, teacher educators, and teachers are intrigued by the plausible concept of core practices, but not all understand the same thing by it. For example, there is no universally accepted "hierarchy" of related concepts. For some, practices are, in a sense, the umbrella, and they are composed of numerous elements that teachers draw on. For others, practices are merely part of a larger, overarching concept.

Another point is that some programs tend toward universally applicable, generic practices that should be part of the profession's DNA, so to speak, regardless of subject or grade level. Others strongly emphasize that practices should be very specific—that is, tied to subject, grade level, goals, and local conditions.

Different views can also be discerned regarding the learning of practices. Some tend toward a structured acquisition of practices in courses, using multiple forms of rehearsal. In this case, practices sometimes appear more as routines and moves that can be used as building blocks for responsive teaching. Others emphasize adaptivity more strongly and want to train how teachers can use practices successfully in open-ended situations (Grosser-Clarkson & Neel, 2020; Kavanagh et al., 2019).

Many who participate in discourses on practices show a rather pragmatic attitude and are not too worried about the strategic, conceptual, and terminological differences. They focus on not only on researching practices but also on teaching them and helping teachers to use them. That's probably a good thing. One can expect that over time certain positions will prevail and become generally accepted, as is, after all, the case in many other disciplines.

SOME PREVIOUS AND RELATED APPROACHES

The basic idea of practices of professional action is not new, nor is it limited to the scholars cited above. Authors have repeatedly approached this idea from many directions. They wanted to find something that guides action in the teaching profession, situated between theory and practice, between careful analysis and reflexive action. In addition, many approaches strive for a concept that connects theory and practice or analysis and reflex so closely that they lead to better solutions in a constant interplay. In this section, a few approaches are described very briefly.

The Schemata and Scripts Approach

Within the field of psychology, the smoothly running processes of everyday life and professional activity have been studied in detail. The underlying concept is that of *schemata* (singuar: schema; e.g., Rumelhart & Ortony, 1977), patterns of acting, feeling, and thinking that one acquires over time and that are automated, so to speak. When it comes to multistep processes in which things happen in a certain way, we speak of *scripts* (Schank & Abelson, 1977).

With reference to teaching, Stigler and Hiebert (1999) in particular have continued developing this concept. They analyzed teachers' patterns in the Third International Mathematics and Science video study and recognized recurring, unconsciously running scripts, which are also partly culturally conditioned (in contrast to scripted lessons, which are detailed scripts of a lesson). From the international comparison of such scripts, they concluded that they are changeable and that a concern of teacher education should be to develop these unconscious scripts in a desirable direction (Stigler, Gallimore, & Hiebert, 2000).

The idea of schemata was repeatedly discussed. Tenorth (2006) proposed to reinterpret teachers' knowledge and to "no longer speak of knowledge, nor of 'tacit knowledge', but of 'professional schemata' and to see the organization of practice, i.e., the accomplishment and success of everyday professional life, as the learning, construction, and procedure of schemata" (p. 589). Again, the practices approach is readily recognizable in these reflections.

The Basic Forms of Teaching Approach

As early as the 1950s, the Swiss psychologist Hans Aebli, an associate of Jean Piaget, pursued the intention of combining the practical demands of the teaching profession with psychological knowledge on teaching and learning. His work *Basic Forms of Teaching* (Aebli, 1961), later developed into *Twelve Basic Forms of Teaching* (Aebli, 1983), took as its starting point the everyday activities and challenges of the teaching profession (e.g., storytelling, the structure of a lesson, concept development) and underpinned it with the psychological knowledge that was current at the time. He showed how these challenges could not only be practiced and mastered but also understood. The professional challenges may have changed since then, but the approach still has its persuasive power even today and can be found in the concept of practices.

The Reflective Practice Approach

In the tradition of American pragmatism, the actual problem to be solved is the starting point of all learning. Challenges are worked through in an iterative process until a stable solution is found. This implies a willingness to try things out and to think critically about the effects of one's own actions in order to improve them in the next step. For John Dewey, the most important representative of American pragmatism, this is the core of all learning, indeed of all thinking in general. As Dewey puts it, "To learn from experience is to make a backward and forward connection between what we do to things and what we enjoy or suffer from things in consequence" (Dewey, 1916, p. 164).

Learning the practices of teaching fits almost seamlessly into this concept. Donald Schön (1987) also describes how reflective practitioners are constantly and almost simultaneously exploring, trying out, and checking things: "When the practitioner reflects-in-action in a case he perceives as unique, paying attention to phenomena and surfacing his intuitive understanding of them, his experimenting is at once exploratory, move testing, and hypothesis testing" (p. 72). This process of learning, quickly adapting, and readjusting during an action is exactly what teachers do when they bring their elaborated practices to bear. They apply them, but they simultaneously reflect and check if they are on the right track. Zeichner (1996) puts it succinctly: "There is no such thing as an unreflective teacher" (p. 207). The focus of Schön's analysis is on the "conversation with the situation" (Schön, 1992, p. 125), whereas it should be critically noted that the aspect of habitualizing, the gradual internalization of practices, hardly plays a role in Schön's work.

The Adaptive Expertise Approach

Following Hatano and Inagaki's (1986) much-cited distinction, there are the routine experts and the adaptive experts. Quite obviously, adaptive expertise is an essential quality of teachers—that is, the ability to adapt and to act appropriately and professionally in a particular and often unpredictable situation (Loughland, 2019).

Most teachers become experts in one way or another during their careers. But what kind of expertise is that? After all, the teacher is expected not only to teach routinely but also to be responsive to students' voices of all kinds and, for example, to allow students to participate actively in discussions, to share their ideas, and to build on each other's contributions (e.g., Kavanagh et al., 2019; Timperley, 2013). Parallels emerge here with the concept of (core) practices that drive precisely this adaptive and professional action.

The question, therefore, is how adaptivity and adaptive practices, in particular, can be learned early on. In teacher education, it would be completely unacceptable and irresponsible to simply wait for expertise to develop quasi-automatically over the years through experience, especially since even this is highly uncertain.

How to achieve expertise? For that purpose, the much-heard comparisons with chess players, musicians, and athletes are constantly mentioned, and the same numbers circulate, according to which it takes ten thousand hours of deliberate practice to achieve expertise (Ericsson, Krampe, & Tesch-Römer, 1993). But to apply this to teachers is a fallacy. That ten thousand hours of practice are needed to achieve expertise may be quite true for top performers, but not everyone wants to become a grandmaster, a golf champion, or a concert pianist. On the one hand, the studies of Ericsson and colleagues are mostly misquoted and misinterpreted, and on the other hand, following Ericsson and colleagues, the earlier one starts and the more one practices deliberately, the faster one achieves expertise.

That means, quite simply, if student teachers start working on their adaptive practices early and intensively in teacher education, they will have a higher level of proficiency when they enter the profession than if they do not (or if teacher education does not give them the opportunity to do so). The consequences are especially fatal for students: unprofessional teachers create a learning loss that can significantly jeopardize students' careers.

The study of a team of researchers from New Zealand, for example, has suggested that learning adaptive practice *during* teacher education is possible. The findings show that practice-based teacher education contributes significantly to building adaptive expertise by placing student learning at the center and providing student teachers with appropriate training and experimentation opportunities (Anthony, Hunter, & Hunter, 2015).

Common Features of These Approaches

What all of these approaches seem to have in common is that they focus on individual proficiency in professional work. It is about empowerment to make the right decisions in order to accompany students in their progress and thus to keep the goal of pedagogical action in view.

This again reveals that efforts have been made from different perspectives to understand professional teaching and to draw conclusions on how to build such practices. The banal call for more practice falls short. It is not the number of hours in a class that is decisive. As is well known, the wrong thing can also be practiced, as an extensive video study by Baer et al. (2011) soberingly revealed. Rather, it is the quality of learning that matters. The time spent in practice should reasonably be used for the serious and conscientious understanding, training, developing, and gaining flexibility of those elements and rapid decision-making processes that we call "practices" here.

Chapter Fifteen

Epilogue
My Own Practices

This book aims to inspire you to address the core practices that are essential to your teaching as a professional. You have been guided, so to speak, to some "hotspots" of professional activities, where professional, flexible, and internalized practices are important and facilitate teaching and learning.

What practices did you find? What next? What practices do you urgently need to develop to become more professional? This is what this last short chapter is about.

Much has been said about practices: an approach to the term, notes on their structure, the concept of "practices" in a larger context, and numerous concrete examples and elaborations. If you skim part I again, you may read it differently and quite fruitfully, because you now understand better what practices are.

You have certainly noticed that practices cannot be conveyed as recipes, tips, and ready-made instructions; such are at best a starting point for trying out. What follows is work: repeated training and optimizing; observing the effects; becoming familiar with variants; rereading, reflecting, researching and discussing; flexibilizing; applying habitually; and yet not being surprised when things turn out differently than expected. And having an intuitively coherent and purposeful response to that, too, is a hallmark of good practices.

Practices become second nature over time, and yet they are not blind routine. You as a teacher or as a student teacher are always awake and self-critical, have your intentions in mind, and use your practices to realize those intentions, mostly to move students forward, because that's what matters most.

A LIST OF ALL PRACTICES?

Numerous practices have been presented and recommended for training. It can be said that some practices are simply indispensable. Without them, a teacher is likely to fail at length. But this book has not presented an exhaustive inventory of professional practices or "core practices," although some authors have done so and have made a good case for it (e.g., teachingsworks.org).

The "Core"

The practices that have been addressed in detail in this book can be considered core, for example, diagnosing, giving feedback, opening a lesson transparently, leading a discussion, giving input, planning a unit of several lessons, planning a single lesson, setting and communicating meaningful goals, designing tasks, using resources, and evaluating fairly, to name a few.

Your Practices Respond to Your Own Unique Challenges

In your job, you will need to use most of these practices, and hopefully you will be good at them. But you will also develop practices that may not be written down anywhere, because they are a response to the specific challenges you face. So you also need to be able to identify and work on practices yourself.

Varying Degrees of Specificity

Practices vary in detail or comprehensiveness, again depending on the teacher. For one teacher, creating a positive and attentive atmosphere at the beginning of a lesson is a demanding practice, while another teacher takes the whole complex of entering a lesson as a practice in which creating a favorable atmosphere is only a small element. No one defines the level of a practice except you yourself as the teacher.

Your Variations of Practices

- Your practices are always individual. Practices become part of your identity as a teacher. You have shaped the practice; you give it indi-

vidual coloration and shaping until it serves you best to implement your intentions.
- Your practices are contextual. You will shape, use, and develop your practices differently depending on the subject, grade level, and topic. A classroom discussion in a foreign language with ten-year-olds requires different practices than a history subject with sixteen-year-olds.
- Your practices depend on your developmental stage. Practices are never fully formed for any teacher. But what is no problem and intuitive for one teacher, another teacher has to work hard at because he or she is repeating the same mistakes and falling into traps over and over again. For example, a teacher who cannot refrain from commenting on the smallest utterance of a learner will probably have trouble bringing an investigative style into a classroom discussion. Some reflexes and spontaneous decisions are sometimes deeply rooted in the teacher's personality, and accordingly he or she must persevere to develop and improve these practices.

WHAT IS MISSING?

Domain- and Grade-Level-Specific Practices

This book has largely confined itself to generic (i.e., domain-unspecific) practices, knowing that each subject has its own core practices that would often be meaningless in another subject. Indeed, there is already a substantial body of experience and studies on subject-specific practices, for example, in science (Windschitl et al., 2012), history (Fogo, 2014), and teaching of foreign languages (Kavanagh & Rainey, 2017; www.actfl.org). In addition, practices vary, of course, depending on the grade level.

Going into detail here is not something this book can do. Teachers and student teachers are challenged to do their own research or turn to the right professionals for advice.

Planning, Setting Goals, Evaluating

You may wonder why lesson planning has not been introduced as a practice. Certainly, it is a core practice, and some aspects have been touched on in passing. Planning is a broad topic that takes up a lot of teachers' time and mental energy. It involves not only planning a specific lesson but also setting goals, dealing with guidelines (standards, curriculum), developing or finding meaningful learning tasks, and evaluating instruction and learning.

All of this cannot be addressed here in a nutshell. Therefore, the practices of planning, goal-setting, and evaluation are covered in more depth in a separate book by the same author.

Classroom Management

Everyone knows that classroom management is an extremely important and emotionally charged topic, especially for less experienced teachers. Why, of all things, was this not addressed here? Three reasons:

- Many problems with classroom management result from bad teaching. This is a fact. Students usually respond to a tense climate and to boring, poorly prepared, or incomprehensible instruction. Good and transparent teaching, on the other hand, based on professional knowledge and good practices, is the best prevention, which can counteract many of the causes of disruptions.
- There is a large amount of mostly good literature and guides on classroom management and disruptions, explaining the basic principles and possible courses of action. Since all teachers have experience in this area, it is easy to obtain advice (the quality of which must be carefully evaluated).
- When dealing with acute disruptions, the circumstances of the classroom and school are very specific, as is the individual situation of the students and of the teacher. While there are certainly some practical rules or mistakes to avoid, the field of possible causes is so broad that the teacher must explore them him- or herself (or with the help of peers) and work out the practices to deal with them.

Thus, handling disruptions is a practice that is ideally suited to be built up by yourself. Proceed analogously as with the other practices. Identify the many facets of this practice, get informed, apply the practice in different situations, and gain experience and refine the practice, all this in several cycles, and seek exchange with peers and professionals.

FINAL REMARKS

Remember (even if you have read and heard it several times), practices are *means to an end*; they have a serving and helping function to facilitate your work and to fluidize teaching in the desired direction.

The goal, however, is always that your students have not come to school for nothing, have not wasted their time, and that they will become more mature, insightful, understanding, and competent in the time they spend with you.

This is now your current state. Building practices is a perpetual work in progress. Stick with it!

Textbox 15.1 ACTIVITIES AND SUGGESTIONS

READY FOR ONE LAST ACTIVITY? YOUR PRACTICES AS THEY ARE NOW

It is now time to make an inventory. Teachers do not necessarily believe that the same situations and practices are important. Building your own (core) practices is a longer process that happens individually.

- Try to distinguish between smaller teacher activities/routines and practices that aggregate a whole group of such activities. For example, you might subsume the teacher activity of welcoming students under a practice called "opening the lesson" or the like.
- You can proceed in two ways, whichever suits you better.

Option 1: Make a List of Subitems

practice A
- teacher activity f
- teacher activity g

practice B
- teacher activity a
- teacher activity b
- teacher activity c

Option 2: Take a Very Large Sheet and Diagram Your Practices

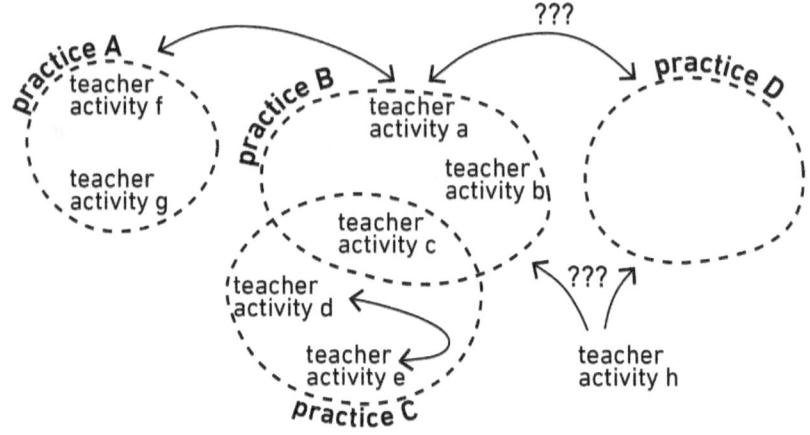

Figure 15.1. Visualizing your practices. *Author created.*

After the first draft, sit back and look at the result.

- Briefly skim the book and your notes again (your "handbook," portfolio, diary, etc.).
- Revise the overview generously or redraw it entirely.
- Also, list practices that were *not* mentioned at all in the book but seem important to you.
- Highlight those areas or practices in which you feel unsure and see a need for development (e.g., by using colors).

References

Abbott, A. (1988). *A system of professions*. Chicago: University of Chicago Press.

Aebli, H. (1961). *Grundformen des Lehrens. Ein Beitrag zur psychologischen Grundlegung der Unterrichtsmethode*. Stuttgart: Klett.

Aebli, H. (1983). *Zwölf Grundformen des Lernens. Eine Allgemeine Didaktik auf psychologischer Grundlage*. Stuttgart: Klett.

Alexander, R. (2001). *Towards dialogic teaching: Rethinking classroom talk*. Cambridge: Dialogos.

Alexander, R. (2017). Developing dialogue: Process, trial, outcomes. Paper presented at the 17th Biennial EARLI Conference, Tampere, Finland, 31 August 2017.

Alexander, R. (2018). Developing dialogic teaching: Genesis, process, trial. *Research Papers in Education, 33*(5), 561–598.

Anderson, L. W., & Krathwohl, D. R. (Eds.). (2001). *A taxonomy for learning, teaching, and assessing: A revision of Bloom's taxonomy of educational objectives*. New York: Addison Wesley Longman.

Angelo, T. A., & Cross, K. P. (1993). *Classroom assessment techniques: A handbook for college teachers* (2nd ed.). San Francisco: Jossey-Bass.

Anthony, G., Hunter, J., & Hunter, R. (2015). Prospective teachers development of adaptive expertise. *Teaching and Teacher Education, 49*, 108–117.

Archer, J., Cantrall, S., Holtzman, S. L., Joe, J. N., Tocci, C. M., & Wood, J. (2016). *Better feedback for better teaching: A practical guide to improving classroom observations*. San Francisco: Jossey-Bass.

Atkinson, R. K., Derry, S. J., Renkl, A., & Wortham, D. (2000). Learning from examples: Instructional principles from the worked examples research. *Review of Educational Research, 70*(2), 181–214.

Ausubel, D. P. (1960). The use of advance organizers in the learning and retention of meaningful verbal material. *Journal of Educational Psychology, 51*, 267–272.

Baer, M., Kocher, M., Wyss, C., Guldimann, T., Larcher, S., & Dörr, G. (2011). Lehrerbildung und Praxiserfahrung im ersten Berufsjahr und ihre Wirkung auf die Unterrichtskompetenzen von Studierenden und jungen Lehrpersonen im Berufseinstieg. *Zeitschrift für Erziehungswissenschaft, 14*(1), 85–117.

Ball, D. L., & Cohen, D. K. (1999). Developing practice, developing practitioners: Toward a practice-based theory of professional education. In L. Darling-Hammond & G. Sykes (Eds.), *Teaching as the learning profession: Handbook of policy and practice* (pp. 3–32). San Francisco: Jossey-Bass.

Ball, D. L., & Forzani, F. M. (2009). The work of teaching and the challenge for teacher education. *Journal of Teacher Education, 60*(5), 497–511.

Ball, D. L., & Forzani, F. M. (2011). Building a common core for learning to teach and connecting professional learning to practice. *American Educator, 35*(2), 17–38.

Barrows, H. S., & Tamblyn, R. M. (1980). *Problem-based learning: An approach to medical education*. New York: Springer.

Barwell, R. (2016). Formal and informal mathematical discourses: Bakhtin and Vygotsky, dialogue and dialectic. *Educational Studies in Mathematics, 92*(3), 331–345.

Bauer, T., Reinartz, A., & Gehrmann, A. (2017). Strukturierung von Unterricht im Rahmen der Stundenplanung von Lehramtsstudierenden. In S. Wernke & K. Zierer (Eds.), *Die Unterrichtsplanung: Ein in Vergessenheit geratener Kompetenzbereich?! Status Quo und Perspektiven aus Sicht der empirischen Forschung* (pp. 77–90). Bad Heilbrunn: Klinkhardt.

Biaggi, S., Krammer, K., & Hugener, I. (2013). Vorgehen zur Förderung der Analysekompetenz in der Lehrerbildung mit Hilfe von Unterrichtsvideos: Erfahrungen aus dem ersten Studienjahr. *Seminar, 2*, 26–34.

Biesta, G. J. J. (2010). Why 'what works' still won't work: From evidence-based education to value-based education. *Studies in Philosophy and Education, 29*, 491–503.

Black, P., & Wiliam, D. (2009). Developing the theory of formative assessment. *Educational Assessment, Evaluation and Accountability, 21*, 5–31.

Bloom, B. S., Engelhart, M. D., Frust, E. J., Hill, W. H., & Krathwohl, D. R. (1956). *Taxonomy of educational objectives. Handbook I: Cognitive domain*. New York: McKay.

Blum, W., Krauss, S., & Neubrand, M. (2011). COACTIV – Ein mathematikdidaktisches Projekt? In M. Kunter, J. Baumert, W. Blum, U. Klusmann, S. Krauss, & M. Neubrand (Eds.), *Professionelle Kompetenz von Lehrkräften:*

Ergebnisse des Forschungsprogramms COACTIV (pp. 329–343). Münster: Waxmann.

Bradbury, N. A. (2016). Attention span during lectures: 8 seconds, 10 minutes, or more? *Advances in Physiology Education, 40*, 509–513.

Bransford, J., Brown, A. L., & Cocking, R. R. (Eds.). (2000). *How people learn: Brain, mind, experience, and school* (expanded ed.). Washington, DC: National Academy Press.

Broadwell, M. M. (1969). Teaching for learning (XVI). *The Gospel Guardian, 20*(41), 641–643.

Brookhart, S. M. (2017). *How to give effective feedback to your students*. Alexandria, VA: ASCD.

Brown, G. T. L., Andrade, H. L., & Chen, F. (2015). Accuracy in student self-assessment: Directions and cautions for research. *Assessment in Education: Principles, Policy & Practice, 22*(4), 444–457.

Bryk, A. S., Gomez, L. M., Grunow, A., & LeMahieu, P. G. (2015). *Learning to improve: How America's schools can get better at getting better*. Cambridge, MA: Harvard Education Press.

Burt, S. (2019). *The art of listening in coaching and mentoring*. Abingdon, UK: Routledge.

Cazden, C. B. (1988). *Classroom discourse: The language of teaching and learning*. Portsmouth, NH: Heinemann.

Cazden, C. B. (2001). *Classroom discourse: The language of teaching and learning* (2nd ed.). Portsmouth, NH: Heinemann.

CCSSO. (2013). *InTASC: Model core teaching standards and learning progressions for teachers 1.0*. Washington, DC: Council of Chief State School Officers.

Cepeda, N. J., Pashler, H., Vul, E., Wixted, J. T., & Rohrer, D. (2006). Distributed practice in verbal recall tasks: A review and quantitative synthesis. *Psychological Bulletin, 132*(3), 354–380.

Collins, A., Brown, J. S., & Newman, S. E. (1989). Cognitive apprenticeship: Teaching the crafts of reading, writing, and mathematics. In L. B. Resnick (Ed.), *Knowing, learning, and instruction* (pp. 453–494). Hillsdale, NJ: Erlbaum.

Compayré, G. (1908). *Herbart and education by instruction*. London: George G. Harrap.

Dann, R. (2018). *Developing feedback for pupil learning: Teaching, learning and assessment in schools*. London: Routledge.

Deci, E. L., & Flaste, R. (1995). *Why we do what we do: The dynamics of personal autonomy*. New York: Putnam's Sons.

Deci, E. L., Vallerand, R. J., Pelletier, L. G., & Ryan, R. M. (1991). Motivation and education: The self-determination perspective. *Educational Psychologist, 26*(3&4), 325–346.

Dewey, J. (1916). *Democracy and education: An introduction to the philosophy of education.* New York: Macmillan.

Dewey, J. (1931). The way out of educational confusion. In J. A. Boydston (Ed.), *The later works* (vol. 6; pp. 75–89). Carbondale: Southern Illinois University Press.

Diesterweg, A. (1838). *Wegweiser für deutsche Lehrer.* Essen: Bädeker.

Dodd, C. I. (1898). *Introduction to the Herbartian principles of teaching.* New York: MacMillan.

Dotger, B. H. (2015). Core pedagogy: Individual uncertainty, shared practice, formative ethos. *Journal of Teacher Education, 66*(3), 215–226.

Ebbinghaus, H. (1885). *Über das Gedächtnis* (2nd ed., 1971). Darmstadt: Wissenschaftliche Buchgesellschaft.

Ebel, R. L. (1970). Behavioral objectives: A close look. *Phi Delta Kappan, 52*(3), 171–173.

Ecroyd, D. H. (1960). *Speech in the classroom.* Englewood Cliffs, NJ: Prentice Hall.

Engelmann, S. Z. (2004). *Learn from the learners!* David Boulton interviews Zig Engelmann. https://childrenofthecode.org/interviews/engelmann.htm.

Eraut, M. (2004). Informal learning in the workplace. *Studies in Continuing Education, 26*(2), 247–273.

Ericsson, K. A., Krampe, R. T., & Tesch-Römer, C. (1993). The role of deliberate practice in the acquisition of expert performance. *Psychological Review, 100*(3), 363–406.

Fend, H. (1998). *Qualität im Bildungswesen. Schulforschung zu Systembedingungen, Schulprofilen und Lehrerleistung.* Weinheim: Juventa.

Feyerabend, P. (1991). *Three dialogues on knowledge.* Cambridge: Blackwell.

Fogo, B. (2014). Core practices for teaching history: The results of a delphi panel survey. *Theory and Research in Social Education, 42*, 151–196.

Forzani, F. M. (2014). Understanding "core practices" and "practice-based" teacher education: Learning from the past. *Journal of Teacher Education, 65*(4), 357–368.

Galilei, G. (1632/1997). *Galileo on the world systems.* Abridged translation of Dialogo dei massimi sistemi, 1632 (M. A. Finocchiaro, Trans.). Berkeley: University of California Press.

Galilei, G. (1638/1914). *Dialogues concerning two new sciences.* Translation of Discorsi e dimostrazioni matematiche intorno a due nuove scienze (H. Crew & A. de Salvio, Trans.). New York: Dover Publications.

Gamson, D. A., Eckert, S. A., & Anderson, J. (2019). Standards, instructional objectives and curriculum design: A complex relationship. *Phi Delta Kappan, 100*(6), 8–12.

Gobet, F., & Chassy, P. (2009). Expertise and intuition: A tale of three theories. *Minds and Machines, 19*(2), 115–180.

Grell, J. (1999). "Direktes unterrichten." In J. Wiechmann (Ed.), *Zwölf unterrichtsmethoden* (pp. 35–49). Weinheim: Beltz.

Grell, J., & Grell, M. (1979). *Unterrichtsrezepte*. München: Urban & Schwarzenberg.

Grell, J., & Grell, M. (2005). *Unterrichtsrezepte* (6th ed.). Weinheim: Beltz.

Grosser-Clarkson, D., & Neel, M. A. (2020). Contrast, commonality, and a call for clarity: A review of the use of core practices in teacher education. *Journal of Teacher Education, 71*(4), 464–476.

Grossman, P. (Ed.). (2018). *Teaching core practices in teacher education*. Cambridge, MA: Harvard Education Press.

Grossman, P., Hammerness, K., & McDonald, M. (2009). Redefining teaching, re-imagining teacher education. *Teachers and Teaching: Theory and Practice, 15*(2), 273–289.

Grossman, P., Herrmann, Z., Schneider Kavanagh, S., & Pupik Dean, C. G. (2021). *Core practices for project-based learning: A guide for teachers and leaders*. Cambridge, MA: Harvard University Press.

Grossman, P., & Pupik Dean, C. G. (2019). Negotiating a common language and shared understanding about core practices: The case of discussion. *Teaching and Teacher Education, 80*, 157–166.

Hage, K., Bischoff, H., Dichanz, H., Eubel, K.-D., Oehlschläger, H.-J., & Schwittmann, D. (1985). *Das Methoden-Repertoire von Lehrern: Eine Untersuchung zum Unterrichtsalltag in der Sekundarstufe I*. Wiesbaden: VS Verlag für Sozialwissenschaften.

Harteis, C., & Billett, S. (2013). Intuitive expertise: Theories and empirical evidence. *Educational Research Review, 9*, 145–157.

Harteis, C., & Gruber, H. (2008). Intuition and professional competence. *Vocations and Learning, 1*(1), 71–85.

Hartmann, M., & Weiser, B. (2007). Unbewusste Inkompetenz? Selbstüberschätzung bei StudienanfängerInnen. In C. Kraler & M. Schratz (Eds.), *Ausbildungsqualität und Kompetenz im Lehrerberuf*. Wien: Lit.

Hascher, T. (2012). Lernfeld Praktikum. Evidenzbasierte Entwicklungen in der Lehrer/innenbildung. *Zeitschrift für Bildungsforschung, 2*(2), 109–129.

Hatano, G., & Inagaki, K. (1986). Two courses of expertise. In H. Stevenson, H. Azuma, & K. Hakuta (Eds.), *Child development and education in Japan* (pp. 262–272). New York: Freeman.

Hattie, J. (1999). *Influences on student learning* (Inaugural Professorial Address August 2, 1999). New Zealand: University of Auckland.

Hattie, J. (2009). *Visible learning: A synthesis of over 800 meta-analyses relating to achievement.* Abingdon, UK: Routledge.

Hattie, J., & Clarke, S. (2018). *Visible learning: Feedback.* London: Routledge.

Hattie, J., & Timperley, H. (2007). The power of feedback. *Review of Educational Research, 77*(1), 81–112.

Herbart, J. F. (1802). Zwei Vorlesungen über Pädagogik. In K. Kehrbach (Ed.), *Johann Friedrich Herbarts sämmtliche Werke in chronologischer Reihenfolge, Band 1 (1882)* (pp. 317–330). Leipzig: Von Veit.

Hiebert, J., Gallimore, R., & Stigler, J. W. (2002). A knowledge base for theteaching profession: What would it look like and how can we get one? *Educational Researcher, 31*(5), 3–15.

Hiebert, J., & Morris, A. K. (2012). Teaching, rather than teachers, as a path toward improving classroom instruction. *Journal of Teacher Education, 63*(2), 92–102.

Hogarth, R. M. (2010). Intuition: A challenge for psychological research on decision making. *Psychological Inquiry, 21*(4), 338–353.

Howe, C., Hennessy, S., Mercer, N., Vrikki, M., & Wheatley, L. (2019). Teacher-student dialogue during classroom teaching: Does it really impact on student outcomes? *Journal of the Learning Sciences, 28*(4–5), 462–512.

Huberman, M. (1983). Recipes for busy kitchens: A situational analysis of routine knowledge use in schools. *Knowledge, 4*(4), 478–510.

Hughes, C. A., Morris, J. R., Therrien, W. J., & Benson, S. K. (2017). Explicit instruction: Historical and contemporary contexts. *Learning Disabilities Research & Practice, 32*(3), 140–148.

James, K. H. (2017). The importance of handwriting experience on the development of the literate brain. *Current Directions in Psychological Science, 26*(6), 502–508.

Johnson, D. W., Johnson, R., & Holubec, E. (2008). *Cooperation in the classroom* (8th ed.). Edina, MN: Interaction Book Company.

Johnson, D. W., & Johnson, R. T. (2009). An educational psychology success story: Social interdependence theory and cooperative learning. *Educational Researcher, 38*(5), 365–379.

Johnson, D. W., & Johnson, R. T. (2016). Cooperative learning and teaching citizenship in democracies. *International Journal of Educational Research, 76*, 162–177.

Kavanagh, S. S., Metz, M., Hauser, M., Fogo, B., Taylor, M. W., & Carlson, J. (2019). Practicing responsiveness: Using approximations of teaching to develop teachers' responsiveness to students' ideas. *Journal of Teacher Education, 71*(1), 94–107.

Kavanagh, S. S., & Rainey, E. C. (2017). Learning to support adolescent literacy: Teacher educator pedagogy and novice teacher take up in secondary English language arts teacher preparation. *American Educational Research Journal, 54*(5), 904–937.

Kazemi, E., Ghousseini, H., Cunard, A., & Chan Turrou, A. (2016). Getting inside rehearsals: Insights from teacher educators to support work on complex practice. *Journal of Teacher Education, 67*(1), 18–31.

Kennedy, M. (1999). The role of preservice teacher education. In L. Darling-Hammond & G. Sykes (Eds.), *Teaching as the learning profession: Handbook of policy and practice* (pp. 54–85). San Francisco: Jossey-Bass.

Kennedy, M. (2016). Parsing the practice of teaching. *Journal of Teacher Education, 67*(1), 6–17.

Kilpatrick, W. H. (1918). *The project method: The use of the purposeful act in the educative process*. New York: Teachers College.

Kluger, A. N., & DeNisi, A. (1996). The effects of feedback interventions on performance: A historical review, a meta-analysis, and a preliminary feedback intervention theory. *Psychological Bulletin, 119*(2), 254–284.

Kruger, J., & Dunning, D. (1999). Unskilled and unaware of it. How difficulties in recognizing one's own incompetence lead to inflated self-assessments. *Journal of Personality and Social Psychology, 77*(6), 1121–1134.

Lampert, M. (2010). Learning teaching in, from, and for practice: What do we mean? *Journal of Teacher Education, 61*(1), 21–34.

Lampert, M., Franke, M. L., Kazemi, E., Ghousseini, H., Chan Turrou, A., Beasley, H., . . . Crowe, K. (2013). Keeping it complex: Using rehearsals to support novice teacher learning of ambitious teaching. *Journal of Teacher Education, 64*(3), 226–243.

Lampert, M., & Graziani, F. (2009). Instructional activities as a tool for teachers' and teacher educators' learning. *The Elementary School Journal, 109*(5), 491–509.

Langer, I., Schulz von Thun, F., & Tausch, R. (2019). *Sich verständlich ausdrücken* (11th ed.). München: Ernst Reinhardt.

Leinhardt, G. (2001). Instructional explanations: A commonplace for teaching and location for contrast. In V. Richardson (Ed.), *Handbook of research on teaching* (4th ed., pp. 333–357). Washington, DC: AERA.

Lemke, J. L. (1990). *Talking science. Language, learning and values*. Norwood, NJ: Ablex.

Lemov, D. (2010). *Teach like a champion: 49 techniques that put students on the path to college*. San Francisco: Jossey-Bass.

Lewis, C. C., Perry, R. R., Friedkin, S., & Roth, J. R. (2012). Improving teaching does improve teachers: Evidence from lesson study. *Journal of Teacher Education, 63*(5), 368–375.

Lipnevich, A. A., & Smith, J. K. (Eds.). (2018). *The Cambridge handbook of instructional feedback.* Cambridge: Cambridge University Press.

Loughland, T. (2019). *Teacher adaptive practices: Extending teacher adaptability into classroom practice.* Singapore: Springer.

Lyle, S. (2008). Dialogic teaching: Discussing theoretical contexts and reviewing evidence from classroom practice. *Language and Education, 22*(3), 222–240.

Lyman, F. T. (1981). The responsive classroom discussion: The inclusion of all students. In A. S. Anderson (Ed.), *Mainstreaming digest* (pp. 109–113). College Park: University of Maryland.

Mager, R. F. (1962). *Preparing instructional objectives.* Palo Alto, CA: Fearon.

Martin-Raugh, M. P., Steinberg, J. H., Reese, C. M., Xu, J., & Tannenbaum, R. J. (2016). *Investigating the relevance and importance of high-leverage practices for beginning elementary school teachers* (Research Memorandum No. RM-16-11). Princeton, NJ: Princeton Educational Testing Service.

Martinez, M. E. (2006). What is metacognition? *Phi Delta Kappan, 87*(9), 696–699.

Mayer, R. E. (1979). Twenty years of research on advance organizers: Assimilation theory is still the best predictor of results. *Instructional Science, 8*, 133–167.

McDonald, M., Kazemi, E., & Kavanagh, S. S. (2013). Core practices and pedagogies of teacher education: A call for a common language and collective activity. *Journal of Teacher Education, 64*(5), 378–386.

Michaels, S., O' Connor, M. C., Williams, M., & Resnick, L. B. (2016). *Accountable Talk® sourcebook for classroom conversation that works.* Pittsburgh: University Institute for Learning.

Mitchell, I., Keast, S., Panizzon, D., & Mitchell, J. (2017). Using 'big ideas' to enhance teaching and student learning. *Teachers and Teaching, 23*(5), 596–610.

Morris, A. K., & Hiebert, J. (2011). Creating shared instructional products: An alternative approach to improving teaching. *Educational Researcher, 40*(1), 5–14.

Muijs, D., & Reynolds, D. (2011). *Effective teaching: Evidence and practice.* London: Sage.

Mullis, I. V. S., Martin, M. O., Foy, P., & Arora, A. (2012). *TIMSS 2011 International: Results in Mathematics.* Boston: TIMSS & PIRLS International Study Center.

Murata, A., & Kim-Eng Lee, C. (2021). *Stepping up lesson study: An educator's guide to deeper learning.* London: Routledge.

National Academies of Sciences Engineering and Medicine. (2018). *How people learn II: Learners, contexts, and cultures.* Washington, DC: National Academies Press.

NCATE. (2010). *Transforming teacher education through clinical practice: A national strategy to prepare effective teachers. Report of the blue ribbon panel on clinical preparation and partnerships for improved student learning.* Washington, DC: National Council for Accreditation of Teacher Education.

Neuweg, G. H. (2016). Praxis in der Lehrerinnen- und Lehrerbildung: Wozu, wie und wann? In J. Kosinar, S. Leineweber, & E. Schmid (Eds.), *Professionalisierungsprozesse angehender Lehrpersonen in den berufspraktischen Studien* (pp. 31–46). Münster: Waxmann.

Nilssen, V. (2009). Encouraging the habit of seeing in student teaching. *Teaching and Teacher Education, 25,* 591–598.

Nystrand, M., Gamoran, A., Kachur, R., & Prendergast, C. (1997). *Opening dialogue: Understanding the dynamics of language and learning in the English classroom.* New York: Teachers College Record.

Ovsiankina, M. A. (1928). Die Wiederaufnahme unterbrochener Handlungen. *Psychologische Forschung, 11*(3–4), 302–379.

Paas, F. G., & Van Merrienboer, J. J. (1994). Variability of worked examples and transfer of geometrical problem-solving skills: A cognitive-load approach. *Journal of Educational Psychology, 86*(1), 122–133.

Pauli, C., & Reusser, K. (2000). Zur Rolle der Lehrperson beim kooperativen Lernen. *Schweizerische Zeitschrift für Bildungswissenschaften, 22*(3), 421–442.

Pestalozzi, J. H. (1801/1894). *How Gertrude teaches her children: An attempt to help mothers to teach their own children and an account of the method* (L. E. Holland & F. C. Turner, trans.). London: Swan Sonnenschein & Co.

Polanyi, M. (1966). *The tacit dimension.* New York: Doubleday.

Pollock, J. E. (2012). *Feedback: The hinge that joins teaching and learning.* Thousand Oaks, CA: Corwin.

Reichmuth-Sprenger, A. (2017). *Struktur und prozedurale Produktivität von Lehr-Lern-Gesprächen im Klassenunterricht.* Zürich: Universität.

Rein, W. (1895). *Outlines of pedagogics.* Syracuse, NY: Bardeen.

Reinhardt, J. (2019). Social media in second and foreign language teaching and learning: Blogs, wikis, and social networking. *Language Teaching, 52*(1), 1–39.

Renkl, A., Schworm, S., & Hilbert, T. S. (2004). Lernen aus Lösungsbeispielen: Eine effektive, aber kaum genutzte Möglichkeit, Unterricht zu gestalten. In J. Doll & M. Prenzel (Eds.), *Studien zur Verbesserung der Bildungsqualität von Schule: Lehrerprofessionalisierung, Unterrichtsentwicklung und Schülerförderung* (pp. 77–92). Münster: Waxmann.

Resnick, L. B., Asterhan, C. S. C., & Clarke, S. N. (2018). *Accountable talk: Instructional dialogue that builds the mind.* Geneva: IBE-UNESCO, http://www.ibe.unesco.org/en/resources/educational-practices.

Reusser, K., & Fraefel, U. (2017). Die berufspraktischen Studien neu denken: Gestaltungsformen und Tiefenstrukturen. In U. Fraefel & A. Seel (Eds.), *Konzeptionelle Perspektiven schulpraktischer Professionalisierung* (pp. 11–39). Münster: Waxmann.

Reusser, K., & Pauli, C. (2010). Unterrichtsgestaltung und Unterrichtsqualität: Einleitung und Überblick. In K. Reusser, C. Pauli, & M. Waldis (Eds.), *Unterrichtsgestaltung und Unterrichtsqualität. Ergebnisse einer internationalen und schweizerischen Videostudie zum Mathematikunterricht* (pp. 9–32). Münster: Waxmann.

Reznitskaya, A., & Wilkinson, I. (2015). Professional development in dialogic teaching: Helping teachers promote argument literacy in their classrooms. In D. Scott & E. Hargreaves (Eds.), *The SAGE handbook of learning* (pp. 219–232). London: Sage.

Richter, D., & Pant, H. A. (2016). *Lehrerkooperation in Deutschland: Eine Studie zu kooperativen Arbeitsbeziehungen bei Lehrkräften der Sekundarstufe I.* Gütersloh: Bertelsmann Stiftung.

Robinson, D. H., & Kiewra, K. A. (1995). Visual argument: Graphie organizers are superior to outlines in improving learning from text. *Journal of Educational Psychology, 87*(3), 455–467.

Ropo, E. (2004). Teaching expertise: Empirical findings on expert teachers and teacher development. In H. Boshuizen, R. Bromme, & H. Gruber (Eds.), *Professional learning: Gaps and transitions on the way from novice to expert* (pp. 159–179). Dordrecht: Kluwer.

Rosaen, C., & Florio-Ruane, S. (2008). The metaphors by which we teach: Experience, metaphor, and culture in teacher education. In M. Cochran-Smith, S. Feiman-Nemser, & K. E. Demers (Eds.), *Handbook of research on teacher education: Enduring questions in changing contexts* (pp. 707–731). New York: Routledge.

Rosenshine, B. (2008). *Five meanings of direct instruction.* Lincoln, IL: Center on Innovation & Improvement.

Rosenshine, B. (2010). *Principles of instruction.* Geneva: IBE-UNESCO, http://www.ibe.unesco.org/en/resources/educational-practices.

Rosenshine, B. (2012). Principles of instruction: Research-based strategies that all teachers should know. *American Educator* (Spring 2012).

Rosenshine, B., & Stevens, R. (1986). Teaching functions. In M. C. Wittrock (Ed.), *Handbook of research on teaching* (pp. 376–391). New York: Macmillan.

Ruhlman, M. (2009). *The making of a chef: Mastering heat at the Culinary Institute of America*. New York: Holt Books.

Ruiz-Primo, M. A. (2011). Informal formative assessment: The role of instructional dialogues in assessing students' learning. *Studies in Educational Evaluation, 37*, 15–24.

Rumelhart, D. E., & Ortony, A. (1977). The representation of knowledge in memory. In R. C. Anderson, R. J. Spiro, & W. E. Montague (Eds.), *Schooling and the acquisition of knowledge* (pp. 99–136). Hillsdale, NJ: Erlbaum.

Ryan, R. M., & Deci, E. L. (2000). Self-determination theory and the facilitation of intrinsic motivation, social development, and well-being. *American Psychologist, 55*(1), 68–78.

Santagata, R., & Guarino, J. (2011). Using video to teach future teachers to learn from teaching. *ZDM Mathematics Education, 43*, 133–145.

Schäfer, S., & Seidel, T. (2015). Noticing and reasoning of teaching and learning components by pre-service teachers. *Journal for Educational Research Online, 7*(2), 34–58.

Schank, R. C., & Abelson, R. P. (1977). Scripts, plans, goals and understanding. An inquiry into human kowledge structures. Hillsdale, NJ: Erlbaum.

Schmidt, H. G., Rotgans, J. I., & Yew, E. H. J. (2011). The process of problem-based learning: What works and why. *Medical Education, 45*(8), 792–806.

Schön, D. A. (1983). *The reflective practitioner: How professionals think in action*. New York: Basic Books.

Schön, D. A. (1987). *Educating the reflective practitioner: Toward a new design for teaching and learning in the professions* (10th ed.). San Francisco: Jossey-Bass.

Schön, D. A. (1992). The theory of inquiry: Dewey's legacy to education. *Curriculum Inquiry, 22*(2), 119–139.

Schultz, K. (2009). *Rethinking classroom participation: Listening to silent voices*. New York: Teachers College Press.

Seidel, T., & Stürmer, K. (2014). Modeling and measuring the structure of professional vision in preservice teachers. *American Educational Research Journal, 51*(4), 739–771.

Sherin, M. G., Russ, R. S., Sherin, B. L., & Colestock, A. (2008). Professional vision in action: An exploratory study. *Issues in Teacher Education, 17*(2), 27–46.

Shulman, L. S. (1986). "Those who understand: knowledge growth in teaching." *Educational Researcher, 15*(2), 4–14.

Sinclair, J. M., & Coulthard, R. M. (1975). *Towards an analysis of discourse: The English used by teachers and pupils*. London: Oxford University Press.

Sipman, G., Thölke, J., Martens, R., & McKenney, S. (2019). The role of intuition in pedagogical tact: Educator views. *British Educational Research Journal, 45*(6), 1186–1202.

Slavin, R. E. (1995). *Research on cooperative learning and achievement: What we know, what we need to know*. Baltimore: Center for Research on the Education of Students Placed at Risk Johns Hopkins University.

Slavin, R. E., & Cooper, R. (1999). Improving intergroup relations: Lessons learned from cooperative learning programs. *Journal of Social Issues, 55*(4), 647–663.

Snow, C. E. (2015). Rigor and realism: Doing educational science in the real world. *Educational Researcher, 44*(9), 460–466.

Stein, M. K., & Kucan, L. (Eds.). (2010). *Instructional explanations in the disciplines*. Boston: Springer.

Stigler, J. W., Gallimore, R., & Hiebert, J. (2000). Using video surveys to compare classrooms and teaching across cultures: Examples and lessons from the TIMSS video surveys. *Educational Psychologist, 35*, 87–100.

Stigler, J. W., & Hiebert, J. (1999). *The teaching gap: Best ideas from the world's teachers for improving education in the classroom*. New York: Free Press.

Stockard, J., Wood, T. W., Coughlin, C., & Khoury, C. R. (2018). The effectiveness of direct instruction curricula: A meta-analysis of a half century of research. *Review of Educational Research, 88*(4), 479–507.

Strelan, P., Osborn, A., & Palmer, E. (2020). The flipped classroom: A meta-analysis of effects on student performance across disciplines and education levels. *Educational Research Review, 30*, 100314.

Stylianides, G. J., & Stylianides, A. J. (2014). The role of instructional engineering in reducing the uncertainties of ambitious teaching. *Cognition and Instruction, 32*(4), 374–415.

Takaya, K. (2003). The method of Anschauung: From Johann H. Pestalozzi to Herbert Spencer. *The Journal of Educational Thought, 37*(1), 77–99.

Tenorth, H.-E. (2006). Professionalität im Lehrerberuf: Ratlosigkeit der Theorie, gelingende Praxis. *Zeitschrift für Erziehungswissenschaft, 9*(4), 580–597.

Tharp, R. G., & Gallimore, R. (1991). *Rousing minds to life: Teaching, learning, and schooling in social context*. Cambridge: Cambridge University Press.

Timperley, H. (2013). *Learning to practise: A paper for discussion*. Auckland: Faculty of Education.

Tobin, K. (1987). The role of wait time in higher cognitive level learning. *Review of Educational Research, 57*(1), 69–95.

van den Ham, A.-K., & Heinze, A. (2018). Does the textbook matter? Longitudinal effects of textbook choice on primary school students' achievement in mathematics. *Studies in Educational Evaluation, 59*, 133–140.

Vygotsky, L. S. (1935/1978). Interaction between learning and development. In M. Cole, V. John-Steiner, S. Scribner, & E. Souberman (Eds.), *Mind in society: The development of higher psychological processes* (pp. 79–91). Cambridge, MA: Harvard University Press.

Wadsworth, B. J. (1989). *Piaget's theory of cognitive and affective development* (4th ed.). New York: Longman.

Wagenschein, M. (2015). The law of free fall as an exemplary theme for the mathematicizability of central natural processes. In I. Westbury, S. Hopmann, & K. Riquarts (Eds.), *Teaching as a reflective practice: The German Didaktik tradition* (pp. 285–294). New York: Routledge.

Wallach, T., & Even, R. (2005). Hearing students: The complexity of understanding what they are saying, showing, and doing. *Journal of Mathematics Teacher Education, 8*(5), 393–417.

Webb, N. M., Franke, M. L., Ing, M., Turrou, A. C., Johnson, N. C., & Zimmerman, J. (2019). Teacher practices that promote productive dialogue and learning in mathematics classrooms. *International Journal of Educational Research, 97*, 176–186.

Whitin, P., & Whitin, D. J. T. (2000). *Math is a language too: Talking and writing in the mathematics classroom*. Urbana, IL: NCTE/NCTM.

Wiggins, G., & McTighe, J. (2006). *Understanding by design* (2nd ed.). Upper Saddle River, NJ: Pearson Merill Prentice Hall.

Wiliam, D. (2018). Feedback: At the heart of—but definitely not all of—formative assessment. In A. A. Lipnevich & J. K. Smith (Eds.), *The Cambridge handbook of instructional feedback* (pp. 3–28). Cambridge: Cambridge University Press.

Wiliam, D. (2019). Some reflections on the role of evidence in improving education. *Educational Research and Evaluation, 25*(1–2), 127–139.

Wiliam, D., & Thompson, M. (2008). Integrating assessment with learning: What will it take to make it work? In C. A. Dwyer (Ed.), *The future of assessment* (pp. 53–82). New York: Routledge.

Winch, M., & Winch, C. (2019). Teaching through textbooks: Teachers as practitioners of a discipline? *Theory and Research in Education, 17*(2), 181–201.

Windschitl, M., & Calabrese Barton, A. (2016). Rigor and equity by design: Locating a set of core teaching practices for the science education community. In D. H. Gitomer & C. A. Bell (Eds.), *Handbook of research on teaching* (5th ed., pp. 1099–1158). Washington, DC: AERA.

Windschitl, M., Thompson, J., Braaten, M., & Stroupe, D. (2012). Proposing a core set of instructional practices and tools for teachers of science. *Science Education, 96*(5), 878–903.

Young, R. (1991). *Critical theory and classroom talk*. Clevedon, UK: Multilingual Matters.

Zander, T., Öllinger, M., & Volz, K. G. (2016). Intuition and insight: Two processes that build on each other or fundamentally differ? *Frontiers in Psychology, 7*, 1395.

Zeichner, K. (1996). Teachers as reflective practitioners and the democratization of school reform. In K. Zeichner, S. Melnick, & M. L. Gomez (Eds.), *Currents of reform in preservice teacher education* (pp. 199–214). New York: Teachers College Press.

Zeichner, K. (2012). The turn once again toward practice-based teacher education. *Journal of Teacher Education, 63*(5), 376–382.

Zeigarnik, B. W. (1927). Das Behalten erledigter und unerledigter Handlungen. *Psychologische Forschung, 9*, 1–85.

About the Author

Urban Fraefel is professor emeritus of the School of Education at the University of Applied Sciences and Arts of Northwestern Switzerland, where he established and coordinated the structures and research activities of Studies on Professional Practice. Moreover, he has held the position of director of the Institute of Secondary Education. Previously, Urban Fraefel was in charge of the teaching and learning of science at the secondary level at the University of Zurich and a member of the founding council of the School of Education Zurich, responsible for the development of field experiences and for the division of educational psychology. Beyond that, Urban Fraefel has a broad experience as a teacher on all levels.

In recent years, Urban Fraefel's research focuses on practice-based education of student teachers in collaboration between universities and schools, assessment of competencies in professional practice, and core practices of teaching especially in initial teacher education. In addition to numerous publications in these fields, he is also a textbook author. Urban Fraefel is furthermore the founder and honorary president of the International Society for Studies on Professional Practice and Professionalization IGSP.

www.ingramcontent.com/pod-product-compliance
Lightning Source LLC
Chambersburg PA
CBHW030319020526
44117CB00029B/130